IN ACTION

Building a Successful Consulting Practice

TWELVE

CASE STUDIES

FROM THE

REAL WORLD

OF TRAINING

JACK J. PHILLIPS
SERIES EDITOR

PATRICIA PULLIAM PHILLIPS
EDITOR

ASTD
Linking People,
Learning & Performance

Ordering information: Books published by ASTD can be ordered by calling 800.628.2783 or 703.683.8100, or via the Website at www.astd.org.

Library of Congress Catalog Card Number: 2002104903

ISBN: 1-56286-331-2

Table of Contents

Introduction to the
In Action Series

Most professionals involved in human resource development (HRD) are eager to see practical applications of models, techniques, theories, strategies, and issues relevant to their field. In recent years, practitioners have developed an intense desire to learn about firsthand experiences. To fill this critical void, the Publishing Review Committee of the American Society for Training & Development established the *In Action* casebook series. Covering a variety of topics in HRD, the series significantly adds to the current literature in the field.

The *In Action* series objectives are:

- *To provide real-world examples of program application and implementation.* Each case describes significant issues, events, actions, and activities. When possible, actual names of organizations and individuals are used. Where names are disguised, the events are factual.
- *To focus on challenging and difficult issues confronting professionals in the field.* These cases explore areas where it is difficult to find information or where processes or techniques are not standardized or fully developed. Emerging issues critical to success are also explored.
- *To recognize the work of professionals in the field by presenting best practices.* Each casebook represents the most effective examples available. Issue editors are experienced professionals, and topics are carefully selected to ensure that they represent important and timely issues. Cases are written by highly respected practitioners, authors, researchers, and consultants. The authors focus on many high-profile organizations whose names you will quickly recognize.
- *To serve as a self-teaching tool.* As a stand-alone reference, each volume is a practical learning tool that fully explores numerous topics and issues.
- *To present a medium for teaching groups about the practical aspects of performance improvement.* Each book is a useful supplement to general and specialized textbooks and serves as a discussion guide to enhance learning in formal and informal settings.

These cases will challenge and motivate you. The new insights you gain will serve as an impetus for positive change in your organization. If you have a case that might serve the same purpose for other professionals, please contact me. New casebooks are being developed. If you have suggestions on ways to improve the *In Action* series, your input is welcomed.

Jack J. Phillips
Series Editor
Box 380637
Birmingham, AL 35238-0637
SeriesEditor@aol.com

Preface

Consulting is a critical, ongoing trend that has both a bright and a dark side. On the bright side, it is one of the fastest growing occupational groups and offers the opportunity for excellent income growth and job satisfaction. It is an exceptionally rewarding occupation and can be very important to the success of other organizations. Many individuals are attracted to this occupation each year, and typically start out as a one-person, independent consultant.

On the dark side, consulting has a tarnished reputation and is often perceived as providing unnecessary services at a high cost. Sometimes consultants are not respected in the organizations they serve, except for the individuals or team who are regarded as clients. Frequently, many of the initial startups of individual consulting practices fail, leaving the entrepreneur devastated—often retreating to a job or career that is completely different from consulting.

This unique book, *Building a Successful Consulting Practice,* will present case studies analyzing the success of consulting organizations. Most of the focus is on small consulting practices, closely related to the human resource development and human resources fields.

Target Audience

This book should be valuable to anyone involved in consulting. The primary audience is those individuals who are interested in starting a consulting practice. This book shows, in much detail, what factors have been and should be considered to develop these successful consulting practices. Any individual who is interested in making this tremendous leap into the consulting occupation should find this an excellent reference to provide the insight necessary to make the leap and land successfully.

The second audience is those individuals actively involved in consulting now. This audience would be interested in finding ways to continue to ensure that their business survives and is successful. These case studies provide insight about how a consulting business is grown and, in some cases, actually sold to other organizations. It should be a helpful guide for continued success for the existing consultant.

The third audience is those instructors and professors who teach others about this important field of consulting. Whether they choose this book for students in university courses who are pursuing degrees in related fields, or use it in internal workshops for professionals or in public seminars on consulting, the casebook would be a valuable reference. It can be used as a supplement to a standard textbook in consulting, such as Peter Block's *Flawless Consulting* (2000). The combination of text and casebook offers the technical details of the consulting process along with examples of successful consulting practices. Together these elements show how to build a successful, viable business.

The fourth audience is the researchers who are seeking ways to understand the success of consulting and those factors that can predict success and failure. The samples in this book offer a cross section of different types of consulting practices. The common thread is that they are all successful, having survived at least two years as the consulting practice developed.

A fifth audience is the entrepreneurs, and those who work with entrepreneurs, who are trying to understand success in various occupations. Many entrepreneurs start a business in some kind of consulting capacity, developing products and services for others. These case studies provide continuing evidence of the success of the entrepreneur in our society.

Each audience should find the casebook entertaining and engaging reading. Questions are placed at the end of each case to stimulate additional thought and discussion. One of the most effective ways to maximize the usefulness of this book is through group discussions, using the questions to develop and dissect the issues, techniques, methodologies, and results.

The Cases

The most difficult part of developing this book was to identify case authors who had developed successful consulting practices, primarily in the human resources, training and development, and performance improvement fields. The editor solicited case studies from about 4,000 individuals. The response was better than anticipated.

The case studies selected met very specific guidelines. Each case study had to represent a consulting practice that met the following seven criteria:

1. had survived a minimum of two years
2. delivered services in the performance improvement, training and development, human resources, and management field
3. had identified the specific techniques, strategies, and tactics that led to success or maintenance of success
4. was successful as demonstrated by both quantitative and qualitative measures
5. involved either internal and external consulting, with most of the focus on external
6. was small in scope and the number of consultants was relatively low
7. had both private and public sector clients.

Although there was some attempt to structure the cases similarly, based on the supplemental guidelines, the actual presentations are not identical in style or content. It is important for the reader to experience the development of the consulting practice from the developers' points of view and identify the issues that lead to success. The result is a variety of presentation styles. All are intriguing and engaging and should offer much insight into successful consulting.

In all cases, the name of the organization is identified, as are the individuals involved. Some of the firms are well-known and should be easily recognized.

Case Authors

It would be difficult to find a more impressive group of contributors than those for this casebook. For such a difficult topic, we expected to find the best, and we were not disappointed. If we had to describe the group, we would say that they are experienced, professional, knowledgeable, and successful. Most are experts, and some are well-known in the field. A few are high-profile authors who have made a tremendous contribution and taken the opportunity to provide an example of their top-quality work. Others have made their mark quietly and achieved success for their consulting organizations.

Best Practices?

In our search for cases, we contacted some of the most respected consultants. We were seeking examples that represent best practices in consulting. Whether or not they have been delivered, we will never know. What we do know is that if these are not best practices, no other publication can claim to have them either.

Suggestions

We welcome your input. If you have ideas or recommendations regarding presentation, case selection, or case quality, please send them to me. You can contact me with your comments and suggestions at Box 380637, Birmingham, Alabama 35238-0637, or email me at thechelseagroup@aol.com.

Acknowledgments

This casebook is a collective work of many individuals, and the first acknowledgment must go to all the case authors. We appreciate their commitment to developing case studies and their interest in the development of the consulting field. We trust the final product has portrayed them as progressive consultants and consulting organizations interested in results and willing to try new processes and techniques.

I would like to thank Francine Hawkins for providing support in developing this casebook. Many thanks also go to Joyce Alff who provided editorial assistance and managed the casebook process to ensure a smooth transition from case author to ASTD.

Thanks also go to Ruth Stadius, ASTD's director of publications. Ruth is always supportive and willing to help to ensure the success of each publication.

Finally, many thanks go to my husband, Jack Phillips, for his continuous support and encouragement. Without his help and assistance, this project, as well as many others, would have gone undone. I am forever thankful for you, Jack.

Patricia Pulliam Phillips
Birmingham, Alabama
May 2002

Reference

Block, Peter. (2000). *Flawless Consulting: A Guide to Getting Your Expertise Used.* San Francisco: Jossey-Bass/Pfeiffer.

How to Use This Casebook

These cases present a variety of consulting organizations representing a wide range of settings, methods, techniques, strategies, and approaches. Most of the consulting practices focus on training and development, organization development, performance management, and leadership. Services offered include direct consulting, publications, workshops, and support tools. The target clients range from local, small organizations to large, multinational organizations. Public sector and not-for-profit organizations are also represented. As a group, these cases represent a rich source of information about the strategies of some of the best consultants in the field.

Each case does not necessarily represent the ideal approach for the specific setting. In every case it is possible to identify areas that could benefit from refinement and improvement. That is part of the learning process—to build on the work of others. Although the settings are contextual, the methods, strategies, and techniques can be used in other consulting organizations.

Table 1 represents basic descriptions of the cases in the order in which they appear in the book. This table can serve as a quick reference for readers who want to examine a consulting practice with a particular type of focus, services offered, and target clients.

Using the Cases

There are several ways to use this book. It will be helpful to anyone who wants to see real-life examples of successful consulting. Specifically, we recommend the following four uses:

1. This book will be useful as a basic reference to professionals who are interested in starting a consulting practice. A reader can analyze and dissect each of the cases to develop an understanding of the factors that contribute to success.

2. This book will be useful in group discussions in existing consulting firms. Individuals can react to the material, offer different perspectives, and draw conclusions about approaches and techniques to improve the practice. The questions at the end of each case can serve as a beginning point for lively and entertaining discussions.

Table 1. Overview of case studies.

Case	Focus of the Practice	Services Offered	Target Clients
Performance Resources Organization	Measuring and evaluating training, HR, and business, including measuring ROI	Publications, workshops, research, and consulting	Private and public organizations worldwide
Redwood Mountain Consulting	Performance improvement	Training, organization development, performance improvement	High-technology companies in Silicon Valley, government, academia, small and large U.S. companies
Hallowell & Associates	Leadership development and evaluation	Defining competencies, program evaluation, 360-degree feedback, instructional design, performance coaching	Primarily large organizations and government agencies
CEP	Full-service performance improvement and training	Consulting, training, workshops, books, and tools	Primarily large companies, including 80% of business with *Fortune* 500 companies
Partners in Change, Inc.	Training and development	Training and development, measurement and evaluation	Various company training and development functions
Management Advisory Services in the Texas State Auditor's Office	Internal consulting practice for a government agency	Help state agencies improve services and identify weaknesses	Texas State Auditor's Office
McCoy Training and Development Resources	One-person training and consulting firm	Customized training and educational programs, external certification programs, team building, books and articles, consulting, and HRD tools	Profit and nonprofit organizations and individuals in the Northeast, primarily Maine

Linneman Associates	Business and university consulting	Consulting in all areas of business, e.g., real estate, finance and investment, human strategy, general business, financial analysis, as well as designing curriculum, hiring staff, marketing programs for universities	Leading U.S. and international companies and universities
Stractics Group, Inc.	Performance improvement	Consulting in process optimization, change management, performance measurement, and management	Companies in U.S., Europe, and Asia
Neil Cerbone Associates, Inc.	Organization development and training	Implementation and delivery of strategic organization development initiatives and learning experiences	More than 50 *Fortune* 400 companies around the world
Lovoy's Team Works, Inc.	Sole-practitioner consulting services	Training in team building, time management, leadership skills, conflict resolution, Myers-Briggs Type Indicator®	Private and public sector companies and individuals primarily in Alabama
The Pyramid Resource Group, Inc.	Corporate coaching for executives and their teams	Individual and team coaching, workshops	*Fortune* 500 and multinational corporations

3. This book will serve as a supplement to other books on consulting. It provides the extra dimensions of real-life cases that illustrate successful consulting practices.

4. Finally, this book will be an extremely valuable reference for consulting staff support. These staff members provide support and assistance and it is helpful for them to understand the results that consulting programs can yield.

It is important to remember that each consulting practice is unique. What works well for one practice may not work for another, even if they are in similar settings. This book offers a variety of approaches and strategies from which to understand the issues involved in successful consulting.

Follow-Up

Space limitations necessitated that some cases be shorter than the author and editor would have liked. Some information concerning background, assumptions, strategies, and results had to be omitted. If additional information on a case is needed, the lead author can be contacted directly. The lead author's address is listed at the end of each case.

Building a Successful Consulting Practice: Opportunities and Challenges

Patricia Pulliam Phillips and Jack J. Phillips

The Consulting Dilemma

This casebook contains 12 case studies of successful consulting practices. They have happy endings. Unfortunately, not all new consulting practices are fortunate enough to have happy endings. Consider these three scenarios of recent consulting experiences. The names have been changed to protect the victims.

Suzanne's high-tech firm recently announced cutbacks of 7,000 employees and offered severance packages to entice volunteers. Suzanne decided to take a severance package and fulfill her long-term dream of building an independent consulting firm. Suzanne had developed excellent skills in team building while serving on the staff of her employer's corporate university. Organizational development assignments and team building projects were her specialties. Using a variety of commercially available tools and expert facilitation, she had accumulated measurable success with teams in her firm. Now, she wanted to take this process public and create her own consulting firm, Team Building, Inc. (TBI). Suzanne went to great lengths to announce her new business and allocated funds for developing brochures and promotional materials. She sent the announcement to every person she knew —even going as far as to purchase a couple of mailing lists. She was eager to tell the world that she was available. Unfortunately, the rest of the world didn't respond. Suzanne had to work very hard to secure even a few assignments and found the competition to be intense in the specialty area she had chosen. She quickly began to realize that it takes years to develop the relationships necessary to build a business and that not everyone was eager to seize the opportunity to use her skills. After nine months of frustration and little revenue,

Suzanne took a job outside of her area of expertise, with much less pay. As a result of her experience, she was very disillusioned about developing an independent business.

With 12 years of experience, Carlos had developed special skills in proposal writing. In his job with a major defense contractor, he developed proposals for new contracts and had earned a reputation as an excellent proposal writer. Carlos's skills were in high demand as he developed winning proposals and advised others on the process. In addition, he conducted internal workshops to improve the proposal writing process. Because of his success, Carlos decided to leave the security of his organization and launch his own consulting practice, Proposal Effectiveness Company (PEC). Carlos struggled desperately in the first few months as he attempted to secure clients. After calling on all his professional colleagues, he managed to land a few assignments and ultimately established a relationship with a competitor of his previous firm. That client, however, failed to drive sufficient revenue to sustain the new business. After a year of struggling, Carlos returned to his familiar industry, securing a proposal writing position with less pay and fewer job perks. Carlos left the situation disappointed and somewhat depressed about his brief effort to build a consulting practice.

John took advantage of an early retirement option to pursue the independent and carefree life of consulting. John had managed several departments and units within his retail store chain and was proud of his managerial and leadership skills. He had always been able to build a great team and gain the respect of his employees within the company. John enjoyed a reputation for being an outstanding manager who always delivered the results, and his work units consistently exceeded goals. Now, John wanted to use these skills to help small businesses develop and grow. With early retirement funds in hand, John launched a consulting practice, Results by Design (RBD). As he explored one opportunity after another, he was surprised by the number of doors that did not open for him. He finally aligned himself with a small business incubator program in his metropolitan area and secured some work through this organization, although most small firms wanted him to donate his time. He also collaborated with a group of retired executives who volunteered their services to assist small businesses. Again, most of the clients expected his services to be provided pro bono. After a year and a half of struggling with his business, John decided to pursue his early retirement a different way and purchased a fast-food restaurant franchise and devoted his time to developing that small business himself. The fast-food option translated into more headaches, longer hours, and less pay than he'd ever dreamed.

These three depressing scenarios paint a picture of the fate of many new consulting businesses. Historically, the failure rate for starting a new business is extremely high, but especially high in consulting. Yet, many individuals are attracted to the consulting business because of potential rewards and the appearance of a self-satisfying profession.

The consulting business represents an interesting dilemma. It has enjoyed tremendous growth in the past two decades, exceeding that of many professions. According to most predictions, the consulting industry will continue to grow in the range of 15 to 20 percent per year. Whether involved in restructuring the business, implementing new systems, developing staff, changing procedures, or bringing new products and services online, consultants are being asked to assist organizations in myriad ways. Companies are fervently seeking consultants for their external perspectives and expert opinions, hoping these consultants can provide solutions to improve their business.

At the same time, clients have become disappointed in the services consultants deliver and often blame them for their problems. Some critics say that consultants are incapable of producing results or supplying a useful product or service. Perhaps this image of consultants is underscored best, or at least in a more visible way, in the role of consultants depicted in the *Dilbert* comic strips. In Scott Adams's best-selling book, *The Dilbert Principle,* which was number one on the *New York Times* best-seller list, nearly 10 percent of the book's coverage is devoted to consultants and consulting. Dilbert depicts the petty and stupid requests and activities of consultants and consulting projects that litter cubicles throughout the corporate world (Adams, 1996). Some of Adams's observations of consultants are:

- A consultant is a person who takes your money and annoys your employees while tirelessly searching for the best way to extend the consulting contract.
- Consultants will hold a seemingly endless series of meetings to test various hypotheses and assumptions. These exercises are a vital step toward tricking managers into revealing the recommendation that is most likely to generate repeat consulting business.
- After the correct recommendation is discovered, it must be justified by a lengthy analysis. Analysis is designed to be as confusing as possible, thus discouraging any second-guessing by staff members who are afraid of appearing dense.

- Consultants use a standard set of decision tools that involve creating alternative scenarios based on different assumptions. Any pesky assumption that does not fit the predetermined recommendation is quickly discounted as being uneconomical by the consultants.
- Consultants will often recommend that you do whatever you are not doing now.
- Consultants do not need much experience in industry in order to be experts; they learn quickly.

Adams continues with his list of advantages that consultants bring to a company:

- Consultants eventually leave, which makes them excellent scapegoats for major management blunders.
- Consultants can schedule time on your boss's calendar because they do not have your reputation as a troublemaker who constantly brings up unsolvable issues.
- Consultants are often more trusted than your regular employees.
- Consultants will return phone calls because it is all billable time to them.
- Consultants work preposterously long hours, thus making the regular staff feel worthless for only working 60 hours a week.

While this is a humorous attack on the consulting field, it unfortunately rings true for many consultants, bringing confirmation on at least some of the points.

The dilemma of an apparently attractive, growing occupation, with its high failure rate and tarnished image, will be explored in this casebook. Each case study describes a successful consulting practice. This introductory chapter focuses on many of the key issues that contribute to success.

The Consulting Business

The best point to begin the discussion about consulting is the definition. A consultant is a person in a position to have some influence over an individual, group, or organization, but has no direct power to make changes or implement programs (Block, 2000).

Internally, most people in staff functions in an organization are really consultants, even if they don't officially have a consultant title. Staff functions such as human resources, training and development, market research, product design, strategic planning, financial analysis, product support, and technical support are all, in a sense, consultant roles. The individual receiving the consulting advice is usually called a client and that term will be used throughout this book. Sometimes the client is an individual; sometimes it is a group or team.

Externally, a consultant provides advice and counsel completely to another organization. A consultant can be an individual operating as a one-person consulting entity or part of a larger consulting organization. The number of one-person consultants is difficult to pinpoint although the actual figure is estimated to be quite large. Statistics for the past year hover around 20 million for independent contractors (Bick, 2001). Many of these solo practitioners are actually consultants, providing advice, assistance, and counsel to organizations. The number of consulting firms is also quite large and can range from a loosely organized group of two or three consultants to giant firms, such as Accenture and PriceWaterhouseCoopers. Both of these firms have more than 50,000 consultants and hold the distinction of being the top two consulting firms in the world in terms of number of consultants.

The focus of this casebook is on those consultants in the smaller end of the category—ranging from the one-person shop to small consulting businesses; this is an area where more insight is needed to identify the success and failure of these smaller firms so they can become larger organizations.

Consultants usually have a particular methodology as they provide advice and counsel to companies. Regardless of the process, they often listen to the client and key members of the client's organization; they explore and investigate a situation, problem, or opportunity; they analyze data, problems, and different scenarios; they recommend alternatives; and, sometimes, they actually implement their solutions (Nelson and Economy, 1997).

Figure 1 depicts a simplistic view of a consulting process, beginning with a client's present status or condition and an objective to change that condition to a desired state. The process uses the consultant's expertise, skills, knowledge, resources, and feedback to move the client to that desired state (Weiss, 1992). All consultants bring a uniqueness to their business with their processes, as they possess expertise, skill, knowledge, or resources that make them valuable. Ideally, this creates a niche opportunity.

Types of consulting projects vary considerably. Some involve specialty and technical projects, such as financial forecasting, environmental compliance, human resources compliance, technical training, system design and implementation, market research, and labor contract negotiations. Other projects are more management-oriented, where the

Figure 1. The consulting process.

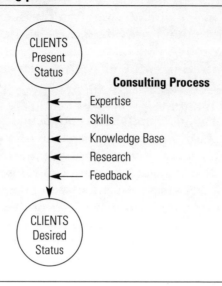

work assists the management team in a variety of issues including strategic planning, organizational development, or retention. Those assignments tend to be longer, requiring an ongoing relationship, and the client typically handles implementation. Still, other consulting projects might fall into the category of international work, such as international relations, government interface, global planning, and global strategy. International consultant assignments are often long term and require a consulting firm that is uniquely qualified and configured. Finally, other consulting projects involve work with troubled companies to assist their management team in a turnaround effort. This also involves marketing, financial, and operation issues where the duration of the engagement is often uncertain and skills have to be unique.

In summary, the types of consulting projects are extremely varied and include all types of scenarios. The particular type of project often defines the operational issues with the consultant, including the duration of the assignment, the nature of the work, and other important issues (Tuller, 1992).

The Myths of Consulting

A variety of myths are associated with consulting that often motivate people to enter the business when it may not be the right choice

(Biech, 1999). These myths are fully explored in this chapter and briefly detailed here.

1. **Consultants don't have to work so hard.** In reality, consulting may be one of the most difficult jobs one can do. It requires a tremendous amount of hard work to be successful and survive. Traditional eight-hour days are replaced with long hours, weekend work, and often no vacation or holidays.

2. **Consultants don't have a boss.** While an independent consultant may not have an immediate manager, there's still a boss in the equation: the client. The client can be more demanding and difficult to please than any direct manager.

3. **Consulting is a respected profession.** As described earlier, the image of a consultant has been severely tarnished in recent years. Many individuals in a client's organization view outside consultants as disruptive, unnecessary, and even harmful as they recommend flawed plans or processes. Add accountability concerns, and the issue of excessive costs, and consultants often suffer images depicted in *Dilbert* (Adams, 1996).

4. **Consultants make large amounts of money.** The daily rates for consulting are often less than imagined. Also, this daily rate is just that— the rate for a particular day. Unfortunately, there are not enough billable days for many consultants. When the daily rates are spread over the costs of providing consulting services, many firms don't have enough income to survive.

5. **Consultants are viewed as experts in their area.** Expertise is not automatically granted with the label of consultant. The consultant must constantly prove him- or herself to every client—in every situation.

6. **Consultants are void of office politics.** Sometimes consultants are placed in the middle of office politics as they attempt to accomplish their assignments. Many find themselves using their political skills as much as their technical, organizational, and management skills.

7. **It's easy to expand a consulting business.** As the number of clients increases, it would seem logical that the business could grow easily. But once the number of clients grows beyond what the original consultant/owner can deliver, it is often difficult to expand merely by adding consultants. Clients may not perceive the same level of expertise with other consultants or the new consultants may not have the same skills.

These and other myths create a flawed perception of consulting, causing many to make the leap into the consulting business, only to fail along the way.

Why Consulting Businesses Fail

As mentioned earlier, consulting has a very high failure rate. Many, if not most, consulting businesses fail in the first year. As the opening scenarios in this chapter illustrate, the reasons for failure vary considerably. An interesting account of the journey to failure is covered in the article *How to Start Your Very Own Consulting Business . . . and Fail* (Hochberger, 1999). In this blow-by-blow account of a failed practice, Hochberger details the ups and downs of the consulting start-up experience. Hochberger harbored many of the common myths about consulting and pursued the business without planning, forethought, or a basic analysis of how the business can succeed.

Many of the current consulting books offer insight on how consultants fail on their assignments. For example, the book *Consulting for Dummies*® offers the 10 biggest mistakes a consultant can make (Nelson and Economy, 1997):
1. not listening
2. failing to establish rapport
3. letting your ego get in the way
4. being inflexible
5. overpricing your services
6. underpricing your services
7. having one primary client
8. turning down work
9. taking current clients for granted
10. failing to market for future business.

These, and other mistakes, emphasize how the consulting process can go astray. Few, if any, consultants detail the fundamental errors made in the beginning when starting a consulting business. The major categories in the remainder of this chapter outline some of the important issues that must be considered as the business is launched—and in the first years of the practice. Without proper attention to these areas, the actual consulting methodology may not have a chance to succeed.

Why People are Interested in Consulting

Each year, many professionals (and nonprofessionals) are attracted to the consulting profession. Some are pursuing a lifelong dream of independence, freedom, and financial success. Others are running away from jobs and situations in hopes of finding something better. The attraction is strong and can usually be summarized in the following scenarios. To a certain extent, these scenarios are almost mirror images of the myths of consulting because what attracts someone to consulting is often based on a myth.

1. **Independence.** Running your own business and managing your own schedule gives you independence not enjoyed in occupations inside conventional organizations.

2. **Freedom.** The freedom to grow the business (or not), accept clients (or not), and travel (or not) is an important issue. This freedom often does not exist in traditional jobs in other organizations. A consulting opportunity seems to be an ideal way to escape the constraints and obstacles of previous jobs.

3. **The nature of the work.** Consulting is a helpful process that adds value to an organization. The consulting process, from exploration and investigation to analysis and recommendation, is exciting work. It is challenging and self-fulfilling.

4. **Rewards.** Consultants help individuals and their organizations. It is rewarding to see the results of a consulting assignment translate into important improvements in an organization. Ideally, the consultant makes a difference—sometimes a significant difference.

5. **Image.** In many cases, consultants are well-respected, the image of their work is a positive one, and they're proud to be a consultant.

6. **Financial rewards.** Consulting appears to be a lucrative profession; consulting rates are often very high, and large consulting projects can be extremely profitable for the individual as well as the firm.

7. **Leveraging talent.** Consulting is an excellent opportunity to leverage the knowledge and expertise of the consultant in an organization. In some cases, knowledge and skills are literally transferred throughout the organization.

8. **Opportunity for growth.** The profession is growing and the use of consultants is growing. The consulting field has the appearance of opportunity for much growth, and the opportunity for individual growth within the profession appears to be great.

9. **Escape mechanism.** Consulting appears to be the way to escape many of the frustrations inherent in corporate bureaucracy and the stifling effect of large organizations. Consulting is a way to move from the present situation to something much better. To go it alone is the ultimate dream of many people.

Those and other issues are attracting people to the consulting business each year. Attempting to determine if consulting is a good fit for an individual can be difficult. Figure 2 shows a slightly modified checklist taken from an important guide to consulting (Biech,

1999). It illustrates the key issues that should be considered to determine if consulting is right for you. The number of checks in the figure is significant; each person must face the reality of each issue. Every box that you are unwilling to check is an indication that you might not be closely matched to this profession.

Making the Transition

Making the leap to consulting is perhaps one of the most critical issues to address. Preparation is essential to success. The process begins with establishing the credentials necessary for a quality consulting service. Documenting your experience with speeches, case studies, articles, and books will ensure that expertise exists and is known to others. A service should be offered that is not readily available from other sources. Providing a niche opportunity that others are not adequately serving will help ensure that there is a demand for your services. It makes little sense to offer a service that is readily available in the market, especially if oversupplied.

Figure 2. The consulting match.

Is Consulting Right for You?

Quick Quiz

- ☐ I am willing to work 60 to 80 hours a week to achieve success.
- ☐ I thrive on risk.
- ☐ I have a thick skin—being called a pest does not bother me.
- ☐ I am good at understanding and interpreting the big picture.
- ☐ I pay attention to details.
- ☐ I am an excellent communicator.
- ☐ I am a good writer.
- ☐ I like to sell my work and myself.
- ☐ I can balance logic with intuition and the big picture with details.
- ☐ I know my limitations.
- ☐ I can say "no" easily.
- ☐ I am compulsively self-disciplined.
- ☐ I am comfortable speaking with people in all disciplines and at all levels of an organization.

(Adapted from Elaine Biech, *The Business of Consulting.* San Francisco: Jossey-Bass/Pfeiffer, 1999.)

Preparing for an assignment from a financial perspective is another critical step. Sufficient start-up funds and cash flow are needed to keep the business afloat during its first few months—perhaps years. The initial financial structure must be in place, including cost control, reporting records, and budgets.

Exceptional management and organizational skills are critical during the early stages of the practice. New consultants must be able to manage projects *and* manage the business, including managing time and having the discipline to routinely stay on track. Managing the financial, strategic, operational, administrative, and even legal contexts are all important and should be considered. Weaknesses should be addressed early so they don't become problems later.

The support of friends and family is crucial when starting a new business. Supportive relationships are necessary because of the stress connected with a new venture, and the long, hard hours that are inherent in consulting. A completely different lifestyle will usually emerge. The business will consume the individual, not only with long hours and hard work, but also the constant attention needed to keep it on track and moving in a proper direction.

Triggering events sometimes motivate an individual to launch a consulting business. A layoff, early retirement, unexpected job loss, or reaching a specific milestone (for example, an "empty nest") are all factors that can trigger the beginning of transition. Preparation for such an event is critical to ensure business survival for the first two years.

Strategy

Developing a strategic plan is often reserved for large organizations. However, it is also needed in small and new businesses. A strategic plan examines long-term goals and details a plan for achieving them. These goals are crucial to the ultimate success of a consulting business. One goal, for example, may be to define the region of operation, whether local, national, or global. Another strategic objective could focus on the type of consulting and related services to offer. Still another could focus on the type of organizations targeted for the practice.

Developing a strategic plan begins with a mission, vision, and values. The mission defines the purpose of the organization, the vision describes the ultimate outcome desired, and the values are the important principles and beliefs needed to achieve success. One example of a mission statement for a team building consulting firm is: To provide a variety of consulting services to develop teams and team-based organizations so that they will achieve the desired success.

An important part of the strategy is to have a business plan. This plan identifies what should happen to make the business successful. At least six critical areas should be addressed in the business plan:

1. *Background information* that thoroughly documents why the business exists and what has transpired to date. This would include statements of expertise and a description of the niche opportunity that exists.

2. *Strategic objectives* detailing what needs to be achieved long term to make the business successful.

3. *Tactical objectives* indicating short-term implementation steps as the business grows and develops.

4. *Resources required* to sustain and grow the business. These include marketing support, new locations, additional funding, and expertise.

5. *Progress and performance* made since the last review of the business plan.

6. *Outlook* showing the realistic prospects of the business and what can be accomplished in the future under different scenarios.

The business plan is a living, workable document. It must be reviewed periodically and updated as necessary. Plan, do, adjust is the philosophy. While the business plan becomes a working document for the consulting staff, it is also an important document for others such as bankers, alliance partners, key clients, prospective staff members, and potential owners.

Attracting and Retaining New Clients

Another critical ingredient in the success of a consulting business is attracting and retaining clients. Along with selling personal services, a consulting practice must focus on marketing processes and concepts. This step involves six key elements:

1. **A marketing plan.** This plan details the type of marketing; the appropriate mix; and how it will be implemented, including the timing, costs, and other issues.

2. **The image of the principal owner.** The image of this individual is very important. Whether the image is created in person in key business development presentations, or documented on paper, it must address the philosophy, mission, approach, expertise, and niche process that the consultant can offer.

3. **Marketing materials.** Presenting the consulting practice on paper—whether on business cards, letterhead, brochures, or handouts is important. Documentation may also include testimonials, articles, or books.

4. **The use of the Web.** The World Wide Web has become an important tool for any consulting firm, regardless of its size. The Website may be the best marketing tool to present your image, approach, and success.

5. **Proposals and contracts.** Written contracts between two groups are critical in terms of how they focus on the client and client satisfaction. Too much legal terminology can often create more problems than it solves.

6. **Building client relationships.** Ideally, the first client will be a long-lasting one. Continuing to build and strengthen existing business relationships, and expanding into new opportunities, is necessary to establish successful, long-term client relationships.

Structure

The structure of a consulting firm involves many issues that must be addressed early in the process. Among the issues is the basic type of legal entity planned, whether it's a sole proprietorship, corporation, or partnership. The extent to which other associates or employees will be involved is another issue as is the decision to have a formal office or conduct business in a home office. The desired scope of operation in terms of local, national, or international is important. If a global strategy is perceived, appropriate representation must be secured in other countries.

The actual organizational structure, in terms of reporting relationships, lines of authority, and working relationships must be designed to be rigid, loose, or in between. Some organizations are structured very loosely, such as Indigo Partners, a Silicon Valley consulting firm with six consultants specializing in marketing for high-tech firms. Indigo has no office, no secretarial pool, no overhead, and no assets to manage. A partner can take off as much time as he or she wants (Bick, 2001). The use of subcontractors is still another issue. Some consulting firms choose to subcontract some of their work, while others do not. Collectively, these structural issues—and others—determine the basic form of the organizational entity for the consulting practice.

Financial Issues

No topic is more important than the financial aspect of a consulting practice. The initial funding is often the very first step in developing the business. The type of ownership in terms of who owns the business and what type of stock they are issued is another important consideration. The need for adequate capital to keep the business going is an essential part of the original plan. Having the appropriate budgeting process to take the organization through its early startup is critical. Fees and pricing structures must be established so they're appropriate, fair, and equitable. Financial reporting must be in place so that the operational results will be known and cash flow can be pinpointed. Later, several issues may surface, such as escalating fees to cover rising prices, the collection of revenue, and addressing bad debt situations should they occur.

Consultants generally don't possess financial and accounting expertise. When that is the case, it is a must to acquire the expertise, having an accountant or CPA to work, at least initially, part-time. Financial issues are critical and must be addressed often and thoroughly to ensure that the business remains fiscally sound.

Managing the Business

For some consultants, the most unpleasant and distasteful aspect of consulting is managing the business. Because most entrepreneurs are not good managers, one classic reason for failure is that they fail to manage the business properly. Various management issues are involved in even a one-person shop. As the practice grows, it may be necessary to employ a business manager, operations manager, or administrative manager. One of the key issues here is not only finding the appropriate person, but also being willing to let go of operational control of the organization. Many consultants/owners are unwilling to let others manage the business, particularly if they're the sole owner. An effective business manager can maintain appropriate control of the business and build the team. The consultant/owner is often absent much of the time, working with clients. The support staff needs direction and someone available to make decisions. A business manager may be the answer for most small consulting businesses.

The Consulting Process

Every consultant has a process that clearly defines the practice, usually an expertise developed over several years. The process is usually in harmony with an accepted methodology and defines the techniques, models, and methods used by the consultant. That process often defines the niche or uniqueness of the practice.

The consulting process must be standardized with procedures and practices documented, ensuring that a defined method is available and is consistent from one project to another. As other consultants use that process, it is important for the same standards and procedures to apply. The documentation of the process may include philosophy as well. For example, in McKinsey & Company, a large strategic consulting firm, a defined approach has been developed to communicate the philosophy of working with clients (Rasiel, 1999):

1. The problem is not always the problem.
2. Don't reinvent the wheel (Part 1).
3. Every client is unique (no cookie cutter solutions).
4. Don't make the facts fit your solution.
5. Make sure your solutions fit your client.
6. Sometimes you have to let the solution come to you.
7. Some problems you just can't solve . . . solve them anyway.

Documenting and communicating the philosophy helps to ensure that the consulting engagement is consistently successful.

Products and Support Tools

Most consultants have an opportunity to develop other products and tools, and there are several advantages to this approach. Without other products and support tools, the only source of revenue is the consultant's time. When the consultant doesn't work (for example, when on vacation or ill), revenue isn't generated. Additional products and services complement the consulting process and make excellent tools to understand and use the processes. Also, products and tools often enhance the credibility of both the process and the consultant.

Support products and tools often fall into these 10 categories:

1. software
2. other supporting technology
3. job aids or templates
4. sample reports and guides
5. article reprints
6. technical bulletins
7. case studies
8. books
9. audio tapes
10. videos.

These tools should complement the consulting process and not be perceived as add-ons to justify charging more fees. More importantly, this approach provides the client with useful tools that can make the consulting assignment more successful, while at the same time, generating other sources of revenue for the consultant.

Writing Proposals and Reports

A well-written proposal can make the difference between attracting and losing a new client. Some consultants prefer to document as little as possible in a proposal, attempting to bind the consulting project commitment with a handshake. That approach can create problems later on. Proposals can avoid misunderstandings and miscommunications. More important, they represent an opportunity to showcase the organization and sell the consulting firm.

A winning proposal begins with clear defining objectives. The elements of a proposal can vary considerably, but should include the following:

1. **Background and situation.** This is a detailed understanding of the problem and the current situation. This is presented so the client and consultant agree on the current situation.

2. **Objectives of the project.** These objectives define what will be accomplished and the ultimate outcome of the project. Figure 3 shows typical project objectives.

3. **Assumptions.** The various assumptions important to the project are developed and listed.

Figure 3. Examples of broad consulting project objectives.

Project Objectives

- Identify the causes of excessive, unplanned absenteeism, and recommend solutions with costs and timetable.
- Evaluate the feasibility of three alternative approaches to new product development and rollout. For each approach, provide data on projected success, resources required, and timing.
- Implement a new accounts payable system that will maximize cash flow and discounts and minimize late payment penalties.
- Design, develop, and implement an automated sales-tracking system that will provide real-time information on deliveries, customer satisfaction, and sales forecasts.
- Enhance the productivity of the call center staff as measured in calls completed, without sacrificing service quality.
- Build a customer feedback and corrective action system that will meet customer needs and build customer relationships.
- Reorganize the sales and marketing division from a product-based unit to a regional-based, fully integrated structure.
- Provide review, advice, and oversight input during the relocation of the headquarters staff. Input is provided by memo each week. The project will address concerns, issues, problems, and delays.

(Taken from Jack J. Phillips, *The Consultant's Scorecard*. New York: McGraw-Hill, 2000.)

4. **Methodology.** The consulting process is outlined and includes steps, techniques, models, and approaches that are clearly defined. This is the heart of the consulting practice.

5. **Deliverables.** Include a list of exactly what will be delivered at the end of the project.

6. **Specific steps.** In addition to methodology, the specific steps needed as the deliverables are developed and presented are detailed.

7. **Project costs.** A detailed listing of costs is presented. Sometimes there is concern about detailing too many costs; however, it is better to show the client the detailed costs in advance than to have added costs at the end of the project. This approach builds credibility and respect for the consultant.

8. **Satisfaction guarantee.** A statement of a guarantee is essential.

Once accepted, the proposal becomes a working document throughout the project. It defines exactly what is delivered, when, and how. It should be reviewed often—and not allowed to collect dust until the end of the project.

A Results-Based Process

In the current economic climate, perhaps one of the most important issues for the consulting process is to focus on the results suitable to client expectations (Schaffer, 1997). Without the proper focus on results, consulting assignments can easily go astray. More important, the client ends up being dissatisfied. This dissatisfaction may result in not only lost business but litigation as well (O'Shea and Madigan, 1997). What is needed is a well-defined philosophy of delivering results. Not only are the ultimate outcomes (expressed as deliverables) necessary, but also a process of meeting client expectations throughout the project. A results-based approach to consulting consists of the following seven elements:

1. Consulting projects are designed with precise measures and are initiated, developed, and implemented with the end in mind.

2. A measurement and evaluation system is in place for each consulting project.

3. Several approaches are used to measure consulting, representing a balanced profile of data.

4. ROI evaluations are developed for a few selected consulting projects.

5. Stakeholders understand their responsibility to make consulting successful.

6. Support groups (management, supervisors, co-workers, and so forth) help to achieve results from consulting.

7. Consulting results are routinely reported to a variety of target audiences.

To determine the extent to which a project focuses on results, it may be helpful to use the checklist shown in figure 4. If only a few of these are checked "no," it sends a danger signal. Ideally, all should be checked "yes" to have a results-based focus on a project and to deliver it to the client.

An important element of the results-based approach, which appears as number two on the checklist, is guaranteed satisfaction and is presented in the book *Extraordinary Guarantees* (Hart, 1993). Christopher Hart shows how service providers can gain a competitive advantage by guaranteeing their work. The following is Hart's own con-

Figure 4. A results-based checklist.

How to Make Sure Your Consulting Focuses on Results

	Yes	No
1. Do you have results from other projects?	☐	☐
2. Will you agree to guarantee results?	☐	☐
3. Have you specified the current requirements for the project?	☐	☐
4. Is there a clear focus on results up-front in the proposal and early discussions?	☐	☐
5. Has there been a detailed analysis and needs assessment indicating the specific business impact and job performance needs?	☐	☐
6. Is it possible to forecast the actual ROI?	☐	☐
7. Have multiple levels of objectives been established for the project?	☐	☐
8. Has an evaluation plan been developed?	☐	☐
9. Have expectations been communicated to all stakeholders?	☐	☐
10. Is there a method to routinely provide feedback to make adjustments?	☐	☐
11. Can you develop an impact study?	☐	☐
12. Can you isolate the effects of the consulting intervention?	☐	☐
13. Have you examined a variety of data from different sources at different times?	☐	☐
14. Are the data collection, analysis, and reporting independent of project delivery?	☐	☐
15. Is there a plan to monitor the long-term effects of the project?	☐	☐

(Taken from Jack J. Phillips, *The Consultant's Scorecard.* New York: McGraw-Hill, 2000.)

sulting firm's guarantee, "Our work is guaranteed to the complete satisfaction of the client. If the client is not completely satisfied with our services, we will, at the client's option, either waive professional fees or accept a portion of those fees that reflect the client's level of satisfaction." At first, this might seem outrageous—a professional firm guaranteeing work! How can you make a guarantee like that when consulting services are subject to so many influences? But it is important to point out that what is guaranteed is *satisfaction*. It is not a guarantee that a specific *result* will be achieved, but rather, a guarantee of the client's complete satisfaction to which most firms say they are dedicated to anyway (Maister, 1997). It is certainly a concept worth pursuing, particularly early in the proposal process.

Ethics

No treatment of consulting would be complete without attention to ethics. Operating ethical standards are often developed as the consulting firm is structured, defined as the value system of the owner/consultant. These standards are often a reflection of personal convictions and define how the consultant will operate in a given situation.

Ethical issues surface in many ways. It may be in the professional area, where the consultant is asked to deliver results completely different than what was planned. It may be personal, where the client is demanding that the work be completed unrealistically. It could be an interpersonal situation, where the client is difficult to work with. It could be organizational, where the culture and dysfunctional practice of the organization interferes with the completion of the project.

When ethical issues arise, they must be dealt with accordingly. Here are seven approaches that may work (Cohen and Reinhart, 2000):
1. Politely pull out of the consulting project.
2. Express your discontent and try to resolve the issue.
3. Decide to complete the project, but refuse to do business with the organization later.
4. Leave without pay.
5. Complete the project and ignore the issue altogether.
6. Wait until the issue goes away, if it does.
7. Confront the client and stand up for your rights.

Those are all approaches to deal with an unethical client. Ethical issues materialize from the perspective of both the consultant and the client. The consultant must establish appropriate ethical standards and communicate them clearly so that the consultant does not become the ethical issue.

Measuring Success

The success of individual consulting projects is directly linked to the overall success of the firm. Success is measured in different ways. Positive financial results are usually the first definition of success. The primary measure involves profits or the reduction of losses extending over an initial time period. It may also include other financial goals, such as the profit per assignment, office expenses, revenue per consultant, and so forth. Without financial success, at least in the long term, the firm will not survive.

In reality, client success must come before financial success. If the client is not satisfied, the business will probably fail. Not only will there not be repeat business, but others will not engage your services.

Another success element is the personal success in delivering consulting services. Consulting is a rewarding process when it operates correctly—the consultant provides counsel that assists the client in measurable ways. Personal success is a powerful motivator to maintaining the discipline and determination necessary to make the practice work.

When measuring the success of a consulting project, six types of measures are necessary. These are shown in figure 5. This approach

Figure 5. Measuring success of consulting assignments.

Consulting Return-on-Investment: The Six Measures

Types	Measurement Focus
Satisfaction/Reaction	Measures the satisfaction/reaction directly involved in the consulting intervention.
Learning	Measures the actual learning taking place for those individuals who must implement or support the process.
Implementation/Application	Measures the success of implementation and the use of the consulting intervention solution.
Business Impact	Measures business impact change directly related to the consulting intervention.
Return-on-Investment	Measures the actual cost versus benefits of the consulting intervention.
Intangible Benefits	Measures important intangible benefits not used in the benefit-cost formula.

reflects a balanced set of measures where data is collected in different categories and at different timeframes, often from different individuals. It is very credible as the process always includes some method to isolate the effects of the consulting. Not all firms are using these six measures, but it is an ultimate goal of many firms (Phillips, 2000).

Exit Strategies

Early in the process, if not from the very beginning, it is important to focus on an exit strategy—the way in which the business will eventually phase out or change hands. Unfortunately, this is not given ample attention in the early phases and problems often arise later. Sometimes a consultant wants to sell the business, but, because of early decisions, finds that the business is not as marketable as expected. Also, as ownership changes hands, even from different members of a family, there are often financial, legal, and tax implications that need to be addressed as early as possible. Six avenues are available that describe the fate of a business:

1. **Sell the business.** Here, the emphasis is on building a consulting practice that is marketable, one that will have some value, either with its intellectual property or tangible assets.

2. **Dissolve the business.** This is the ultimate fate of many consulting firms, as the business is dissolved or phased out. Still, there are some legal and tax implications with that outcome.

3. **Merge the business.** Consultants sometimes merge, creating a larger, more viable consulting practice. A possible merger needs to be explored early, and planning for this should be made throughout the process. A merger has its own share of difficulties and problems. In most cases, mergers are not successful.

4. **Take the practice public.** Some consultants build a practice and take it public through an initial public offering (IPO). Although few make it to this level, it is a viable option. Careful planning is necessary to ensure that the business can be sold to the public and investors will buy shares.

5. **Transfer the business to a family member.** Here, planning is critical because of the legal and tax implications.

6. **Let it die naturally.** Sometimes a consulting practice should be allowed to disintegrate quietly and phase out of existence. Still, if it is a legal entity, such as a subchapter S corporation, there are some legal implications, and the planning should be addressed for this approach as well.

Conclusions—Keys to Success

While there is no absolute prescription for achieving success in a consulting business, this chapter has attempted to underscore some of the key issues involved in developing a successful consulting practice. The focus is on small consulting practices, even a one-person operation. Many issues are explored that can have an impact on the viability of a business. While no prescription is perfect, it may be helpful to end this chapter with a list of 10 success factors from one important consulting reference (Kintler, 1998):

1. Be persistent.
2. Focus on the client's needs.
3. Develop your unique selling proposition.
4. Project a professional image.
5. Have financial reserves available.
6. Develop and expand your contacts.
7. Never miss an opportunity to spread the word.
8. Focus on results.
9. Get testimonials.
10. Provide more value than expected.

The individual case studies presented in this book delve deeply into the various reasons for success. The message here is simple: If you are considering consulting, thoroughly explore all your avenues and plan properly, addressing all the issues in this chapter. If your consulting business is ongoing, these issues will need your attention to make it successful. Good luck!

References

Adams, Scott. (1996). *The Dilbert Principle: A Cubicle's-Eye View of Bosses, Meetings, Management Fads & Other Workplace Afflictions*. New York: Harper Business.

Bick, Julie. (November 2001). "The New Face of Self-Employment." *Inc.*, pp. 84-91.

Biech, Elaine. (1999). *The Business of Consulting: The Basics and Beyond*. San Francisco: Jossey-Bass/Pfeiffer.

Block, Peter. (2000). *Flawless Consulting: A Guide to Getting Your Expertise Used*. San Francisco: Jossey-Bass/Pfeiffer.

Cohen, Stephen L., and Carlene Reinhart. (May 2000). "Fifty Ways (More or Less) to Leave Your Client and Have Closure." *Training & Development*, pp. 86-89.

Hart, Christopher W. (1993). *Extraordinary Guarantees: Achieving Breakthrough Gains in Quality & Customer Satisfaction*. New York: AMACOM.

Hochberger, Joel. (March 1999). "How to Start Your Very Own Consulting Business. . . and Fail." *Training*, pp. 44-48.

Kintler, David, with Bob Adams. (1998). *Independent Consulting: Your Comprehensive Guide to Building Your Own Consulting Business.* Massachusetts: Adams Media Corporation.

Maister, David H. (1997). *True Professionalism: The Courage to Care About Your People, Your Clients, and Your Career.*. New York: The Free Press.

Nelson, Bob, and Peter Economy. (1997). *Consulting for Dummies®.* IDG Books.

O'Shea, James, and Charles Madigan. (1997). *Dangerous Company: The Consulting Powerhouses and the Businesses They Save and Ruin.* New York: Times Business/Random House.

Phillips, Jack J. (2000). *The Consultant's Scorecard.* New York: McGraw-Hill.

Rasiel, Ethan M. (1999). *The McKinsey Way: Using the Techniques of the World's Top Strategic Consultants to Help You and Your Business.* New York: McGraw-Hill.

Schaffer, Robert H. (1997). *High-Impact Consulting: How Clients and Consultants Can Leverage Rapid Results into Long-Term Gains.* San Francisco: Jossey-Bass.

Tuller, Lawrence W. (1992). *Cutting Edge Consultants: Succeeding in Today's Explosive Markets.* New Jersey: Prentice Hall.

Weiss, Alan. (1992). *Million Dollar Consulting: The Professional's Guide to Growing a Practice.* New York: McGraw-Hill, Inc.

Further Resources

Bellman, Geoffrey M. (2001). *The Consultant's Calling: Bringing Who You Are to What You Do* (2d edition). San Francisco: Jossey-Bass, Management Series.

Connors, Roger, and Tom Smith. (1999). *Journey to the Emerald City: Achieve a Competitive Edge by Creating a Culture of Accountability.* New Jersey: Prentice Hall.

Dauphinais, G. William, and Colin Price. (Eds.). (1998). *Straight from the CEO: The World's Top Business Leaders Reveal Ideas that Every Manager Can Use.* London: Brealey.

Dembitz, Alex, and James Essinger. (2000). *Breakthrough Consulting.* London: Prentice Hall.

Donovan, John, Richard Tully, and Brent Wortman. (1998). *The Value Enterprise: Strategies for Building a Value-Based Organization.* Toronto: McGraw-Hill/Ryerson.

Hiebeler, Robert, Thomas B. Kelly, and Charles Ketteman. (1998). *Best Practices: Building Your Business With Customer-Focused Solutions.* New York: Simon & Schuster.

Lu, Maggie. (Ed.). (2001). *The Harvard Business School Guide to Careers in Management Consulting.* Boston: Harvard Business School Press.

Mitchell, Donald, Carol Coles, and Robert Metz. (1999). *The 2,000 Percent Solution: Free Your Organization from "Stalled" Thinking to Achieve Exponential Success.* New York: AMACOM/American Management Association.

Redwood, Stephen, Charles Goldwasser, and Simon Street. (1999). *Action Management: Practical Strategies for Making Your Corporate Transformation a Success.* New York: Wiley.

Sadler, Philip. (Ed.). (1998). *Management Consultancy: A Handbook for Best Practice.* United Kingdom: Kogan Page.

Sheth, Jagdish, and Andrew Sobel. (2000). *Clients for Life: How Great Professionals Develop Breakthrough Relationships.* New York: Simon & Schuster.

Trout, Jack, with Steve Rivkin. (1999). *The Power of Simplicity: A Management Guide to Cutting Through the Nonsense and Doing Things Right.* New York: McGraw-Hill.

Building a Global Consulting Practice in a Niche Market

Performance Resources Organization

Patricia Pulliam Phillips and Jack J. Phillips

This case describes the development of a global consulting practice focusing on a defined niche market. From the outset, the practice was developed to operate globally and with the objective to take it public with an initial public offering (IPO) or sell to another organization. Seven years after its creation it was sold to a much larger, well-known consulting firm.

The Practice

Performance Resources Organization (PRO) was formed in January 1993 to provide workshops and consulting services in human resources accountability to all types of organizations. The practice grew out of successful efforts with measurement and evaluation processes, including the return-on-investment (ROI) process, developed by Jack J. Phillips, and was based on publications written by Phillips. As shown in figure 1, the ROI process collects and develops six types of data revealing the impact and success of programs.

The firm provided a variety of services to implement measurement and evaluation systems including research to discover new applications and improved options with the process. As shown in figure 2, the services provided were supportive and integrated. Publications, which were developed around the measurement and evaluation processes including ROI, built the awareness of the process and became the how-to books for the workshops. The workshops became the principal avenue for consulting. Most of the consulting projects were generated from workshop participants when they realized assistance was needed with

This case was prepared to serve as a basis for discussion rather than to illustrate either effective or ineffective administrative and management practices.

Figure 1. The ROI process defined.

The ROI Process Provides Six Types of Data

A comprehensive and systematic performance-based process that generates six types of measures:

- Reaction and Satisfaction
- Learning
- Application and Implementation
- Business Impact
- Return-on-Investment
- Intangible Measures

This balanced approach to measurement includes a technique to isolate the effect of the program or solution.

the process. Consulting assignments represented opportunities to conduct applied research, review the status of the process, and develop improved methods. The research and experiences from consulting were reported in additional publications.

Essentially, PRO was a consulting firm but used research, publications, and workshops to drive the consulting business. Typical consulting activities fell into four categories:

1. Conduct impact studies to determine the contribution of a training program or human resources program.

2. Assist organizations with implementing the ROI process and help them build comprehensive measurement and evaluation systems.

Figure 2. Integrated products and services of PRO.

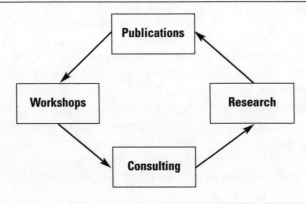

3. Review the current status of training and development and human resources functions to determine the extent to which there is a focus on accountability.

4. Assist organizations to keep the ROI process on track through regular reviews and meetings.

Making the Transition

The development of PRO extends from the early work of Jack Phillips in a variety of organizations where he developed and fine-tuned the ROI process. Serving in roles of training and development manager, HR executive, and operating executive, Phillips had the opportunity to experiment with the process. Four essential drivers led to the creation of PRO:

1. The development of a niche product. As far back as the 1970s, Phillips developed an ROI study on a supervisor-training program and reported it to a senior executive team. The reaction was excellent and what followed was a successive string of impact studies on different programs in three organizations. That ultimately led to presentations, articles, and a book on the process. In 1983, *Handbook of Training Evaluation and Measurement Methods* was published. (Now in its third edition, this was the first U.S. book on training evaluation.)

2. The demand for consulting assistance on comprehensive measurement and evaluation processes, as reported in the initial book, began to grow. Essentially, the handbook was used all over the globe as a major reference for training and development functions. In addition, it was adopted by dozens of universities and became a standard reference for measurement and evaluation, particularly in graduate classes. Thus, a strong demand for assistance was slowly developing during the 1980s.

3. Economic forces began to create more concern about accountability. In the 1990s, many executives were searching for increased efficiencies and productivity in their organizations. They were examining ways to reduce costs and enhance output to compete in a global economy. The top executives were demanding that new processes, functions, programs, or solutions show a contribution. These forces created a need for increased accountability, including measuring return-on-investment.

4. There was little or no competition for these processes. No organization appeared to be offering assistance with measurement and evaluation in a comprehensive way—the field was "wide open."

With these drivers developing, it appeared that the decision to create a consulting practice was an easy one to make. But not being much of a risk taker, Phillips was not willing to leave the comfortable surroundings of the corporate environment. Meanwhile, he had been elevated to president of a regional banking organization. It wasn't until the banking group was sold and Phillips received an economic windfall from stock options that he had the courage (and the funding) to develop the practice. His ambitious plans, conceived some 15 years earlier, became a reality with the founding of Performance Resources Organization.

Four personal influences helped him make the transition, in addition to having the financial capability of initiating a consultant practice:

1. The desire to operate independently and move out of the typical corporate structure that was becoming more bureaucratic, political, and less productive.

2. The desire to make a contribution, particularly in training and development and human resources, the areas where Phillips spent most of his working life.

3. The satisfaction that comes from helping others and watching "the lightbulb go on" as individuals see how the ROI process can be used to add value to their own work.

4. The desire to build a successful business with a limited staff of people who shared a similar vision.

Finally, years of preparation were in place and the funding was secured. PRO began as a low-risk opportunity with ambitious plans.

Strategy

From the beginning, several strategic objectives were developed that later proved to be a cornerstone of PRO's success. Although the strategies were fine-tuned in the early months and years, the following objectives were essentially developed at the beginning of the business:

- *To offer integrated products and services.* The products and services should complement each other. PRO began first with a workshop, followed immediately with consulting services, all built on the reputation from the handbook. Thus, the concept of integrated products and services began almost immediately with the launch of PRO.

- *To launch the consulting practice globally.* Recognizing that there was some pent-up demand for products and services in many parts of the world, Phillips responded with the first consulting and workshop opportunity in Johannesburg, South Africa. The trip was sponsored by Eskom, South Africa's largest electric utility. Phillips took a short leave of absence from the bank to provide consulting services and workshops, not only for Eskom, but also for the South African community. The positive reaction to this visit provided the encouragement needed to start the consulting practice. Within three months, the practice was launched. The second assignment was in Asia; the fifth was in Canada. Consequently, from the beginning, the effort to build a global organization was part of the strategy.

The desire to launch globally was important because many of the organizations targeted for this process were large, multinational corporations operating in many countries. Phillips recognized the need for a service provider that could offer assistance in different countries. Also, there was a perceived need for services in many of these countries. A new firm should be able to tap into the needs in other countries. The process quickly developed in most of the Asian countries, while at the same time, its use was growing in Europe, Canada, and the United States. Moderate growth has been experienced in Africa and South America. Today the firm operates in 33 countries.

- *To select a name for the organization that reflected the services offered.* With the combination of workshops, consulting, and publications offered, the term "resources" became an important consideration in selecting a name. Because the programs and processes were aimed at improving performance of individuals, teams, and work units in an organization, the term "performance" also became a consideration. It was also important to select a name that did not represent any particular individual, such as Phillips and Associates, The Jack Phillips Group, or Jack Phillips, Inc. The combination of Performance Resources Organization was selected because the abbreviation PRO was easy to recognize and remember. PRO began as an organization providing a variety of performance services.

- *To build a practice that could be sold.* Initially, it was envisioned that the practice would be developed so it could be sold to a larger group or taken public through an initial public offering (IPO). A strong demand for the services appeared to exist, and Phillips felt that a team could be developed to provide those services and that it would be ultimately attractive to a larger group.

- *To develop products, not just services.* With the advice of other consultants in the field, the firm focused on developing products that could be sold instead of relying on selling the time of the owner and other consultants. This included books, related support material, diskettes, a variety of packaged workshops that could be conducted by others, and standard consulting processes that could be delivered by other individuals. This effort was designed to have continuing income that would not rely on the principal owner.

- *To develop a process that would be recognized as the standard throughout the globe.* This noble objective required Phillips and the team to develop standards, publish more articles, develop case studies, create a database of impact studies, and write additional books—all for global distribution.
- *To evolve the application of the process from one function to another.* The application of the ROI process began in the training and development area, quickly migrated to human resources, and then moved on to consulting interventions such as organizational development. Eventually the process was applied to technology, change, and quality.

Collectively, these initial strategic initiatives provided PRO's direction and, through refinement over the years, provided the basis for growth as a niche firm in accountability. A business plan was developed around the objectives and included history, progress, plans, and major events. The plan was reviewed regularly and revised every six months. That plan was considered one of the most important vehicles to keep PRO focused and on track.

The Process

Because the consulting practice focused on the ROI process, it is important to understand more detail around this unique approach to evaluation. The overall ROI process, which was trademarked and is now owned by the Franklin Covey Company, consists of five elements, as depicted in figure 3. The consulting practice focused on all the elements, with most of the effort devoted to the actual use of the ROI process model.

The basic framework for evaluation consists of the levels of evaluation. This framework, originally introduced by Don Kirkpatrick in the late 1950s with four levels of evaluation, was expanded to include a fifth level. All five levels are shown in figure 4. The fifth level is the actual ROI calculation where the cost of the program or solution is compared to the monetary benefits from that program. In addition to inserting a level, Phillips and the PRO team adjusted other levels to make them more appropriate for a wide variety of applications.

The heart of the practice was the ROI process model, which provided a step-by-step method to collect, process, and analyze data, and report it to various target audiences. Depicted in figure 5, the com-

Figure 3. The ROI process.

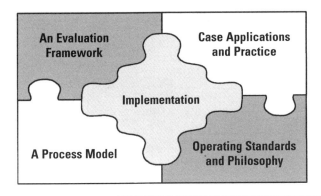

Figure 4. The levels of evaluation.

Level		Measurement Focus
1	Reaction and Planned Action	Measures participant satisfaction with the program and captures planned actions.
2	Learning	Measures changes in knowledge, skills, and attitudes.
3	Application	Measures changes in on-the-job behavior.
4	Business Impact	Measures changes in business impact variables.
5	Return-on-Investment	Compares program benefits to the costs.

plete ROI process model became the primary tool for consulting and teaching a comprehensive measurement and evaluation process. The content and detail around the processes will not be explored here as they are reported in several other publications.

Structure

The structure of the organization evolved over time. Initially, it was one person (Jack Phillips full time) with a full-time assistant. From this beginning, in the attic of his house, the company grew. Independent contractors, who could apply the processes and function as a network with PRO, were added. These contractors became associates of PRO. Later, the company added more employees and moved into nearby offices, establishing a structure that endured for several years. Figure 6 shows how the organization evolved with key officers driving each of the major product lines and processes. Workshops developed

Figure 5. The ROI process model.

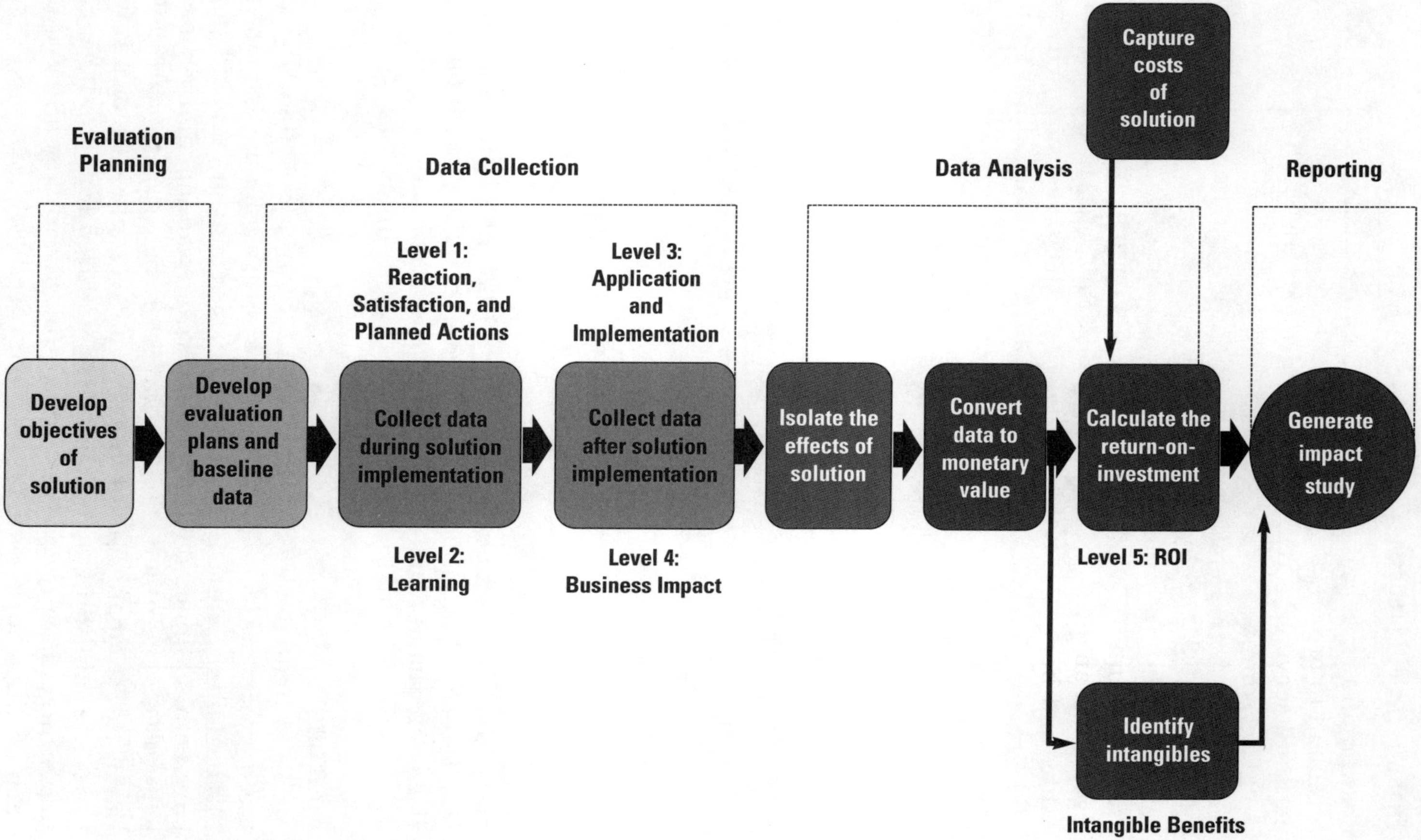

consulting assignments, and all professionals provided input into publication and research. An office staff supported each individual vice president to provide a cohesive team, focusing on accountability products and services.

The company was incorporated as a subchapter S corporation with five board members. The initial board members were Jack Phillips (chairman and CEO), Ron Stone (vice president of consulting), Patti Pulliam Phillips (vice president of marketing, planning, and operations), Ann Akins (vice president of finance, administration, and legal), and an external board member, Frank Ashby from New York. Ashby had been a longtime colleague, client, and supporter of the ROI process. The structure evolved to include a technology leader and an individual to develop alliances. Several individuals changed roles. In the end, Stone and Pulliam Phillips were the key executives working with Phillips.

Attracting and Retaining Clients

Part of the early PRO philosophy was to provide complete customer satisfaction. Most of the proposals developed by PRO contained this statement: If you're not completely satisfied with the products and services delivered by PRO, there is no charge.

In its entire history, PRO never had to cancel an invoice or render services pro bono. In only two cases, a refund was given to workshop participants, when one of the facilitators did not meet expectations. That is a remarkable track record for an organization that trained more than 5,000 individuals in its workshops in a seven-year period while its principal business was consulting.

Figure 6. Organizational structure in the late 1990s.

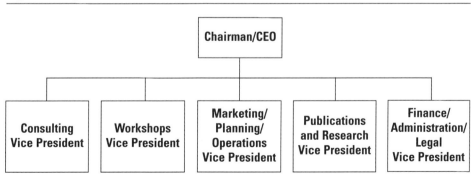

The commitment to client satisfaction translated into customer loyalty. PRO's original client, Eskom, is still a client, with services rendered as recently as 2001. PRO's second and third customers are still clients today, as are most of the original clients. Typically, an organization will engage PRO's services and continue to use PRO to provide additional training, assistance with implementation, assessment reviews, and follow-ups. In many cases, the principal client in the organizations may leave or the philosophy may change, but most of them will return for additional services and support.

An important ingredient for attracting and keeping customers was PRO's philosophy of abundance mentality. PRO consultants distributed material freely, gave away publications, and sometimes diskettes of a workshop session. Participants involved in certification were allowed to use all the materials within their organization, and were provided diskettes to help with the internal training and briefings. Tools, case studies, and templates were provided to participants to help them with application—all of this without an additional charge. The philosophy of the approach was to remove barriers and assist with implementation, and not let continuous, repeat charges stand in the way of an organization's use of the material.

An important client development issue was the philosophy of staying in touch, but not interfering with the client's progress. The approach taken was to inform the client that the PRO staff was available for assistance, along with the best way to contact them. Scheduled follow-up calls to the customer were not part of the plan. The desire to leave clients alone and allow them to make their own decisions overshadowed plans to provide routine follow-up phone calls. Some will argue that PRO's approach was extreme.

PRO's marketing approach was also helpful with new client development. The strategy involved consultants speaking at conferences, writing articles for publication, and responding to requests. Essentially, the market developed in response to customer requests. The number and variety of foreign countries visited depended on interest in that country. The plan was to develop the market based on "who called" and "who wants to pursue the partnership" in that area. That was not always the best way to expand, as the firm lost control over where it should be in a particular market, area, country, or type of organization. The advantage was that it was a low-cost approach, which was important with a limited marketing budget.

PRO's brand recognition was helpful in attracting clients. Seven terms used by PRO were trademarked and displayed on materials, with the ROI process being the most prominent one. The trademarks helped validate the success of the process, provided name recognition for potential clients, and protected some of the intellectual property.

A final strategy for customer retention was to obtain high profile clients. Success breeds success. As one major client began using the process, several others would follow. In the package delivery industry, for example, DHL Worldwide Express (a Belgium-based company) became interested in ROI when FedEx and UPS began using the process. Figure 7 shows a sample of the private sector clients using the process in 1999.

Certification

To further build client loyalty and attract new clients, certification for the ROI process was introduced publicly in 1995. The process involved prework and preparation prior to attending a one-week workshop. The comprehensive workshop was designed to build 10 essential skills needed to apply and implement the ROI process. Those skills are listed in figure 8. The workshop was followed by implementing individual projects and a project review.

During the workshop, the participants plan a project for ROI evaluation, develop the data collection and ROI analysis plan for the project, and present it to the team for feedback. In addition, they develop and present a plan to show how they will help implement the ROI process in their organization, addressing the issues under their control. The typical participant was charged with the responsibility of implementing ROI in his or her division or organization. Sometimes, participants were part of a team and the entire team attended.

The public version of certification followed two successful internal projects (both outside the United States) aimed at the same objective. The public version was offered in 1995 when it became apparent that many organizations wanted to send one or two individuals to this type of session—to develop the skills to lead the implementation of ROI—but did not have the resources to send the entire team.

The concept of certification was simple. Teach the participants all we know about the ROI process and its implementation in a one-week workshop. Initially, this concept met with some resistance from the PRO staff. There was a fear that the consulting process might disappear if we equipped participants with the skills necessary to implement ROI. Our fears proved to be unfounded when we realized that, as more people became involved in certification, they demanded more services from PRO. Thus, the consulting business grew.

Figure 7. A sample of private sector clients.

(Excludes consulting firms, nonprofit organizations, universities, and government organizations)

- Air Canada
- Accenture
- Alaska Petroleum Contractors, Inc.
- Allstate Insurance Company
- Amazon.Com
- Amoco
- AmSouth Bank
- Apple Computer
- Asia Pacific Breweries
- AT&T
- Bank of America
- Bank of Central Asia
- Banner Health Care
- Baptist Health Systems
- BE&K
- Bell Atlantic
- Blue Cross & Blue Shield of Maryland
- Boeing
- Bristol-Myers Squibb
- Caltex—Pacific
- Canadian Imperial Bank of Commerce
- Canadian Tire
- Chevron
- CN Rail (Canada)
- Commonwealth Edison
- Compaq
- Delta Airlines
- DHL Worldwide Express
- Deloitte & Touche
- Duke Energy
- Entergy Corporation
- Eskom (South Africa)
- Federal Express
- First American Bank
- First Union National Bank
- Ford Motor Company
- Glaxo Wellcome, Inc.
- Guthrie Healthcare Systems
- Harley Davidson Motor Company
- Hewlett-Packard
- Honda of America
- Hong Kong Bank
- IBM
- Intel
- Illinois Power
- Lockheed Martin
- M&M Mars
- Mead
- Microsoft
- Motorola
- Mutual Assurance
- NCR
- National Computer Systems (Singapore)
- Netscape
- Networks
- Nextel
- Nortel
- Novus Services
- Overseas—Chinese Banking Corp
- Pfizer
- PriceWaterhouseCoopers
- Public Bank (Malaysia)
- Raytheon
- Rolls Royce
- Singapore Airlines
- Singapore Technologies
- Sprint
- Standard Bank of South Africa
- Telkom Indonesia
- Texaco
- Toronto Dominion Bank
- United Parcel Service
- UNOCAL
- VodaPhone
- Volvo of North America
- Waste Management Company
- Whirlpool
- Xerox

Figure 8. Ten skill sets for certification.

Skill Areas for Certification

- Planning for ROI calculations
- Collecting evaluation data
- Isolating the effects of training
- Converting data to monetary values
- Monitoring program costs
- Analyzing data including calculating the ROI
- Presenting evaluation data
- Implementing the ROI process
- Providing internal consulting on ROI
- Teaching others the ROI process

To date, almost 1,000 individuals have attended a certification workshop, representing 35 countries. The certification has been conducted on several continents and still enjoys internal and public success.

ROI Network

In 1996, the ROI network was created to exchange information among the graduates of the certification workshop. The certification workshop is an intensive, focused, weeklong activity where participants immerse themselves in the ROI process. During this process, the participants bond and freely exchange information with each other. The ROI network is an attempt to meet the need to exchange information across the different groups of graduates from the certification.

The professional organization was created with a board of directors and office support, and continues to this day. The ROI network claims about 400 members. The network operates through a variety of committees and communicates with members through newsletters, a Website, a listserv, and annual meetings.

The ROI network represented an opportunity to build a community of practice around the ROI process. It was a subtle marketing tool that promoted the ROI process, branding the name, and stimulating the application of the process internally. The members of the network, the officers in particular, served as ambassadors of PRO and supporters of the ROI process. For the first five years of its existence, the ROI network was supported by PRO, but eventually was given the opportunity to be completely independent and operate as a professional society.

Publications

From the launch of PRO, publications were perceived as an integral part of the firm. The cycle of activity, depicted in figure 1, continued to be the focus as more publications were produced in subsequent years. Two important series of publications were developed during this time. In 1994, the American Society for Training & Development (ASTD) published the first casebook, *Measuring Return On Investment*. This unique publication contained actual case studies of how organizations developed ROI. Because of the interest in ROI and this type of publication, a series was launched from this book and became known as the *In Action* Series published by ASTD. The books captured human resource development in action and covered a variety of topics important to human resource development today. This series continues to grow with the number of titles published reaching 30.

The series was important to PRO because eight casebooks focused directly on the processes used at PRO. Three volumes of *Measuring Return On Investment* were developed, along with two casebooks on front-end analysis offered by PRO (*Conducting Needs Assessment* and *Performance Analysis and Consulting*). Another was developed to focus on two levels of evaluation (*Measuring Learning and Performance*). Still another casebook focused on implementing the ROI process (*Implementing Evaluation Systems and Processes*). A final casebook focused on government and education applications (*Measuring Return on Investment in the Public Sector*).

The casebook series allowed many of PRO's clients to publish their success stories—enhancing their credibility and success—while at the same time presenting best practice approaches for the processes offered by PRO. This has been ASTD's most ambitious project. The series has developed into an excellent publishing venture and became very successful, based on sales alone. In 2001, four casebooks were among the top 10 best-sellers with two enjoying the number one and number two slots (*Measuring Return on Investment*, volume 2 and volume 1, respectively).

In addition to case studies, others books were developed on the ROI process (*Return on Investment in Training and Performance Improvement Programs*), measurement and evaluation (*Handbook of Training Evaluation and Measurement Methods*), accountability (*Accountability in Human Resource Management*), and developing scorecards (*The Consultants Scorecard* and *The Human Resources Scorecard*). Most of these were published by Gulf Publishing, which has been acquired by Butterworth-Heinemann. These books became the textbooks for workshops and calling cards for consultants delivering consulting services. Jack Phillips became editor of a successful, new series, *Improving Human Performance*, which brings accountability to human performance in organizations.

Collectively, these comprehensive books explain and illustrate the processes offered by PRO. More than anything else, the books developed in these two series, along with other books from McGraw-Hill, Jossey-Bass, and Crisp Publications, enhance PRO's reputation and provide recognition for ROI and measurement and evaluation.

Managing the Business

Managing the operations and business aspects of PRO was a challenge. Phillips did not have the time nor did he want to take the time to manage a business. However, in the early stages of operation he was forced to take the time because he could not afford the luxury of an office manager. As the practice developed, an office manager, vice president for operations, and chief financial officer were eventually appointed. It became apparent that more attention was needed for controlling costs, accounting for sales, and developing the appropriate financial and operating statements. The decision to recruit a chief financial officer was a tough one—but necessary to manage the financial operations. This individual made a tremendous difference, ensuring that the company was operating profitably and efficiently.

All the funding for PRO came directly from the owner's capital. Stock was not sold, although it was distributed to board members. That approach created some restrictions on expanding, as growth was funded by revenue rather than venture capital. Phillips made a conscious decision not to pursue venture capital for fear that the direction and control of the company might be lost. In 1996, a goal was established to take the firm public or sell it to another firm in five years.

The Acquisition of PRO

With the increasing name recognition and expanding use of the ROI process, several larger consulting firms began to take interest in PRO. Strategic alliances were developed with PriceWaterhouse-Coopers in Europe and Deloitte & Touche in the Asia Pacific area. In addition, other firms desiring to expand consulting services expressed an interest. PRO responded to an initial request for potential acquisition and began to entertain the prospect of selling the business, although the timing was earlier than anticipated. Phillips wanted to take advantage of the market possibilities and the name recognition that the company enjoyed. Consequently, he informed the board members and strategic partners about the decision to be considered as an acquisition candidate. This stimulated other offers and, during the summer of 1999, five firms were involved in due diligence with the intention to acquire PRO.

During the same time period, PRO developed an informal alliance with the Franklin Covey Company. Two members of Franklin Covey's Measurement and Evaluation Center attended a two-day workshop and developed a one-day version for their own use, crediting Jack Phillips for some of the material. The reaction with clients was very favorable, and Franklin Covey wanted to enter a formal alliance with PRO. Those discussions led to Franklin Covey's interest in acquisition. Ultimately, an offer was made that was acceptable to both parties. The decision to be acquired by Franklin Covey was based on several important conclusions:

1. The desire to be with a firm with an excellent reputation for its relationships and ethical behavior.
2. To operate as an independent continuing unit to grow and develop the business.
3. To continue employment on a contract basis and help develop the business.

Franklin Covey's offer met the requirements and PRO was acquired on September 1, 1999. Franklin Covey's Center for Research and Assessment was folded into PRO's organization and renamed the Jack Phillips Center for Research. Since the acquisition, the Center still thrives as an independent division of Franklin Covey, providing products and services for assessment, measurement, and evaluation for a global community. At the same time, the members of the Center staff assist clients with measuring the success of Franklin Covey programs and help them address specific measurement and evaluation issues. The intent is to build a significant database on the effectiveness of Franklin Covey products and services.

Keys to Success

The keys to success for this business can be summarized in the following eight points:

1. *Developing a global strategy early and staying focused.* The ROI process has been implemented in 33 countries.
2. *Following a carefully documented business plan.* From the launch until the business was sold, updates and reviews of the business plan helped PRO stay on track.

3. *Integrating research, publications, and workshops into the consulting business.* These processes complemented each other and provided excellent marketing, image building, and branding for the firm.

4. *Relentlessly pursuing promotion through conferences and workshops.* All key staff members were required to conduct workshops and encouraged to make presentations at conferences as often as possible.

5. *Having a niche product that no one had exploited.* Although many individuals had experience in evaluation, no individual or firm had developed a feasible, sound ROI process. Also, no firm offered a complete range of assessment, measurement, and evaluation services, including workshops, consulting, and publications.

6. *Offering total client satisfaction.* PRO's commitment to provide excellent client satisfaction helped to build both important and lasting relationships with key clients.

7. *Developing the certification process.* Ultimately, certification workshops provided a way to transfer the process to organizations with minimal barriers.

8. *Creating the ROI network.* Essentially, the network served as a marketing tool and a source for case studies, associates, and speakers.

Lessons Learned

With any success there are always ways to improve. The following lessons were learned through the development of PRO:

1. *Place more emphasis on publishing by PRO's partners and key consultants.* Although publishing was encouraged, it should have been a requirement for those joining the business early in its development. Later, this became an issue, as more firms wanted to consult only with the person who had his or her name on the books. Sometimes it was difficult to hand off clients to those who were not identified as an author and might be perceived as "not as knowledgeable" as the author of a book.

2. *Pay more attention to the financial aspects and operational issues.* This is probably true for any entrepreneur. The person who creates the niche opportunity and drives the process for clients is not always the best person to run the business. Trying to manage the office took precious time away from client development, publications, and strategic issues.

3. *Put more emphasis on software development.* A failure to develop the appropriate technology early was a problem. Several aborted attempts to develop appropriate software to support the process were made

but, for a variety of reasons, were unsuccessful. Primarily, the company did not want to allocate the necessary capital to develop the comprehensive software. This proved to be a barrier to significant growth after the acquisition.

4. *Develop a cohesive team.* To deliver products and services, a highly focused team was needed. Most of the attention was focused on providing excellent customer care and not enough attention was paid to developing the appropriate infrastructure and support necessary for a growing consulting business.

5. *Make appropriate use of independent contractors.* The use of associates (independent contractors) proved to be troublesome. At times, more control was needed to provide consistent, quality services. In some situations, associates ignored their noncompete agreements and created a competing practice.

Questions for Discussion

1. Critique PRO's strategy and suggest changes, if appropriate.
2. Evaluate PRO's approach to client development. Offer other solutions or suggestions.
3. Examine the potential weaknesses of PRO as a consulting firm and suggest how they could have been overcome.
4. Could this practice be replicated? Explain.
5. Describe the process of taking PRO public. Discuss the various issues, concerns, and ramifications.
6. Examine the consequences of selling the business and remaining employed.

The Authors

Patricia Pulliam Phillips is chairman and CEO of The Chelsea Group, an international consulting company focused on implementing the ROI process. She has provided consulting services and support for the ROI process for several years and has served as author and co-author on the topic in several publications.

Jack J. Phillips is with the Jack Phillips Center for Research, a division of the Franklin Covey Company. Phillips developed and pioneered the use of the ROI process and has provided consulting services to some of the world's largest organizations. He has written more than 12 books on the subject. The Phillipses can be reached at SeriesEditor@aol.com or TheChelseaGroup@aol.com.

The View from Redwood Mountain

Redwood Mountain Consulting

Jeanne Farrington and Jim Fuller

Redwood Mountain Consulting (RMC) is a performance improvement consulting firm. Founded in 1997, RMC is a generalist practice that employs expert consultants who assist clients in improving their business results. Major decisions in developing RMC included keeping the firm small, aiming for strategic projects, and developing an integrated approach to life and work. This case illustrates that developing even a small firm requires attention not only to meeting a client's needs, but also to meeting the needs of the business itself.

The Practice

Redwood Mountain Consulting (RMC) is a small consulting firm in San Jose, California, that offers training, organization development, and performance improvement services. Its clients range from small to large organizations, many of them high-technology companies—which is not surprising, given RMC's location in Silicon Valley. In addition to the high-technology sector, RMC works with clients in government, academia, and other business sectors across the nation. Their consultants' expertise is in human performance technology (performance improvement) and instructional design. RMC takes a results-oriented, systems approach to making improvements in an organization. Its purpose is always to help people—a company's executives, managers, and employees—to achieve their goals.

This case was prepared to serve as a basis for discussion rather than to illustrate either effective or ineffective administrative and management practices.

When there is something keeping people from doing their best work—
a lack of knowledge, skills, motivation, tools, structure, or processes—
RMC's consultants identify what the barriers are to their achievement
and then create solutions to remove those barriers. Their products and
services include specific individual projects to answer specific customer
requests, ongoing consulting or coaching services, and workshops to
teach others various aspects of the training and performance improvement
field. See table 1 for an illustration of the range of RMC products and
services.

A Brief History

About a year before incorporating RMC and leaving corporate life
to work on their own, Jeanne Farrington and Jim Fuller were both working in senior positions in corporate education at Hewlett-Packard (HP).

Table 1. RMC products and services.

Service Area	Example Projects	Typical Results
Strategies and Methodologies	• Corporate University Design • E-Learning Strategy • Knowledge Transfer or Knowledge Management Strategy	Blueprint for action, development of a business plan, strategy, or methodology so that the client can proceed on a new course of action
	• Evaluation Protocols	Proof of concept projects
Assessments	• Performance Needs Assessment • Training Needs Assessment/Analysis • Small Business Triage	Recommend solutions to bridge gaps and eliminate barriers between what is currently happening and desired results
Development Projects	• Performance Improvement • Organization Design and Development • Training Development • Coaching Protocols • Meetings and Conferences	A completed project with business or learning goals attained; for example, increased sales, a well-implemented change, a successful merger, an improved process, or increased knowledge and skills
Coaching	• Executive Coaching • Individual Performance Improvement • Business Consulting	Defined goals, more effective and efficient approach to their accomplishment
Workshops	• Performance Improvement • Human Capital Management • Managing for Performance	Participants improve their knowledge and skills in these areas

Fuller was the director of learning and performance engineering, where he was responsible for creating HP's performance consulting group and implementing the company's first performance technology projects. Farrington was responsible for the development of HP's worldwide education community. The education community included about 1,500 employees who were primarily responsible for internal or external training, performance consulting, change management, or related performance improvement activities. Fuller had been working at HP for 18 years in a number of functions, including engineering, sales, product marketing, project management, training, and performance technology. While Fuller's career was more varied by function and roles within a company, Farrington's work history was more varied in terms of working for different companies. She had been an executive for a well-established consulting company, and she held management positions in training at Sun Microsystems and Silicon Graphics before coming to HP.

Having worked within large, established organizations, Fuller and Farrington wanted the freedom to work on their own. After years of managing groups and hiring contractors, they wanted to spend more time putting their own skills to work helping clients meet their goals. They were looking forward to challenging opportunities and to making a broader contribution working with different organizations, clients, and projects. And as independent professionals, they could share their expertise more generally with others in their field.

In 1997 Farrington and Fuller launched Redwood Mountain Consulting. News of the company spread fast, and clients began requesting assistance from the first day of operations. Within a few weeks there was a challenging amount of work.

Since then, they have continued to work on a variety of projects, including needs assessments, performance improvement, training, learning methodologies, assessment strategies, organization development, executive coaching, and workshops. RMC has met its revenue goals each year, allowing the company to invest effort in volunteer activities that contribute to the field through professional organizations. RMC's founders take time for volunteer work that contributes to society using the skills they have acquired in business.

Market Niche

At the beginning of the practice, and occasionally after that, people asked whether the company has a specialty. Many consulting firms specialize in specific areas, such as needs assessment, meeting facilitation, or instructional design. Specialization can help a consulting firm to build customer awareness and to increase its business in that area. However, too narrow a focus can decrease opportunities to find work: If a company can't find anyone who needs its change management process or its Web-based design skills right now, the overly specialized firm may go wanting for work.

RMC decided not to limit its consulting beyond the general categories of training and performance improvement. As a result, the types of clients have ranged from individuals to *Fortune* 20 companies. The clients have included high-tech, consumer goods, insurance, academic organizations, and government agencies; and they have ranged in age from brand-new startups to companies more than 100 years old. The diversity of projects has spanned a wide range as well, within the categories previously listed, giving RMC consultants an ever-broader perspective and a growing ability to help new clients achieve their goals.

Success as a Consulting Practice

Although Farrington and Fuller knew from the beginning that most new businesses fail, they were determined to make RMC work. Success is measured at RMC according to three basic criteria: the customers, the money, and the lifestyle.

1. The customers must achieve their goals, RMC must receive high marks from customers, and the firm must generate repeat business as well as referrals.
2. RMC must meet or exceed revenue goals, which includes a careful watch on the ratio between expenses and salaries.
3. RMC's consultants, although they often work intensely for long hours and for days on end, must have a sense of personal satisfaction in their work and a corresponding sense of freedom to pursue personal goals.

So far, the track record on all three criteria has exceeded original expectations.

Making the Transition

Why decide to start a consulting firm? Taking careful note of the known difficulties in starting a new business, there were still four compelling factors that influenced the decision to start RMC:
1. ability to work together and with experts in the field
2. opportunity to use and continue developing expertise
3. opportunity to make a substantial contribution to the field as well as to client success

4. ability to create a different lifestyle from the typical *Fortune* 500 experience.

The decision to make the move was made easier because the founders possessed a combination of seven important qualifications:

1. Both Farrington and Fuller were widely known within the performance improvement profession and across multiple organizations where there were potential clients.

2. Both founders possessed extensive experience implementing performance improvement while working inside organizations, which many other consultants do not have.

3. Fuller had extensive management experience in a number of functions outside the performance improvement field, which would lend credibility with clients.

4. Farrington possessed extensive experience working in all aspects of small businesses.

5. Both founders had advanced academic credentials that enhanced their practical experience.

6. They both had noticed a general shortage of experienced and successful performance improvement professionals.

7. The economy was fairly robust at the time of the company's startup.

Skills and Knowledge

RMC was built by employing broad expertise in consulting, training, and performance improvement. Each of those three areas is composed of many interrelated skills, such as contracting, analysis, design, project management, presentation, facilitation, interpersonal skills, writing, negotiation, and keeping one's composure when confronted by the occasionally difficult customer experience. RMC's consultants have advanced degrees in relevant fields as well as many years of practical experience that can only be gained working inside other companies. In addition to the technical skills required to complete the consulting work, it was also essential to have knowledge, skills, and experience building and running small businesses. Technical skills of consulting and performance improvement are necessary but not sufficient to construct and maintain a successful consulting business.

The Transition Itself

RMC wasn't built or even started overnight. The idea of going into business changed from being an idle thought to something that seemed worth serious consideration. Farrington and Fuller spent time talking through and planning to implement the business, asking and answering multiple questions in more and more detail. They decided on the name, Redwood Mountain Consulting, talked about what products and services to offer, who their first clients would be, estimated necessary and potential revenues and expenses, and made a list of things to do to get started, which included:

1. Define and contact potential customers and advisors.
2. Define products and services.
3. Figure out how to win the business.
4. Decide on the business's structure.
5. Make a list of supporting infrastructure requirements.
6. Start planning for business development.

Before going into business, the founders both wrote extensive vision-mission statements, which were taped to the office wall. After the first week, Fuller put a big Post-it® over his long paragraph of a statement with two words, "Kick Butt," written in big block letters. *Merriam-Webster* (2001) defines the term as "to succeed or win overwhelmingly." This became the unofficial company slogan, repeated with smiles to each other as they dug into a pile of work or headed off to meet with clients. It really means, "Win the business. Succeed in meeting customer goals. Make the best impression possible. Do your best."

A home office made the most sense. As external consultants Farrington and Fuller would almost always meet with clients at the clients' office or on the telephone. Setting up a more formal, external office seemed an unnecessary expense and time sink. One advantage to having just one office (not one at home and one at work) is that all reference materials and files reside in the same place. One is never in the office where the book or file is not.

During the first week or so there was a daily trip to an office supply store to buy one more essential bit of office equipment or some other necessary item. New business owners frequently overlook and underestimate the extensive infrastructure a large organization provides.

Making the change from driving 45 minutes or more to work and back each day was not a problem. Determining how to transition from "being at work" to "being at home" took several days. Knowing when to stop working on any particular day, especially when there were so many start-up tasks in addition to client work, was a challenge. At first the partners worked all the time. Five years later many days are still like that.

The shift from a large organization to a small business created a qualitative difference to each day. Without extraneous meetings, email, voice mail, telephone calls, and casual interruptions from co-workers, more time was available for real work. The result was an improved work environment. Focusing, writing, or coming up with a creative idea all seemed infinitely easier.

On the other hand, the social aspect of working in a larger company was gone. So to make sure they made time for friends, the partners set up dinner meetings with their academic colleagues, set aside family time, and started a book club.

Another big difference in working for oneself versus working for someone else is that a person can have an unproductive week or two inside a big corporation and still take home the same paycheck. But when invoicing a client becomes dependent on completing the next milestone or deliverable, "pay for performance" takes on a whole new meaning. Also, if a company's regular employee is late or fails to contribute to a meeting now and then, colleagues tend to forgive the employee unless this behavior becomes habitual. He or she will still be included as the work moves forward. As a consultant, though, one must constantly add value—or there will be no more work with that client. Consultants must prove themselves repeatedly—with every new client and even with each new project.

Table 2 lists some generalized differences between working for others and working independently. All in all, the transition for RMC's principals went fairly smoothly. In most work situations, there are concerns and advantages. Working internally and becoming an independent consultant both have positive, beneficial aspects and also those things that keep one up at night.

Strategy

Redwood Mountain Consulting's overall strategy for the business is straightforward: to offer clients access to highly successful, educated, and experienced performance improvement professionals on an as-needed basis. When implementing major performance improvement projects, most organizations want assistance from experts with significant capability and a demonstrated track record for results. Organizations may not have such resources on staff, and many of the bigger consulting firms employ large numbers of inexperienced consultants who are still learning the profession. RMC is distinctive because its clients always receive the services of experts in the field, most likely Fuller or Farrington.

Table 2. Factors in transition.

	Working for Others	Working Independently
Customer Satisfaction	• Often, one's manager becomes the primary client; focus on internal or external clients is frequently secondary	• Clients and potential clients are unquestionably the main focus all the time
The Work Itself	• As assigned or negotiated with one's manager, usually bounded by role, job function, and department charter	• Depends on customer desires as well as consultant's ability and preferences, probably has more variety and a broader scope
Money	• Usually a set salary, perhaps a bonus or profit sharing	• Directly tied to personal decisions and ability of the firm to generate revenue—can be "feast or famine"
Benefits	• Usually a menu of different benefit choices available • Costs are frequently borne by the company or require small cost sharing	• Can be difficult for small consulting firms to secure benefits, such as medical coverage, at reasonable costs or without expending a great deal of time setting them up
Reputation and Recognition	• Important for the individual within a narrower scope, perhaps as small as one's department or company • Somewhat based on one's department or company reputation	• Essential to develop—both for the individual and for the firm itself • Networking, visibility, and positioning become keys to success
Social Aspects	• Often complex, sometimes distracting friendships and other relationships form with co-workers	• Fewer people in the work environment, perhaps more work done individually rather than in teams
Infrastructure	• Easy to take for granted, often robust and complex, even though there is often room for improvement	• Must be created and maintained by the small firm at significant financial and time costs
Training and Development	• Often provided or funded by the company within parameters set by company goals	• Funded by the new company's revenues, approval fairly automatic, time to invest is scarce
Internal Company Politics	• Can easily be a quagmire, slowing down one's ability to make decisions and get things done	• Simple to apparently nonexistent

Table 2. Factors in transition (continued).

	Working for Others	Working Independently
Internal Company Bureaucracy	• May be counter-productive or even stifling	• Almost nonexistent
Client Company Bureaucracy	• Not a concern	• Can be a daunting experience to navigate through purchasing and finance department processes
Work-Life Balance	• Dependent on company culture, management practices, current projects, and individual boundaries	• Can be more difficult to attain, in the sense of working long hours, but work and life can seem more integrated, easier to take time off if determined to do so

Initial clients sought to offload performance improvement projects to RMC because they lacked either the internal resources or capability to implement those projects themselves. Over time, clients became interested in developing their own internal performance improvement resources, and they turned to RMC for assistance. The strategy and services of RMC expanded to meet these requests. In addition to implementing performance improvement projects, RMC offered workshops to develop performance consultants and worked alongside the new consultants as mentors and coaches. A new service product called Consulting on Demand™ was introduced, providing internal performance consultants at client organizations with easy access to an experienced and successful mentor at RMC.

Redwood Mountain Consulting's business strategy continues to develop with the needs and business directions of its clients. Each discussion with clients is an opportunity to explore and discover emerging needs that RMC can meet through new or expanded services.

Structure of the Practice

One of the early questions was how to organize or structure the company. Initially, one may view this as a simple task with a two-person consulting firm, but there are actually many roles that need to be filled in a small business, regardless of the number of employees.

As an organizing model, RMC adopted concepts presented by Michael Gerber (1995). The "E Myth," he says, is that entrepreneurs start small businesses. But in reality, most small businesses are started by individuals who are experts in the technical aspects of their job, such as consulting. To have a successful small business, the roles of entrepreneur (build the business, seek new customers) and manager (set business controls, watch the finances, and manage the infrastructure) are required. To ensure the success of RMC, all the necessary roles were identified and then divided between Farrington and Fuller, based on interest and expertise.

It did not take long for business volume to grow, and the founders needed to maximize the time available for providing consulting services. They hired a part-time assistant to deal with administrative and logistical tasks, increasing the overall consulting time available for Farrington and Fuller.

Although occasionally thinking about becoming a larger company, RMC continues the strategy of not adding additional consultants. During large or complex projects, trusted associates are brought in to participate because a project needs more resources or additional expertise. RMC has developed an extensive network of associates who are experts in various performance improvement specialties. This approach allows RMC to offer its clients access to significant thought leaders and practitioners in the field.

Attracting and Keeping Clients

A small consulting business must always be mindful about finding new clients, new projects, more work. Although it requires consistent effort, the process of attracting clients has not been difficult for Redwood Mountain Consulting. Existing clients frequently recommend RMC to other organizations that have performance improvement needs. Both Farrington and Fuller are fairly visible in the performance improvement field based on their networking, speaking, and writing efforts.

RMC uses technology to provide information to existing and potential clients. In addition to a detailed Website, they also publish an electronic newsletter called *HPT Notes*. This newsletter covers recent developments in the performance improvement field as well as summarizes some of the latest research on performance issues.

Writing not only increases visibility, but it also establishes credibility in the minds of potential clients. The partners co-authored *From Training to Performance Improvement: Navigating the Transition* (Fuller & Farrington, 1999). Fuller wrote a chapter for *The Handbook of Human Performance Technology* edited by Stolovitch and Keeps (Fuller, 1999), which is considered *the* reference book for the field. Farrington writes articles for professional journals, and they both write chapters for their own and others' books. Currently, RMC is developing a series of white papers on emerging performance improvement topics. There is always a writing project in the works at RMC.

Speaking has been another successful awareness-building method. Both Farrington and Fuller have been frequent speakers at major training and performance improvement conferences and events. By focusing on important topics and bringing solid research and practical experience to the presentations, their sessions are usually crowded. One speaking engagement often generates requests for another, or an encore, which perpetuates the process from one presentation to the next. And for RMC's business, the presentations frequently result in new referrals and clients.

To increase the likelihood of repeat business, or client loyalty, RMC works on two fronts: 1) exceeding customer expectations and 2) developing good relations with its clients. In reality, RMC's consultants care about its clients as people, and it shows. Maintaining a professional relationship does not have to be a series of stiff or overly formal encounters. Relationships that work are built by creating trust, helping others, and fostering friendship.

Trust is developed by keeping commitments, delivering on time, exceeding quality expectations, telling the truth, and maintaining confidentiality within and between different clients. A consultant can also enhance a sense of mutual confidence by demonstrating trust in the client.

When developing relations with friends, clients, and partners, it is essential to continually act on opportunities to help, even if a particular action does not specifically result in new business or income. For example, being well networked in the performance improvement field provides RMC with the opportunity to connect clients with candidates for job positions and to connect professionals with new employment opportunities. Making a few phone calls or sending someone a promising resume can assist an organization to find much-needed talent or make a big difference in someone's life.

And being friendly with clients can result in actions like the following examples: keeping in touch without an agenda, just to see how things are going; meeting for lunch to share experiences, ideas, and companionship; or showing up at a client's site with a soothing tea to ease a cold-like flu. Why? Of course it is good business to keep in touch and to care about one's clients. But it is also great for the consultant personally to work with clients he or she cares about as people. Relationships are two-way streets. Loyalty to a client tends to engender loyalty to the consultant in return.

Measuring Success

Determining whether RMC is successful includes looking at success for individual consulting projects and also at the success of the business itself. RMC's consulting methodology automatically builds in project success measures. The measures may be more or less explicit, depending on the type of project and customer preference. At the beginning of an engagement, RMC consultants focus on the question, "What are the clients trying to achieve? What results will indicate success for this project?" Defining the answers to those questions at the beginning assists in determining whether the project was a success at the end.

Measuring RMC's success as a company means looking at its own business results, which include the following: client satisfaction, company finances, growth in company experience, and internal satisfaction. Table 3 outlines these measures.

Keys to Success

There are three major factors contributing to the success of Redwood Mountain Consulting: 1) a range of professional expertise, 2) experience with a broad range of clients and companies, and 3) attention to the business itself. Professional expertise includes practical and research-based knowledge and skills to tackle a variety of projects, consulting and interpersonal skills, and knowledge of how businesses work. Having a broad range of experiences to draw from not only assists the consultant in completing a project, it also inspires client confidence. Potential clients often look for consultants with relevant past experiences: similar business sectors, size and stage of development of the company, work with similar client groups, or matching project content or methodology. And beyond knowledge and experience in one's field, consultants must invest effort in the nuts and bolts of developing their own business: customer care, sales and marketing, watchful accounting, process development, infrastructure management, and employee development and satisfaction.

Lessons Learned

Naturally, the volume of work in a small consulting firm increases and decreases in cycles throughout a year. When exceptionally busy,

Table 3. Measuring success of the business.

Category	What to Measure	Measurements
Client Satisfaction	• Repeat business and referrals by current and previous clients	• Average number of projects per client, percentage of clients with multiple projects • Ease of obtaining references, feedback on the strength and content of those references • Number of instances that a new client was referred by a former or existing client
Revenue	• Meeting revenue goals profitably	• Actual revenue versus revenue goals set according to expected salaries, expenses, and profits
Client Base	• New clients, new types of industries or projects	• Number of new clients per year • Note new industries, new types of projects
Working Smarter	• Improved infrastructure for efficiencies and effectiveness	• Periodic review of internal tools, processes, equipment, and the environment • Continuous improvement of effectiveness with reduced costs and time requirements
Internal Satisfaction	• Interesting and rewarding work • Employee and partner motivation	• Opinions of founders, consultants, staff, and partners

it is easy to let marketing fall off the list of things to do. However, clients sometimes change their priorities. Occasionally they cancel projects. During one exceptionally busy time, RMC's consultants were concerned about an increased workload. Four new projects were scheduled to start during the next month. But at the last minute, all four clients cancelled their projects. The clients were from four separate companies, and they each had their own internal reasons. This was an unusual coincidence, but it illustrates the point. Make marketing a habit; find ways to do it consistently, even when it seems like there is more than enough work.

Another important lesson has to do with how to react when a client doesn't take good advice. There are times when a consultant can see a disaster in the making. "If they do this, or they don't do that, bad things will happen." The consultant may know for sure what action must be taken and apply reasonable powers of explanation and persuasion. Even so, sometimes the clients don't take the advice. It is possible to lose sleep over such situations, but that is not helpful. A year after advising against some unnecessary floundering in a start-up company, RMC received a call from the now ex-CEO. Chagrined, he outlined a list of RMC's suggestions that he now wished he had heeded. And he asked for help in his new venture, promising to take more of RMC's advice this time. Losing sleep does not help. Sometimes clients have to learn the hard way, as much as you want to make things easier for them.

Of course, there are lessons to be learned every day. "I should have asked this. I should have known that. When he said that, he really meant . . . . I should have seen that coming." Gerber (1995) suggests developing strategies to capture lessons learned in all aspects of the business, such as job aids and desk descriptions—a cookbook for the business. For example, RMC hired someone once who did not need an income. She was excited to work with RMC's consultants, but the company and the work was more of an adventure or hobby to her. She came in late, left early, and took long lunches. RMC updated its list of "Useful Questions to Ask in Interviews."

In another example, Farrington was halfway through writing a fairly complicated proposal when she discovered that a total of 20 consultants had been invited to submit proposals for the same project. If she had known that, she would have thought longer before participating in that proposal process. RMC updated its list of "Things to Ask Before Responding to an RFP." Documenting lessons learned along the way is a great way of developing the business.

Questions for Discussion

1. If you are thinking about starting your own consulting firm, are you clear about your motivations for doing so? What are they?

2. What are the capabilities that you would bring to the crowded consulting market that would make you unique? What is your value proposition?

3. What are the barriers that might prevent you from starting your own firm? What can you do to overcome or minimize each one?

4. Have you developed a network of colleagues who could assist with large or complex projects? Is it adequate? What can you do to round out your network of resources?

5. Starting a new venture has significant impact (positive and negative) on your personal lifestyle and work-life balance. Be completely honest and list all the positives and negatives you can anticipate. What does the list tell you about your decision or plans?

6. How will you fill all the roles necessary to sustain a business? Who will act as the entrepreneur, the manager, and the technician? If it is you, how will you accomplish this? Do you have the capability and capacity to do so?

7. In addition to talking to people who have been successful building new consulting firms, have you talked to any people who have failed? Why not? Go learn from their experience as well.

The Authors

Jeanne Farrington is president of RMC. She has many years of experience creating performance improvement initiatives, developing training programs, and providing business consulting. She has created a wide variety of programs, methodologies, and strategies for many different organizations. She also teaches instructional design and performance consulting. Farrington has an M.A. in instructional technology from San Jose State and an Ed.D. in educational psychology and technology from the University of Southern California (USC). She is an adjunct professor at USC. She can be reached at Redwood Mountain Consulting, 1657 Fairorchard Avenue, San Jose, CA 95125; phone: 408.448.6704; email: jeanne@redwoodmtn.com.

Jim Fuller is Redwood Mountain Consulting's principal consultant. He is a recognized expert in assisting organizations to create performance consulting strategies and conducting projects to improve human performance. Previously, Fuller was the director of learning and performance engineering at Hewlett-Packard, where he created HP's first performance consulting group. He led the development of performance technology practices and developed HP's performance improvement consultants. Fuller holds an M.S. in instructional and performance technology from Boise State University. He is currently an Ed.D. candidate in performance technology at the University of Southern California.

References

Fuller, James. (1999). "From Training to Performance." In *Handbook of Human Performance Technology: Improving Individual and Organizational Performance Worldwide,* edited by Harold D. Stolovitch and Erica J. Keeps. San Francisco: Jossey-Bass/Pfeiffer, pp. 281-297.

Fuller, Jim, and Jeanne Farrington. (1999). *From Training to Performance Improvement: Navigating the Transition.* San Francisco: Jossey-Bass.

Gerber, Michael E. (1995). *The E-Myth: Why Most Small Businesses Don't Work and What to Do about It.* New York: Harper-Collins.

Merriam-Webster's Collegiate Dictionary, http://www.merriam-webster.com /cgi-bin/dictionary., s.v. "kick butt."

Managing the Transition from Academics to a Full-Time Consulting Practice

Hallowell & Associates

Kirk Hallowell

Hallowell & Associates is an independent consulting firm providing corporations with leadership development and evaluation services. This case documents the successful transition from an academic career to this full-time consulting practice. The case highlights the challenges and strategies used to navigate this transition including financial planning, migrating from an academic to business mindset, and building strategic relationships as the basis of a solid practice. The case also includes the description of a virtual business model based on collaborative relationships with other consultants and consulting organizations.

Background

It is not unusual for university faculty to move from full-time academic positions to full-time consultants. As academics develop theories and concepts that grow in application, some of these individuals shift their primary affiliations from university settings to private, external consulting organizations. In these cases, an external consulting practice has often afforded the flexibility, scalability, and entrepreneurial opportunities not accommodated by academic institutions.

A transition from academic to external consulting is not without its challenges. Academic environments offer a great deal of stability and an array of resources to support the development of theory and applications. An academic in a university setting may enjoy years of logistical support, grant monies, strategic relationships, and a steady

This case was prepared to serve as a basis for discussion rather than to illustrate either effective or ineffective administrative and management practices.

income while developing intellectual capital. Support structures such as sabbaticals and differentiated course loads allow academics the time to focus on their research and writing.

In contrast, a private, independent consulting practice may offer little support for research and writing and no regular source of income while the practice is being developed. Demands for products, services, and results can quickly assume immediate priority over conceptual development. The result is that the independent consultants may spend much of their time and energy re-creating the resources to which they had become accustomed in an academic setting. That dynamic adds considerable challenge in transitioning from the relatively stable academic environment to the unpredictable world of running an enterprise.

Another challenge of transitioning from an academic to a business setting is adapting to the differing mindsets of a business environment. Some of these differences are summarized in table 1.

An academic moving from a university to a business setting will find that values and behaviors revered in an academic setting may have considerably less value in the business world. For example, the goal of academic research is ostensibly to create new truths that can be generalized to a wide variety of settings and populations. The reward structure in an academic environment prizes empirical research driven by scientific methodology over specific applications and case studies. In business, the valued outcome of any activity is the positive impact on business results, preferably with direct financial implications. The academic who wishes to serve business in a consulting capacity should keep these different perspectives in mind and adapt accordingly.

This case describes one successful transition of an individual from a full-time academic appointment to the leadership of a successful,

Table 1. Academic versus business perspectives.

	Academic Perspectives	Business Perspectives
Outcomes	Truth	Results
Methods and Resources	Scientific	Financial
Focus	General	Specific

independent consulting practice. The case chronicles the transition and how essential support resources were re-created. The chapter also captures key learnings in the transition and includes significant setbacks and challenges encountered along the way.

The Practice

Hallowell & Associates (H&A) is a growing organizational consulting firm serving primarily large organizations and government agencies. The practice is in its fourth year of operation. H&A services are organized by six major disciplines with each discipline including specific services. The development cycle, shown in figure 1, shows these disciplines in their sequential relationship.

The practice begins by joining with clients to identify specific needs in a client's learning and development systems. This process is typically achieved through a structured needs analysis with key stakeholders in the organization. H&A then develops a proposal based on the six disciplines and identifies specific services that are most appropriate to meet these needs. The proposal includes personnel, performance outcomes, and a delivery timeline. If necessary, H&A contracts with other consulting or educational resources to address needs that the firm does not offer.

Figure 1. The development cycle.

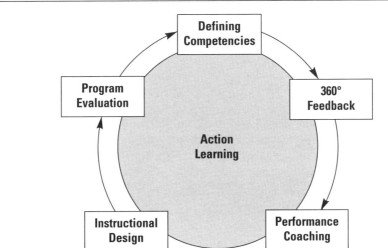

The six disciplines that drive Hallowell & Associates include:

1. *Competency profiling*—determining what skills and knowledge sets are needed for individual and organizational success
2. *360-degree feedback process design*—designing systems to assess competencies and identifying both individual and organizational strengths and opportunities for improvement
3. *Coaching teams and individuals*—working with teams and individuals to build capacity in specific competency areas and to produce meaningful results
4. *Instructional design*—developing performance-based learning interventions to develop individuals and teams
5. *Performance-based evaluation*—determining the impact of learning on business results
6. *Action learning*—creating a comprehensive action-based initiative that balances individual and team learning with sustainable business results. Action learning is the core discipline of the practice in that successful implementation of action learning requires incorporation in each of the other five disciplines.

In addition to providing consulting services related to these six disciplines, H&A offers a suite of train-the-trainer courses related to five of the six disciplines. For example, "Learning for Results" is a two-day course on performance-based evaluation for advanced practitioners. Each of these courses is customized based on a needs assessment and includes case study and application to a client organization. Whenever possible, participants are encouraged to bring active projects to the class as the basis of learning. The result is that participants are able to get real work done in the course of the workshop.

Making the Transition

Perhaps the single, most significant challenge encountered in moving toward a full-time, independent consulting career was managing the transition from an existing career. The process caused the author to reinvent his professional identity and his source of income. The transition demanded a great deal of soul-searching and reflection. In leaving an academic institution, the author gave up stability, recognition by colleagues, and a strong commitment to students. To justify the decision, the potential positives had to thoroughly outweigh the barriers.

Several factors led to the decision to leave a faculty position. As an assistant professor in the counseling department at Northern Illinois University, the author developed a growing interest in organizational dynamics. Teaching courses in group dynamics, psychological assessment, and organizational development led to research and writing interests focused on organizations. At the same time, the author became involved in an external leadership development program through the university. The program provided team-oriented content through an experiential learning process to corporate clients. The program offered experiences in instructional design and interaction with corporate clients while providing an opportunity to put group and organizational theory into practice.

As the author moved through the tenure process, he found great personal satisfaction in applied work with corporate clients. The result was that increasing amounts of time and energy were focused on developing consulting projects than on performing traditional research and writing. Realizing that a long-term faculty appointment would not be consistent with these interests, the author considered the alternative of starting an independent consulting practice. Listed in table 2 is a decision analysis capturing the top three drivers and barriers that the author considered in his decision to leave the university.

Perhaps the most compelling draw for leaving the university was the opportunity for autonomy afforded by an independent practice. Endless committee appointments, faculty meetings, and weight of the academic hierarchy consistently burdened life at the university. The lure of working day to day without a bureaucratic system looming above was most attractive. The associated barrier for leaving the university was the loss of a support structure—the first and foremost of which was a steady income. Along with the regular income were vital benefits such as matching retirement funds and health insurance. In addition, the university provided valued collegial support, an office, and logistical support resources that would be lost in a transition. The loss of each of these benefits needed to be weighed in the decision to leave the university.

Table 2. Drivers and barriers for the transition.

Drivers	Barriers
Need for Autonomy	Loss of Support
Desire to Increase Income	Instability of Income
Valuing of Tangible Results	Travel Demands

The opportunity to increase income also weighed in the decision to leave the university. One of the advantages of transitioning out of a position as an assistant professor is that it is not difficult to exceed the associated level of income. For example, billing for a two-day consulting contract would regularly exceed the entire compensation for a semester-long course taught on overload within the university. Not only did an independent consulting career offer potentially more money, but also there was no arbitrary cap on income as determined by salary increments. Of course, the significant barrier associated with this benefit was the potential for unstable or no income. With a family to support, this was a challenging consideration.

The third driver for making the transition was the need to see more tangible and immediate results based on specific interventions. The author experienced much of his efforts in an academic position as conceptual and indirect. He would usually not see the direct impact or outcome of teaching, research, or service activities. While those activities were eventually tied to positive results, the direct impact was not typically observed. In contrast, consulting offered an opportunity to provide services in such a way as to see, participate in, and measure impact more immediately.

The final barrier to making the transition decision was the anticipation of an extended travel schedule often required by a consulting practice. The author's commitment to family and personal time were challenged by the potential of excessive travel. An academic position offered limited and predictable travel demands. The author made a decision in advance that he would limit travel to no more than six nights a month. In retrospect, this commitment has been kept with few exceptions.

As the transition came to fruition, three supporting factors led to a successful negotiation of these barriers. First, the opportunity to gain six years of consulting experience within the university was invaluable. These experiences provided the track record, references, and self-assurance that were necessary to make the initial plunge. Without this level of experience, the transition would be nearly unthinkable. Second, Harold Hillman, director of Amoco's Management Learning Center, offered the author a half-time position as a research coordinator for the center. That position provided the author with a regular income for a year while building a client base. The author also used this year to establish strategic relationships with other consultants and other consulting organizations that would be the foundation of the practice.

The third supporting factor was the opportunity to continue to teach advanced courses in organizational development for Northern Illinois University's Division of Continuing Education. Preparation of coursework closely paralleled the work done in consulting, and consulting experiences provided real-time case studies to present in class. Teaching provided the opportunity to develop instructional skills while maintaining visibility in the business community. Several important client relationships were formed during this teaching experience. These opportunities combined to make the first year of transition very successful.

Strategy

The key to the success for H&A is captured in the organization's mission statement: Our mission is to establish learning partnerships with our clients to create healthier and more productive workplaces.

H&A does not supply off-the-shelf learning interventions or prescriptive solutions. Instead, the firm establishes mutually beneficial learning relationships with clients with a long-term engagement in mind. The goal of H&A's partnerships is to impart strategic capabilities to the client organization so that the organization can move forward independently as quickly as possible. This approach is more time consuming and far less efficient than a product-based offering. The advantage of this strategy is that it has resulted in a positive reputation for the firm. This reputation has enabled the practice to compete successfully with much larger and more established consulting firms.

H&A operates as a virtual organization. Kirk Hallowell serves as principal of the practice, and the practice does not have additional, full-time employees. H&A taps necessary capacity by identifying other contractual relationships with individuals and organizations as the need arises. The current network of resources includes relationships with six independent consultants (each with complementary capabilities), three larger consulting firms, and the resources of Northern Illinois University's Division of Continuing Education.

Maintaining a relationship with the other independent consultants as associates has proven to be highly effective. Identifying individuals with complementary skill sets has allowed H&A to take on a broader array of services while ensuring an appropriate depth of expertise is represented to a client. Having these resources also provides the opportunity to expand the principal's knowledge and experience base. Finally, the process of running an independent consulting operation can be isolating at times. A network of associates provides meaningful opportunities for encouragement and support—particularly when business is slow.

Here is an example of how the organization works: H&A was awarded a contract to produce a developmental planning guide for a government agency. One of our associates with considerable experience in this area was briefed on the proposal and accepted the position of co-author. At the same time a project assistant and a layout/copy editor were contracted for the job. H&A negotiated a contractual agreement for each party's contribution and established a budget and project plan. The guide was successfully executed and H&A collected and distributed the proceeds. At the end of the project, an informal debrief was conducted with each contributor to identify opportunities for improvement and the relationship and services provided.

H&A has also benefited from relationships with larger consulting organizations including Lominger Consulting, Inc., and the Center for Creative Leadership. These relationships allow the firm to join in large-scale projects as a subcontractor or as a partner. One example of this kind of upward relationship is a contractual relationship with TalentGenesis, Inc., a Chicago-based leadership development and performance management firm. As TalentGenesis has developed contract requirements that have required special skills, it has included H&A as a subcontractor. This relationship has been particularly beneficial in that the author has gained experience with a process design developed by another firm. While respecting of TalentGenesis's intellectual property, the author invariably gained new insights, learned new tools, and participated in new approaches to learning and development interventions.

There are considerable advantages to running a virtual business model. The most important is managing overhead. Using this model, H&A does not pay for contractual services unless it is charging a margin on those services contracted. If there is a slack in business for a period of time, H&A does not incur any ongoing salary expense. All associates meet federal tax requirements as independent contractors or as corporations. This means that H&A does not pay payroll tax or benefits to associates. In addition, not having a standing workforce allows the practice to forgo typical office, travel, communication, and insurance expenses associated with full-time employees.

Another major benefit is the scalability this model affords. Given a wide range of talents and capabilities available in its talent pool, H&A can create a custom blend of skills and experiences to meet the clients' needs. In this way the firm is able to provide skills and capabilities well beyond those of the owner. If needed, H&A can bring together all the resources necessary to execute a major project and then dismantle the temporary organization when the project is completed. H&A charges consulting associates 15 percent of their day rate to cover operating and advertising overhead.

A third advantage of the virtual model is that the approach provides a degree of flexibility in work and life balance. Not having full-time employees to keep engaged, the author is free to flex the client load and select among projects he wishes to pursue. As this business model matures and the client base increases, it is not uncommon for the author to engage in eight to 10 client contact days per month with only three to four nights of travel. The result is that the author can build in flexibility for alternative workloads and schedule time for external interests and family.

The virtual business model is not without its drawbacks. Because the contributing associates each have their own businesses and competing priorities, there is no guarantee that these resources will be available on the time frame required by H&A. In some cases, project deadlines and specific deliverables have been renegotiated with the client based on the availability of these resources. Advance planning, accurate communication, and good project management skills minimize that challenge. The bottom line is that the ability to marshal and direct resources is more limited and more time consuming than in a traditional, employee-based organization.

Attracting and Keeping Clients

Client relationships are fundamental to the success of H&A. In addition to delivery of services, attracting and keeping clients are the most time and resource intensive activities of the practice. Without the opportunity to develop new client relationships and the capacity to provide additional services to existing clients, the practice would soon be out of business. Fortunately, H&A has identified a successful blend of client development activities.

H&A has established four primary means of promoting the business: informal networking, professional presentations and writing, an Internet Website, and direct mail. Table 3 indicates the approximate percentage of revenues generated from each kind of promotion over the past two years.

Clearly, networking is the key to the success of H&A. The ability to establish a relationship, do good work, and garner the support

Table 3. Revenues generated by each type of promotion.

Type of Promotion	Percent of Revenues Generated
Networking	65%
Professional Presentations	20%
Website	10%
Direct Mail	5%

of a client is essential to building the business. When clients have been pleased with their experience with H&A, they have shared the contact with colleagues within and outside of their organization. The result has been sustained relationships with organizations over several years and multiple contact points within several of these organizations as well. About 75 percent of H&A's revenues are accounted for by repeat business.

The advantage of networking is clear: the process is highly effective and there are no additional costs associated. Clients who have received excellent service are generally pleased to offer a referral or serve as a reference. While networking has provided the core of H&A's growth, networking alone has not been sufficient to generate new business. Networking is not predictable and is a relatively time-consuming way to develop new client contacts. While networking is a highly effective means to grow business within an organization, it is a less effective strategy to develop contacts outside that organization. Other means of developing customer relationships are essential.

Another successful strategy to engage new customers has been making presentations at professional conferences. The author has consistently sought opportunities to make presentations or present workshops for professional organizations. Local chapters of the American Society for Training & Development, Association for Quality and Productivity, and the Organizational Development Network have hosted conferences that bring practitioners and potential clients together. In addition, H&A has benefited greatly by presenting at large, proprietary conferences hosted by organizations such as the International Association for Quality and Productivity and Linkage, Inc. These events have enabled H&A to demonstrate its capability while establishing face-to-face contact with potential clients.

Another successful strategy in building the business is to develop a comprehensive Website. While the Website does not bring substantial new business, the few relationships established on the Internet have been very important. Clients have said they appreciate the posting of articles related to the topics addressed by H&A. These clients value the Website as a source of information more than just another advertisement. The Website has also generated several inquiries from academics, graduate students, and other consultants, which has led to valuable dialogue, if not sales. Unfortunately, the Website produces a fair number of inquiries from unqualified or nontarget clients and unsolicited commercial email advertisements. Over all, this is a reasonable price to pay for the breadth of exposure.

The fourth business development strategy used by H&A is direct mail. Working with an advertising company, H&A has developed a series of direct mail pieces and mailed them to a target audience of HR decision makers in a three-state region. The results have been less than spectacular. The direct mail campaigns have been costly, time-consuming, and produced few results. In fact, the few client contacts initiated from direct mail campaigns were already aware of H&A through some other form of advertising or networking. The experience has taught that direct mail requires expertise and client knowledge to be effective. For H&A, direct mail pitches a small consulting practice in direct competition with myriad big-budget advertising firms for the limited attention of a highly specialized market. Future use of direct mail will be limited and only for highly qualified distribution at best.

Managing the Business

Close management of business-related expenses has been a key to the success of H&A. When cash flow is positive, there is always the temptation to buy a new computer, invest in some new software application, or draw additional income from the practice. Experience has shown that it is best to keep capital expenses to a minimum and to avoid business-related debt at all costs. The result is H&A invests in top quality resources when the practice can well afford the expenditure.

The primary financial challenges encountered by H&A have been managing cash flow. One of the first challenges in adapting to an independent consulting practice is managing to the irregular rate and frequency of income. It typically requires three to six months from an initial point of contact to the actual receipt of a first payment on a consulting contract. Despite efforts to bill on a net-30 day basis, many large companies typically take 45 to 60 days to pay their contractors. H&A has become adept at making inquiries with account payable departments to expedite payments. In some cases, the typical payment cycle has been shortened considerably with an expeditious call to the right administrative personnel. In other cases, the accounts payable department has never received the original invoice from the department that received services. An expeditious and friendly call has often saved weeks or months of waiting for a check. Companies rarely make exceptions to their payment practices unless a specific request is made.

Another unanticipated consequence of running a business is the inordinate amount of taxes paid on a quarterly basis. Tax bills have included the 33 percent federal rate, a 15.3 percent self-employment tax, and a 3 percent state tax. Consequently, about half of all funds drawn off the business are devoted to paying taxes. To accommodate this demand, funds to pay taxes have to be identified and dedicated well in advance of payment dates. Irregularity of workload, delayed payment, and quarterly tax burdens have made H&A receivables follow the proverbial "feast or famine" routine. This unpredictability of cash flow has made it necessary for H&A to continually keep enough cash reserves to run the practice for two to three months without income.

Measuring Success

H&A serves primarily large corporations and government agencies although it has served several growing manufacturing and service organizations. To date, the practice has served 32 organizations with some clients establishing long-term, multiproject relationships. The average amount of contract dollars and length of services rendered has increased substantially since the firm's inception. The network of contacts and resources developed by H&A has grown exponentially. In addition, the breadth of services and content offered by H&A has expanded consistently.

Two important metrics of Hallowell & Associate's financial success include yearly growth in sales revenues and gross margins. Both of these important indicators are shown by year in table 4.

As these figures indicate, the numbers reflect significant and consistent growth in the business coupled with high efficiency of operating budget. The most rapid growth of the business took place in the second year of operation. A large, ongoing contractual relationship with a big client allowed H&A to increase billing and expand service offerings in this second year.

Table 4 also indicates that H&A operates on relatively high gross margins compared with traditional organizations. With the business centered in a home office, business-related expenses are maintained at a minimum. Primary costs include nonreimbursed travel, advertising, office equipment, and communications expenses. By avoiding

Table 4. Increase in revenues and gross margins.

Year	Percentage Increase in Revenues	Gross Margins (pretax)
1998	——	82%
1999	33%	78%
2000	22%	76%
2001*	18%	72%

*Projected

the temptation to open an external office with a full-time reception-ist and related expenses, H&A operates on a relatively modest monthly budget. The result is that cash flow strains are minimized and need for business-related borrowing has been eliminated.

Another method of measuring the success of H&A is the impact the firm's interventions have on its clients. H&A endeavors to measure the impact of its interventions at all five levels of evaluation. Table 5 shows some of the typical methods and measures used to evaluate the impact of its offerings.

Table 5. Typical approaches used in each level of evaluation.

Level of Evaluation	Question of Interest	Approach to Evaluation
Level 1	Did participants value the learning experience?	End of session surveys, individual interviews
Level 2	What did participants learn?	Pre- and post-self-assessments, objective tests, simulations
Level 3	Do participants translate learning to new behaviors on the job?	Self-assessment, supervisor's assessments, link to performance appraisal
Level 4	Have participants applied the learning to make a business impact?	Action learning reports, focus groups, performance metrics, learning journals, team debrief
Level 5	Did the investment in learning pay off?	Cost of learning versus documented outcomes

H&A has enjoyed consistent success in the reception of its services and workshops over the years. Level 1 and Level 2 evaluations reflect that participants value the quality of the intervention and demonstrate learning. The most significant opportunities for improvement have been the long-term implementation of the skill and knowledge the firm has imparted to clients. In some cases, Level 3, 4, and 5 evaluations conducted one to three months after a learning intervention have shown limited application of learning in the workplace. While those kinds of results are not atypical, H&A strives to improve these outcomes. Among the various process improvements that H&A has used, four strategies have proven effective:

1. *Get buy-in from top leadership from the start.* Many times a consulting process is initiated in the middle of an organization's hierarchy. For example, a midlevel HR director may be creating a learning intervention for one of his or her client business units. In those cases, it is essential to get the business unit leadership involved in the needs assessment and design process as early as possible. Failure to do so has resulted in unanticipated resistance to the intervention down the road. When a client is reluctant to involve leadership in the process, careful and direct communication is needed to convey the importance of buy-in from the top.

2. *Be explicit about accountability.* A great deal of learning interventions seem to be based on the implicit assumption that if we give people good tools and processes, they will simply use them. With a few exceptions, this has not been the experience of H&A. Consulting interventions that have been most successful and sustained long-term impact on the organization have consistently been linked to specific accountability in the workplace. For example, a manager is far more likely to follow-through on a development plan if he or she is required to hold quarterly reviews on progress with the supervisor and direct reports.

3. *Use action-based opportunities with feedback.* Action and feedback are essential to create and sustain organizational change. The practice has found that learning interventions are more robust and effective when they include the opportunity for application of learning in the workplace with an opportunity for reflection and feedback. For example, H&A now uses a learning structure where its two-day workshops include a one-month application period between classroom sessions. The second day of the class is a debrief of the participants' experience in applying concepts in the workplace.

4. *Plan from the beginning to be involved in follow-up.* In all cases, H&A strives to be involved through the duration of the consulting assignment and builds this commitment in project proposals. Evaluation

is a natural process to define a role in follow-up activities and H&A advocates follow-up evaluations of all interventions when appropriate. Assessing the impact of an intervention several months after it was initiated includes significant benefits for both the client and the practice. Also, H&A offers phone consultation support for its learning activities without exception.

The combination of these four strategies has yielded significant increase in the successful transfer of learning and sustained performance improvements.

Lessons Learned

Looking back at the transition, the three drivers leading to the decision to leave the university have been realized but each with important limitations. The initial desire for autonomy has been realized to a greater degree than anticipated or desired. The practice provides opportunities to make fundamental decisions about self-determination and priorities every day. The demands of a step-by-step contractual obligation are seen as a welcome degree of structure in an open and sometimes chaotic system. There are days when the author would welcome someone else making some of the decisions or setting priorities. It is easy to lose sight of the scope and boundaries of where the practice is and where it is going. Occasional reflective conversations with other practitioners and clients are helpful in this respect.

The financial impact of the transition has been positive overall. With an annual income exceeding even a highly paid academic salary, the practice has afforded significant financial benefits. The practice has also afforded a great deal of lifestyle flexibility. While travel can sometimes be extensive, there are also periods when time spent at work is limited. There have also been difficult periods when business has stalled or an important contract has been lost. During some of these periods the author has had ample time to question the reasonability of this career path. In time, there has always been a financial recovery and the author has become more adept at taking business setbacks in stride.

The third driver to enter full-time consulting centers on the opportunity to participate in the impact of a learning intervention. The outcome of this objective is mixed. The opportunity to see the impact of the work is more immediate; however, many consulting interventions do not bear fruit immediately. In many cases, H&A is able to be involved with the entire consulting process through its completion. In these cases, the author has been able to see dramatic impact based on the client's initiative and commitment. In many cases, however, H&A

is engaged briefly for one facet of a much larger change process. In these cases, the author is left wondering if the intervention had lasting impact and value for the organization.

Looking Forward

The future of Hallowell & Associates appears bright. Several new strategic relationships have afforded the practice a great deal of leverage in marketing, business development, and collaborative delivery. In terms of business strategy, H&A is focusing on more product-based rather than service-based offerings. Products, such as workshops and seminars, tend to be easier to sell on a conceptual basis to clients. Once the client relationship has been formed, there are opportunities to introduce services such as program design and a 360-degree feedback process. This approach has proven effective in a number of cases.

A network-based organization may grow slowly at first, but as it grows, the number of contacts and associations grows exponentially. While the temptation still exists to build a traditional, employee-based organization around this growing source of business, H&A is deeply committed to the virtual business model. The goal of H&A is to create a sustainable business model that does not demand excessive amounts of time or resources to operate effectively. Based on the success of the transition to date, the author is confident that this goal will be achieved.

Questions for Discussion

1. In addition to the drivers and barriers list in table 2, what other factors might one consider before leaving an academic position?
2. What other alternatives could the author have considered besides starting an independent practice? For example, what might the advantages be for joining an established practice or developing a consulting practice within the university?
3. If you were to consider moving from your current occupation within an organization to becoming a full-time consultant, what drivers would support the transition? What would be the most serious risks associated with the change?
4. What resource or supports would you need to garner in order to make a successful transition to full-time consulting? How would you navigate the financial and logistical support challenges through the transition?

5. What other approaches might the author consider in developing a client base and marketing the services of Hallowell & Associates?
6. What are the inherent risks and rewards associated with working a virtual business model?

The Author

Kirk Hallowell is an independent consultant specializing in leadership development, program evaluation, and organizational learning. Hallowell brings more than 17 years of leadership and teaching experience serving corporations, educational institutions, and government agencies. He has worked with a variety of corporations to develop short- and long-term projects focused on creating and assessing development. Hallowell has served as the lead designer for the Next Generation Executive Education Series, serving the top 600 executives of Prudential. That program currently uses an action learning process to drive developmental and business results. In addition, Hallowell has served as a 360-degree feedback specialist and an executive coach to business leaders in several corporations. His clients include BP, Motorola University, and Lucent Technologies Learning and Performance Center, in addition to more than 40 other organizations. Hallowell was formerly a full-time faculty at Northern Illinois University. He earned his Ph.D. in education with an emphasis in statistics from the University of Iowa in 1990. Hallowell has published several articles and presented internationally on organizational learning and transfer of learning. He can be reached at Hallowell & Associates, 27640 Gerry Lane, Sycamore, IL 60178; phone: 815.895.4049; email: Hallowell2@aol.com.

The Role of People and Relationships in Building a Successful Consulting Practice

CEP

Seth N. Leibler, Ann W. Parkman, and Paula M. Alsher

CEP (The Center for Effective Performance, Inc.) is a full-service performance improvement and training consulting firm specializing in helping organizations achieve their strategic business objectives through improved human performance. This case study underscores the importance of quality personnel and business relationships in establishing and maintaining a successful consulting practice. It examines key strategies for competing successfully against larger, well-known consulting firms—including the need for a performance-based methodology and proven bottom-line business results to secure both new and repeat clients. It also explores the benefit of complementary product lines—in this case, train-the-trainer workshops and books and tools—to help attract new consulting prospects.

The Practice

CEP (The Center for Effective Performance, Inc.) provides customized performance improvement and training solutions to organizations worldwide, including upfront analysis, strategic training assessments, and custom instructional design and development services. While each consulting project is unique, CEP's services generally follow the performance improvement process shown in figure 1, which begins by conducting analysis to identify job-critical tasks and skills, to clarify management's expectations with respect to desired performance, and to uncover all of the potential barriers to desired performance. Based on the analysis results, CEP's solutions may include custom

This case was prepared to serve as a basis for discussion rather than to illustrate either effective or ineffective administrative and management practices.

instructional design and development and the development of non-training recommendations to eliminate motivational or environmental inhibitors to desired performance. All of CEP's solutions are focused on helping its clients achieve their strategic business objectives.

The concept of CEP originated in the public sector, when Seth Leibler (CEP's president and CEO) and Ann Parkman (CEP's executive vice president) headed the Center for Professional Development and Training at the Centers for Disease Control (CDC). During their time at this prestigious public health organization, their department had racked up an enviable number of awards, including, on three separate occasions, recognition as an "Outstanding Training Organization" by the International Society for Performance Improvement (ISPI), an award given to organizations that contribute significantly to the field of performance and instructional technology for three consecutive years. They also earned ISPI awards for outstanding performance systems, outstanding application of a management system, outstanding instructional development, and outstanding application of human performance technology to an instructional situation. In addition, the American Society for Training & Development (ASTD) recognized their work through its "Human Resources Development Award."

The idea of establishing a privately owned practice that would provide consulting services and performance improvement workshops to support the health-care industry seemed a natural fit, and in 1985, Leibler, Parkman, and five of their CDC staff left to form CEP. Much to their surprise, their professional reputations attracted a large and diverse, non-health-care-related client base. Within its first year, CEP's consulting practice—which "resided" in the living and dining rooms of Leibler's house to save on rent—included such clients as A Beeper Company Associates, Budget Rent a Car, Mountain Bell, and Anchor Hocking. Due to the number of consulting projects they quickly acquired, their idea of developing and conducting proprietary performance improvement workshops while the consulting business grew was shelved.

In 1986, Leibler received an unexpected phone call from long-time associate Robert F. Mager. "I've got an offer you can't refuse," he said, and in classic Mager style, launched into his sales pitch. "Some people are good at building 'factories'; some are good at running them. Why don't you buy my 'factories' so I can continue building new ones?" With that, CEP suddenly launched itself into the train-the-trainer workshop business.

The well-known Mager workshops would help provide CEP with a steady source of income over the years. But, initially, the

Figure 1. CEP's performance improvement process.

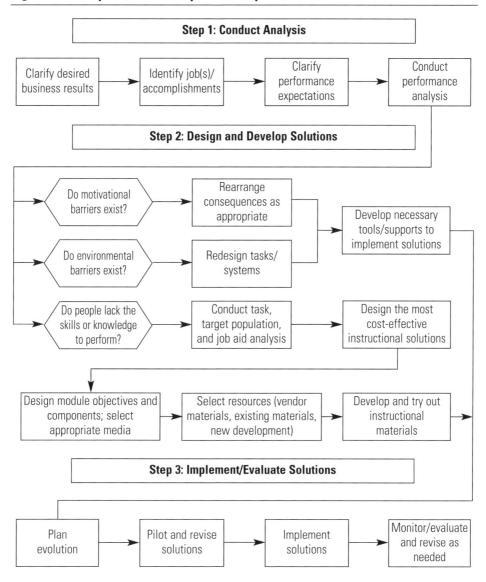

Reprinted with permission from The Center for Effective Performance, Inc., © 2000, CEP, Atlanta, GA (www.cepworldwide.com).

workshops also forced CEP's eviction when neighbors complained about the 18-wheeler, filled with workshop materials, parked in front of Leibler's home.

The company, now in the professional surroundings of an office complex, quickly grew. In 1988, CEP realized its first million-dollar year. In 1989, the company began one of its most ambitious projects—working with the Carter Presidential Center to train special education teachers in China to work with blind and deaf students. And in 1992, Leibler and Parkman were married!

Four years later, a third division of CEP emerged when the company purchased the rights to Mager's books. This would serve as a prelude to CEP Press, a wholly owned subsidiary of CEP, that now publishes high-quality, practical books and tools from some of the most successful performance improvement practitioners in the industry.

CEP's three distinct profit centers—consulting, workshops, and books and tools—offer the company a number of advantages. For example, consulting revenue can vary greatly from one year to the next, depending on the number of projects secured and the size of those projects; on the other hand, the Mager workshops and book sales have generally remained constant from year to year. In addition, the company has witnessed a high percentage of crossover sales—for example, book purchasers who attend workshops and then become consulting clients. This synergy has proven instrumental in helping CEP secure large-scale consulting projects from a broad range of *Fortune* 100 companies, companies that have traditionally relied on the "Big Five" accounting firms for their training and performance improvement solutions.

Making the Transition

While still at CDC, Leibler and Parkman began toying with the idea of establishing a private performance improvement and training practice. They had three key advantages: 1) they knew that, based on the results of their interventions, the Criterion-Referenced Instruction (CRI) methodology they had learned from Mager worked; 2) because of the number of awards they had won, they enjoyed a strong professional reputation within the industry; and 3) they had a phenomenally talented staff of instructional systems specialists. At the same time, Mager was actively encouraging them to go into practice for themselves. So much so that, when Mager was approached by Karl L. Adam to head a new management consulting division within IMS America to deal with performance problems in the health-care industry, Mager recommended that Adam talk to Leibler and Parkman.

After much discussion, they declined Adam's offer to manage the IMS America start-up division, still preferring the idea of establishing their own practice. But the relationship formed from this negotiation proved invaluable. When, a few months later, Adam resigned his position with IMS, he agreed to help finance the start-up of CEP, and he became CEP's chairman of the board.

Strategy

The initial mission of CEP—to improve workforce performance by using the CRI methodology to guarantee that people have the job-relevant skills and the self-efficacy to apply those skills to management's expectations—remains unchanged. What *has* changed is CEP's market niche. While the company has worked on a number of health-care projects over the years, including projects for the World Health Organization and the Centers for Disease Control, CEP's clients include more than 80 percent of the *Fortune* 500.

The majority of these projects have consisted of technical skills training, including call center, system, and enterprise-wide software training—all areas in which companies have made substantial financial investments and recognize the critical need for a skilled workforce. For example, Budget Rent a Car invested millions of dollars on a new reservation system. Budget knew that if its 1,400 reservation agents weren't fully trained to use the new system proficiently on the first day of cutover, the company stood to lose millions of dollars from lost or mismanaged reservations.

CEP bid on that project against the big accounting firms and won. There were three areas that distinguished them from the competition: 1) CEP was the only company to guarantee that learners would master the job-critical skills needed to use the new system proficiently on the first day after training; 2) CEP was the only company to recommend performance analysis as a means of uncovering *all* of the potential barriers to desired performance, including both training and nontraining barriers; and 3) CEP was the only company that focused on providing learners with the self-efficacy (or self-confidence) to apply their newly learned skills back on the job.

Those three distinguishing factors stem directly from their use of the CRI methodology. Originally developed by Robert F. Mager and Peter Pipe, CRI is based squarely on the latest behavioral-science research on human performance, including how people learn, what motivates them to learn, and what motivates them to perform to expectations (an overview of the distinguishing features of CRI can be found in figure 2).

Figure 2. Why CRI-developed training works.

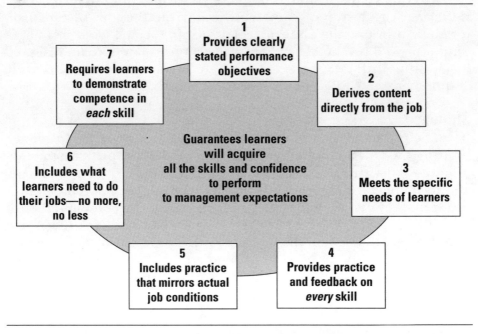

Upon implementing its CRI-based training solution, Budget reported a number of positive findings. Total training time averaged between 10 and 20 percent less than the training required for comparable systems. More important, agents who completed all of the training modules proved proficient in using the new system on the first day after training. "This was the smoothest cutover to a new system in Budget's history, due in no small part to the training," commented the director of reservations for Europe, the Middle East, and Africa.

In the months after the new system was implemented, Budget also reported an additional benefit from CEP's training solution—the average talk time (the time agents spend on the phone with each customer) had dropped by almost 10 seconds per call. Considering the fact that the rental car agency handled more than 16 million calls annually, this proved a significant time savings. As a result of performance analysis, CEP also recommended a number of nontraining solutions. Implementing just one of these recommendations resulted in increased revenue of $130,000 a year to Budget.

While CRI can be applied just as effectively to soft skills training, CEP has found it harder to prove the bottom-line value and impact of their custom instructional solutions to senior management—especially with the plethora of off-the-shelf training products in existence. Hence, while CEP's initial strategy was to support both soft and technical skill training needs, its focus has shifted to the latter, where the firm has more relevant experience and can more easily demonstrate significant bottom-line business results.

Structure of Practice

CEP is incorporated in the state of Georgia and headquartered in Atlanta. Funding of the company to date has come from private loan agreements, established lines of credit, shares of stock held by CEP's four-person board of directors (consisting of CEP's president, executive vice president, chairman, and legal counsel), and income generated by sales.

CEP's management structure consists of a management team made up of Leibler, Parkman, and the departmental heads of each of CEP's major divisions—consulting, workshops, CEP Press, client solutions, and finance/management information systems (MIS). The management team is responsible for all decisions related to the strategic direction of the company. (See figure 3.)

Within the consulting practice, CEP employs a core group of full-time project managers and performance improvement consultants and about 80 independent contractors who are expert in applying CRI to the performance problems facing today's organizations.

CEP also maintains strategic alliances with consulting organizations that offer complementary solutions, such as training return-on-

Figure 3. CEP's organizational structure.

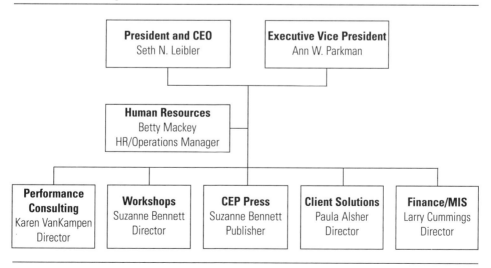

investment (ROI), performance process improvement, and technology solutions. Many of these alliances originated through publishing agreements with industry experts secured through CEP Press.

With respect to its workshops, CEP also has relationships with various international distributors. These workshop distributors, currently located in Japan, Australia, Singapore, and the Netherlands, have been fully trained to apply the CRI methodology to the performance improvement and training problems facing their clients, to conduct the Mager workshops, and to distribute Mager materials. Through CEP Press, they also work with a number of international book distributors to make their books available throughout Europe, South America, and Asia.

Attracting and Keeping Clients

There are three primary sources of consulting prospects and clients: 1) workshop graduates, 2) CEP's Website and e-newsletter, and 3) referrals by existing CEP consulting clients. The first source — workshop graduates—depends on frequent, high-volume direct mail communication (including catalogs, brochures, and letters) to encourage inquiries—both toll-free and online—to CEP. The CEP e-newsletter, which offers practical advice, tips, and guidelines for guaranteeing effective performance, has also proven an effective means of driving traffic to the CEP Website—interested parties can sign up for the free e-newsletter from virtually any page of the site.

The third source of consulting clients—referrals—is arguably one of the biggest keys to CEP's success. While CEP may be much smaller than its competitors and less recognizable to key decision makers— especially those outside of the training arena—the company has secured a number of consulting projects on the strength of the referrals from existing clients. For example, during an industry conference, Hilton Hotels Corporation asked for recommendations for a training partner, and Marriott International, a longtime client, recommended CEP.

CEP worked with Hilton to develop Revenue Management University (RMU), a training program designed to give newly hired directors of revenue management (DRMs) the analysis and decision-making skills needed to succeed at Hilton's properties. After implementing the program, Hilton reported that: 1) the company's industry ranking increased from a C to a B+; 2) the company grew in market share and penetration in all major markets; and 3) 40 percent of the individuals who graduated from RMU earned promotions within six months of completing the course. Since working on this project, CEP has been called back to work on additional projects for Hilton, including developing a human resource candidate selection tool and a revenue management project for the company's catering division.

One reason CEP receives such strong referrals is, of course, the positive bottom-line business results it generates on behalf of its clients. But another key reason is that CEP prides itself on being a people-oriented company: "We have always been cognizant that, because we are so much smaller and less well known than the Big Five, our clients are going out on a limb in recommending us to upper management. We therefore understand that our clients' success is our success," says Karen VanKampen, CEP's consulting director. "It really strikes home when you hear something like 'I owe my new promotion to senior VP to the work that CEP has done.'"

CEP is also flexible in working with clients to meet their deadlines and budget constraints. Depending on their clients' needs, CEP can manage the project from start to finish, it can provide partial support (such as for analysis only), or it can provide coaching/mentoring services to help clients build internal expertise. That flexibility has proven instrumental in helping CEP establish a viable working relationship with its clients.

Managing the Business
Profitability
CEP maintains a five-year business plan containing specific growth strategies for each division of the company, along with targeted revenue and earnings before interest, taxes, depreciation, and amortization (EBITDA) growth. In addition to this growth plan, CEP also maintain profitability targets specific to each consulting project, workshop, and book. Those plans and targets are reviewed on a regular basis, and adjusted as necessary, to help control costs and ensure profitability.

Growing Pains and Crises
By 1996, CEP found itself squeezing two people per office, with one unlucky employee actually working in a hallway "office." After a year of diligent searching, CEP relocated to its current facility. The new office boasted two and a half times the square footage of the previous office, more space than the company actually needed. But the increase in space would accommodate CEP's plans for continued growth over the long term. At the present time, the unused space is being

occupied by one of CEP's strategic partners in exchange for free technology support.

Another growing pain, which CEP's technology partner has helped them to manage, is data. Before that assistance, CEP had multiple databases of record—a consulting database, a customer service database for workshop enrollments and book orders, and a separate accounting database. Combining all three into one integrated database has been key in helping CEP track all of its consulting clients, workshop graduates, and book purchasers, and to leverage this information for cross-selling purposes.

Yet another challenge is how to effectively manage ever-increasing workloads as the company continues to grow. CEP has addressed this issue in two ways. First, in 1997, it restructured the organization to better service each of the profit centers. As part of that reorganization, CEP created a separate Client Solutions division to support the sales and marketing of all consulting clients, workshop graduates, and book purchasers. CEP also split off the product development function from the consulting division in order to ensure the timely and continuous development of new workshops and resources.

Second, CEP developed a structured candidate selection process to help find the most qualified people to continue to fuel the company's growth. As a means of identifying individuals with the right mix of skills and knowledge, CEP uses a performance-based candidate selection tool that includes specific, relevant qualities required for each position. Some obvious characteristics include "Does the candidate have relevant work experience? Relevant training or education? Relevant computer experience?" and so on. But assuming candidates meet those types of requirements, CEP then takes the candidate selection process a step farther.

Generally during the second or third interview, interested candidates must complete relevant work-related exercises or simulations to demonstrate their proficiency in job-critical areas. For example, candidates for CEP's project management position must demonstrate their ability to: 1) perform a task analysis by choosing a simple task and determining all of the critical steps and decision paths related to that task; 2) conduct a performance analysis by interviewing a CEP employee who role-plays the part of a client with a performance problem; and 3) scope out a project approach, estimated timeline, and required resources based on information on a consulting lead provided by CEP and additional questions about the project that the candidate feels are required.

The candidate selection tool has proven invaluable in helping CEP select the most qualified applicants for any given position. In a few instances, it has actually helped speed the selection process, but in most cases, CEP has found that the candidate selection tool requires patience and time. But the investment in time is worth it. After all, if you are not staffed with the right people, you don't have to worry about managing the business because you probably won't have a business to manage. This holds especially true in small business, where every individual must pull his or her weight.

Maintaining Work and Life Balance

Starting up any new enterprise requires sacrifice. In the case of CEP, it took an extreme commitment for the first five years to establish the company. While the commitment required to service CEP's consulting clients is no longer 24/7, it still remains an ongoing challenge to maintain an acceptable work/life balance.

"It's hard to schedule your life when your clients need you," says VanKampen. "Here's a perfect example. In order to get a new project off the ground, we need to first interview a key subject matter expert who is a senior VP-level person. Because of his tight schedule, he only had two openings—tomorrow afternoon and two weeks away. Our project manager couldn't interview him tomorrow because she had another CEP commitment, so she asked if I could handle the interview so we wouldn't delay the project. The only way I could be available is if I cancelled a doctor's appointment I had scheduled.

"In this case, the decision was easy—cancel the doctor's appointment. But it is a much harder decision when you have an important family obligation that you have to meet. Basically, it is a judgment call."

It helps to have other individuals who can step in and take care of client commitments when conflicts like this arise. It also helps to have a corporate culture that acknowledges the importance and value of having a healthy, balanced life outside of the office.

"CEP has always been a very flexible company," says Human Resource Manager Betty Mackey. "We realize that our employees are our greatest asset, and we try in every way to help them blend their home and work life. This means being as flexible as possible in allowing employees to work from home when there is a sick child, adjusting work schedules so they can 'be there' for school events, and so on."

It is more challenging to balance work and life when the two are inseparable, as is the case with Leibler and Parkman, who are not only CEP's leadership team but also a married couple. There are two keys to maintaining an acceptable balance that has worked effectively for these business/life partners: 1) Don't discuss work at home, and 2) if you can't spend the entire weekend away from work, at least reserve one full day that is non-work-related.

Obstacles to Success

Arguably the biggest obstacle that CEP faces on a constant basis is client disbelief. "I can't believe all of our training isn't being done this way," is something CEP hears all of the time, often accompanied by "Why doesn't everyone know about CEP and CRI?" The answer to that question is that CEP is and has always been composed of practitioners, not salespeople. That disadvantage often comes to the forefront at the finalist stage of a request for proposal (RFP), when upper management must make a final decision on a training partner.

Senior executives seldom understand the critical business value of effective performance-based training. They are attempting to change the strategic direction of their companies by installing enterprise-wide software, improving business processes, or rolling out new products. They are often working with the Big Five firms to help implement these major initiatives. So why would they turn anywhere else for their training?

In most cases, CEP's success in such situations rests on the intervention of its training clients—clients who may have attended one of CEP's workshops, were referred to them by another client, or with whom they have worked on a prior consulting project. Often, these training clients serve as CEP's salesforce to "sell" CEP to upper management.

Ethical Issues

One of the reasons why CEP is able to maintain such strong client relationships is its commitment to ethics. CEP will never lowball an investment estimate just to get in the door and then tack on unexpected fees. The company does not accept projects just to make money; in fact, CEP has actually turned down jobs because it did not believe that what it was being asked to do would provide value to the client.

CEP also strives to involve its training clients in every project decision made. CEP considers this a critical element in forging a positive, long-term client relationship. Ongoing project involvement, especially when the project meets or exceeds the desired business objectives, helps to foster a sense of pride and ownership in the solution, thereby making the client's success the company's success.

Measuring Success
Financial Measurements

CEP's management team reviews progress toward the five-year growth plan on a quarterly basis, and any negative variances to the plan are aggressively acted upon. In addition, CEP reviews financial measures for each consulting project, workshop, and book on a monthly basis. This continuous measurement of results to plan allows CEP to quickly take necessary action to address potential shortfalls. With respect to consulting, financial metrics include specific revenue targets, average gross profit targets, and an acceptable ratio of billable in-house staff to independent contractors.

Nonfinancial Measurements

After a consulting project has ended, CEP conducts a client debrief to assess the client's overall satisfaction with the project, the solution, CEP, and CEP's project management. The company also interviews the CEP project team for a balanced perspective of the project. This information has proven helpful in establishing long-term relationships with both new clients and repeat clients.

Repeat business is another indicator of success that the company tracks on an ongoing basis. For example, in 2000, 69 percent of CEP's consulting projects came from repeat clients. In 2001, this percentage dipped slightly to just over 65 percent.

Evaluation

CEP's custom instructional solutions automatically incorporate Kirkpatrick's evaluation Levels 1 and 2. Level 1 evaluation—learner reaction—consists of a performance-based feedback form that measures such critical elements as whether the training objectives were clear, whether ample opportunities for practice were provided, and how confident learners felt about their ability to apply their new skills on the job.

Level 2 evaluation—skill acquisition—is measured by a skill check at the end of each instructional module. All learners must demonstrate competence by successfully completing the skill check before moving on to the next module of instruction.

CEP also works with its clients at the beginning of a project to set up metrics before, during, and after implementing training, which will allow CEP to evaluate the remaining two levels of Kirkpatrick's evaluation model—skill application and business results. For example, CEP worked with Delta Air Logistics to determine ways to measure the success of new-hire acceptance agent training. Metrics included:

- pennies-per-pound productivity (how much it cost the air carrier to move a pound of freight)
- the number of insurance claims related to lost or damaged goods
- the number of FAA fines and letters of investigation based on regulatory infractions
- the rate of acceptance agent turnover.

By measuring that data while the analysis phase of the project was taking place, Delta has a baseline upon which it can evaluate the training solution when it is rolled out.

Keys to Success

When CEP was still in the start-up phase, Leibler asked Mager for advice on how to find good employees. Mager's response was "Find someone with a good sense of humor. People who take themselves too seriously wind up being a pain in the _ _ _." While, of course, there's no substitute for "smarts," CEP has taken Mager's advice to heart and firmly believes that the quality of the people employed at CEP has been instrumental to its success. CEP therefore places more value in having the right people for each position than in having each position filled.

Mager himself has also been key to CEP's success. Even when potential clients did not recognize the CEP name, they often knew Mager's name. Especially as a start-up, the ability to leverage the name of the most well-known and respected figure in the industry served as a definite advantage. At the same time, Mager wanted CEP to succeed. Not only did he refer consulting projects to CEP, he also agreed, on more than one occasion, to serve as a project advisor as a way to help CEP secure business.

Last but not least, the CRI methodology is another critical key to CEP's success because it allows the company to distinguish itself from the competition. To this day, CEP is the only performance improvement organization to *guarantee* that learners will master *each* skill its instruction is designed to teach or CEP will fix the training at its own expense. Especially in these days of economic uncertainty, this guarantee is a powerful differentiator.

Lessons Learned
Lesson 1

While rare, within the past five years CEP has encountered a few individuals—both employees and contractors—who have valued personal gain to the detriment of CEP. The company now requires employees and contractors to sign noncompetition and confidentiality agreements that define and legalize the ownership of clients, employees, and all work done on behalf of CEP.

Lesson 2

Traditionally, all strategic company decisions are reached through consensus by the CEP management team; no one person dominates the decision-making process. This "management by consensus" is a carryover from the CDC days. CEP has found that this decision-making process offers both advantages and disadvantages. On the plus side, the company believes that the quality of the decisions it makes is greatly improved because all potentially affected divisions are involved in the decision-making process. CEP honestly believes that no one person can match the collective wit of a group of competent people. At the same time, being involved in each key decision creates a sense of ownership among the management team, which in turn helps to drive a sense of ownership in the outcome.

On the downside, reaching consensus can sometimes take longer than anticipated, especially when disagreements occur. While disagreements are inevitable in any business, it is important to see value in a disagreement. A quotation by William Wrigley Jr. helps drive this point home: "When two people in business always agree, one of them is unnecessary."

Another challenge of "management by consensus" is that this approach will only be effective when: 1) all members of the team genuinely respect each another and what each person brings to the table, and 2) when the entire team is focused on the same goal—the success of the organization as a whole. In large measure, CEP attributes the synergy of its management team to the effectiveness of its candidate selection tool. Again, the importance of hiring the right people cannot be overstated.

Lesson 3

Nothing in business ever stays the same; things are always changing. Therefore, the question is whether you want to steer change in the direction you want to go. Prior to 2001, CEP had never worked from a growth plan. The effect of this lack of focus began to materialize in the past couple of years when its level of sales began to flatten out. So in 2001, CEP launched its first-ever growth plan and established regular review meetings with the management team to continually measure results to plan and to make needed adjustments. While it is a five-year plan, CEP is already witnessing the results—2001 was the best year ever both for CEP's consulting division and for the company as a whole.

Questions for Discussion

1. What are the criteria you use to hire employees?
2. Who do you consider your primary competition and how do you distinguish yourself from them?
3. What methodology do you employ for your instructional solutions?
4. How do you ensure that your instructional objectives are tied to your client's business needs?
5. How do you address nontraining barriers that could prohibit people from performing as desired?
6. How do you leverage client relationships to gain referrals and repeat business?
7. Are there well-known names in the industry to whom you can turn for referrals or other support?

The Authors

Seth N. Leibler, president and CEO, is a cofounder and managing partner of CEP. He has served as an executive and consultant in the business of improving human performance for more than 25 years. Recent publishing credits include a chapter (with Ann Parkman and Karen VanKampen) in *What Smart Trainers Know* (Jossey-Bass/Pfeiffer, 2001). He has also co-authored (with Ann Parkman) a chapter in the second edition of the *Handbook of Human Performance Technology* (ISPI/Jossey-Bass/Pfeiffer, 1999); *The Guidebook for Performance Improvement* (Pfeiffer, 1997); and *Introduction to Performance Technology* (NSPI, 1986). He has been published extensively in *Workforce Training News* and served as a contributing editor to *Corporate University Review*. Leibler is a past president of the International Society for Performance Improvement. He has a doctorate in educational psychology from the University of Rochester. He can be reached at CEP, 2300 Peachford Road, Suite 2000, Atlanta, GA 30338; phone: 770.458.4080; email sleibler @cepworldwide.com.

Ann W. Parkman, executive vice president, is a cofounder and managing partner of CEP. She has more than 20 years' experience in working with organizations to improve workforce performance. Parkman works with clients to identify strategies for improving job performance. The work of Parkman and her staff has been recognized by many professional organizations and has earned numerous national and international awards. Parkman is a certified Mager Associate who delivers Robert F. Mager's renowned train-the-trainer workshops. She is past president of the International Society for Performance Improvement and a past president of the Atlanta ISPI chapter. She has published widely on different aspects of the field of performance technology.

Paula M. Alsher, director of client solutions, has more than 25 years' experience in the training and performance improvement field. Alsher works closely with clients to identify strategies for supporting them in achieving their performance improvement goals. She is also responsible for the overall marketing of CEP's workshops, books, and tools. Alsher has been with CEP since 1990. Prior to joining CEP, she worked in a variety of human resources, training, and employee communications positions in both for-profit and nonprofit environments.

Making the Leap into Consulting

Partners in Change, Inc.

Dana Gaines Robinson and James C. Robinson

Many experienced and successful HRD and HR practitioners within organizations have considered transitioning to the role of an external consultant. But what are the pitfalls that make such a transition difficult? This case study looks at the strategies, the challenges, and the keys to establishing a successful consulting practice. The case demonstrates how a passion for consulting can be combined with business savvy to become a successful external consultant.

The Practice

In January 1982, Dana Robinson was faced with a critical choice regarding her career within the HRD field. Dana and Jim Robinson were married on the 17th of that month. Prior to the wedding they had used a logical problem-solving process to determine that they should live in Pittsburgh, Pennsylvania, where Jim was in a leadership role at Development Dimensions International (DDI). That decision left Dana with a dilemma about what she should do regarding her career. She was moving to the "Steel City" which, during the recession of the early 1980s, was known as the "rust belt." After surveying the local job market, she learned that there were no jobs of a comparable level to the position that she previously held as director of training and development at Merck, Sharp & Dohme. While the poor job market of the early 1980s was one factor to consider, she also had a strong desire to make a difference within the training and

This case was prepared to serve as a basis for discussion rather than to illustrate either effective or ineffective administrative and management practices.

development community. She discussed these factors with her husband and a number of colleagues. By February 1982, she became an independent external consultant. That was the beginning of a consultancy named Partners in Change, Inc. The name reflected her concept that training and development functions must partner with managers to bring about real change in organizations. This partnering would enable training departments to have more impact within their organizations.

Making the Transition

Once Dana made the decision to become an external consultant, she interviewed about 10 successful external consultants to learn how to make the transition. She learned that when making the move from an internal training director to an external consultant, she would need to decide whether to leap or slide. The leap approach is one in which the person resigns the internal position and within a few days is a full-time external consultant. The slide approach is one where a person gradually obtains external clients, while still handling the responsibilities of an internal position. When there are sufficient external business opportunities, the person resigns the internal position and becomes a full-time consultant.

Because Dana was relocating to a different city, she chose to leap into external consulting. The advantages of leaping were that she could concentrate full time on growing her business and she would have more flexibility to respond quickly to prospective clients. The disadvantages of the approach were that there would be nine to 12 months when incoming cash would be limited. In addition, she was leaving a busy full-time position where she interacted with many people to one where she would be working by herself and having much less interaction with people. During the first year as an external consultant the loneliness of this new role had a major impact on her. At times she felt anger when she contrasted her loneliness with her husband's busy schedule at DDI. While discussions between the two helped her cope with these feelings, it was only when consulting assignments became more numerous that the loneliness was replaced by the enthusiasm of creating a new organization. Early in her third year of business (1984), the consulting assignments increased and her husband decided to join her in Partners in Change.

Strategy

Dana Robinson's initial strategy was to create a consultancy that focused on proving that training makes a difference. To do this, she intended to consult with clients as they developed measurement and evaluation systems for their training programs. The consultancy would not only provide clients with an evaluation architecture, but also customize tools to support the measurement efforts.

Marketing these consulting services was her first major challenge. She soon learned that as an unknown external consultant it is very difficult—almost impossible—to sell an intangible such as consulting. Her first year consisted of sending letters to the key training and development people within target markets. The letters were followed by telephone calls to set up face-to-face visits. When that effort resulted in little work, she realized that she needed to attract clients through other means. Therefore, in year two, her strategy changed to developing a "Proving Training Makes a Difference" workshop and using mass mailing of brochures to bring participants into the workshop. A mailing of more than 10,000 brochures resulted in about 10 participants in two workshops. Fortunately, two of these participants became clients for consulting services, thus moving her in the right direction. These two individuals, each from *Fortune* 500 organizations, remained clients for several years.

By year three, when Jim Robinson joined Partners in Change, it became clear that the two would need to establish national recognition if they were to grow the consulting business. Thus they actively sought opportunities to make presentations and conduct workshops at national conferences. In addition, they wrote articles for various magazines and journals, including *Training & Development* and *Training,* to create greater visibility. As the consulting assignments became more numerous and more complex, the Robinsons realized that the consulting assignments were really a research and development lab for advancing their technology. This action research was providing them with an abundance of tips, techniques, and stories regarding "proving training makes a difference." Also during this period they encountered numerous situations where training by itself did not make a difference. In addition to training, clients needed to ensure that the work environment supported the type of performance that the training was expected to generate.

Thus the focus of their consulting evolved to where they were working with clients to conduct front-end assessments that identified both training and work environment needs. This assessment coupled with measurement and evaluation resulted in a system called "training for impact." Their action research in this area enabled them to publish their first co-authored book in 1989, entitled *Training for Impact: How to Link Training to Business Needs and Measure the Results.* That book led to increased consulting assignments and the need to add an additional consultant to the business.

The action research also highlighted the reality that performance assessment and evaluation capability were only part of being an effective training professional. Another important element was skillful partnering and consulting with clients. Therefore in the early 1990s, the Robinsons researched and perfected a set of skills called performance consulting for internal practitioners. That resulted in a second co-authored book entitled *Performance Consulting: Moving Beyond Training*. The book also had a positive impact on the number of organizations that were their clients.

In the late 1990s the Robinsons found that they were working most frequently with internal training departments or HR functions that wanted to transition to a more consultative, strategic way of working with line management. Their action research also identified the infrastructure that must be in place for this transition to be successful. Thus in 1998, they co-edited a book of contributions from successful training managers and performance consultants. That book was entitled *Moving from Training to Performance: A Practical Guidebook*. It resulted in more work with clients. They continued to obtain data regarding the job of performance consultants, including job outputs, best practices, selection criteria, and compensation data. That information was shared with the profession through numerous presentations and articles.

Structure of Practice

By year three, the Robinsons realized that Partners in Change, Inc., had the potential to grow into a small consulting firm. They also realized that to grow the business they would need the help of people in other areas of expertise; specifically, they would need the help of an accountant, an attorney, a marketing consultant, and a strategic planner. In addition to these external resources, there was a need to add support staff that would provide customer service, support the consultants, and create materials for consulting assignments and workshops. At this point, Partners in Change was transformed from a sole proprietorship to a corporation in which the Robinsons were the only stockholders. They were responsible for generating sales and managing the projects resulting from those sales, and they were supported by an excellent internal staff and external resources. In addition, they subcontracted to external consultants and had one or two consultants on staff. For all client projects, one of the Robinsons was the project manager.

While both the Robinsons managed client projects, they almost never worked on the same ones. When more than one person was required on a project, they would use an outside consultant or a staff consultant. They also found that it worked best for them to divide the major aspects of managing the business. Building on the strengths of each, Dana took the lead in marketing the consulting services, while Jim took the lead in the financial management of the organization.

Attracting and Keeping Clients

As discussed earlier, visibility became key in attracting new clients. The Robinson's strategy was to create name recognition through speaking engagements and writing books and articles. In addition to visibility, referrals from current clients became a major source of new clients. To encourage these referrals, the partners established client satisfaction as a core value of the consultancy. On each client project, they established open communications with the key person in the organization. Their collaborative style ensured that they worked as partners with the clients during all phases of the project.

When something did go wrong on a project, service recovery became critical. For example, during a major assessment project, about 100 sales representatives and account managers were asked to respond to an electronic survey and send that information directly to Partners in Change, Inc. Because of a flaw in the software, the information from all respondents was deleted when "read into" the computer. Dana Robinson, who was project manager, took full responsibility for the problem when she spoke with the client. She offered to complete the assessment at no fee to the client if the client was willing to have the individuals complete the survey a second time. As it turned out, each person did complete a second survey. The data was interpreted and reported at no cost to the client. This "lost data" project became the first of several that Partners in Change, Inc., worked on with that client.

Managing the Business

Early on when the Robinsons spoke with other successful external consultants, they repeatedly heard that it was critical to define an area of expertise and then focus on that area. Using that advice as a guideline, they concentrated first on training for impact, and later on performance consulting and the transitioning of training departments and HR functions to a performance focus.

While focusing on areas of expertise can be fun and can lead to success, there is a flip side—knowing when to walk away from work even when the work would be financially lucrative. Thus, a second guideline became to use their expertise to ensure a "win" for both themselves and their clients. That meant that some projects that clients were willing to fund would be declined. That decision was relatively easy when negotiating with a prospect regarding a new project. The Robinsons established criteria for a successful project, and their internal salesperson was able to screen inquiries and move ahead only with those where the win-win criteria were in place. The more difficult situations were those where the Robinsons were already working with a client and it became apparent that the project would not provide a win for the client. Lack of management support or lack of a supportive infrastructure were the most frequent causes of failure. Several times, the internal training director or HR manager wanted to move ahead, while the Robinsons realized they could not achieve the desired results. In most cases, it took several discussions in which they compared the progress of the project against predetermined criteria before the client was willing to let go. However, this approach was critical to ensure a win-win result for all client work.

Measuring Success

The Robinsons used several metrics to measure the success of Partners in Change, Inc. These metrics included revenue, expense control, and profitability. The firm's financial system regularly supplied this information.

Additionally, there were two measures that provided soft data—namely, client satisfaction and the firm's culture. At the end of each client project, the Robinsons would debrief the project with a client organization key person. In a 30- to 45-minute phone conversation, they would discuss each of the project's major deliverables. They would determine the client's perceived value of each deliverable and the client's satisfaction with the process by which that deliverable was accomplished. That approach enabled them to implement service recovery in any situation where the client was less than satisfied. For extended projects, they maintained a "client satisfaction" dialogue with the key contact throughout the project. Many times these discussions would take place on site or over lunch or dinner. While these discussions could highlight opportunities for service recovery, they also identified ways of working that clients valued and should be retained in future work assignments.

The Partners' culture was another key measure of success. By the late 1980s, the Robinsons and their employees had established a set of Partners' values, including respect for the total person, quality of work life, working as a team, and employees as stakeholders. The latter value resulted in establishing a profit-sharing plan and financial information that was available to all employees. The Robinsons monitored the culture by informal discussions with managers, team leads, and employees. However, the reality of the consulting business often had both Jim and Dana out of the office many days each month. At least one time, this absence from the office resulted in a breakdown in the culture of which the Robinsons were unaware. The hard lesson learned is that the breakdown of the culture can result in the loss of good employees and can require an extraordinary amount of effort to reestablish a positive culture. The Robinsons learned that they must be vigilant in keeping in touch with how it feels to work in their organization.

Keys to Success

There seem to be several factors that have contributed to the long-term success of Partners in Change, Inc.:

1. *Focus on a few areas of expertise about which the consultants have passion.* The focus areas are carefully selected. They must be strategic, long-term areas that will be supported by all aspects of the business. This single-minded focus drives business decisions in all areas. For example: The focus drives decisions about the marketing strategy, including the look and feel of marketing messages and pieces. The books and articles that the Robinsons write focus on their areas of expertise. In addition, the sales process is designed to result in projects in those areas of expertise and thus provide a win for both the client organizations and the firm.

2. Implement strategic planning. A thoughtful strategy is required to successfully build the business based on areas of expertise. Each year the Robinsons and the Partners' managers create a business plan of tactics and actions that support the strategy. The Robinsons form the core of this strategy over several weeks. They set aside quiet times for the two of them to have discussions about the future direction of the business. Those discussions result in a core strategy to be fleshed out during a planning meeting. Often this planning session is facilitated by an external consultant. The managers within Partners help form the tactics and activities needed to make this strategy a reality. The Robinsons then brief employees about the plan ensuring that

everyone knows how he or she contributes to it through performance. Jim and Dana continue to refer to the strategic plan at staff meetings and in discussions with employees to ensure that everyone keeps his or her eye on the target.

3. *Foster an open culture.* The Robinsons work hard to maintain an open culture. Essentially all information is available to every employee. Any employee can ask any question at any time and receive an honest answer. This approach has enabled Partners in Change, Inc., to maintain many employees for more than 10 years. As indicated earlier, one or two breakdowns in the employee culture occurred when this openness was not maintained. It is important to monitor the organizational culture on an ongoing basis.

4. *Be quick to respond.* By being a small organization co-managed by the principals, the Robinsons are able to respond quickly to the internal and external environment. That means that they can muster resources for projects on tight timetables. It also means that they can reduce expenses rapidly during times of economic slowdowns. This hands-on, agile approach has enabled them to maneuver between the various hazards faced by small businesses.

Lessons Learned

In summary, the lessons learned include the following:

- It is difficult to sell intangible services when the consultants are relatively unknown. Therefore, it is critical to establish visibility in the marketplace very early in the life of the business when desiring to sell consulting services.
- It is crucial to accept accountability when things go wrong. Things can go wrong anytime. When there is joint accountability between the client organization and the consultant, "Go wrongs" are likely to occur more frequently. Even in these situations—and maybe most importantly in these situations—it is critical for the consultant to initiate corrective action and bring the project back on course. These situations call for the consultant to take accountability for correcting the situation, no matter what or who is the major cause of the problem.
- Focus on the consultancy's areas of expertise. A selling process that uses criteria to qualify those projects within the areas of expertise is critical. The willingness to walk away from lucrative projects that will not provide a win for the client is also crucial. The Robinsons' experience has been that turning away work that is outside their area of expertise is more efficient than trying to get a win out of

that type of project. A focus on areas of expertise has the benefits of maximizing the productivity of the consultants and concentrating the organization's resources on a few areas rather than spreading over many areas.

- Promote an internal climate of customer service and employee support. Establish the value of customer satisfaction as the number one priority and everyone's accountability. Also establish internal values of teamwork and collaboration as a way to achieve customer satisfaction. Recognize and celebrate those situations in which employees have provided extraordinary customer service.

The Most Important Lesson Learned

When asked about the most important lesson learned, the Robinsons respond, "Follow your passion." Their passion included two elements:

1. Make a difference in the training and human resources field. They want the HRD and HR disciplines to be a little better because of their work and research. This is reflected in their hands-on consulting and writings.

2. Spend much of their time as hands-on consultants. Jim and Dana had managed departments and business units previously. They now wanted the thrill and challenge of encountering client problems for which the answers were not apparent. They found the ambiguity of such situations to be exciting.

These passions motivated them to create Partners in Change where the number of employees, including themselves, never exceeded 10. Working directly with clients on real problems provides a sense of satisfaction and excitement that outweighs the travel and long hours.

Questions for Discussion

1. What factors would encourage an internal person to leap into external consulting? To slide into external consulting?
2. What resources does a person need to start up a consultancy?
3. What resources does a person need to grow a consultancy?
4. What are the factors that are critical to the long-term success of a consultancy?
5. What things went wrong in spite of the Robinsons' best efforts?

The Authors

Dana Gaines Robinson is founder and president of Partners in Change, Inc. Prior to becoming an external consultant, she was an internal human resource development professional for nine years. She is a recognized leader in the area of performance technology and assisting organizations in defining performance as it needs to be for an organization to attain its business goals. Dana has a bachelor's degree in sociology from the University of California, Berkeley, and a master's degree in psychoeducational processes from Temple University. She has served on the ASTD Board of Directors.

James C. Robinson is chairman of Partners in Change, Inc. He is a recognized leader in the area of human resource development and performance consulting. He has consulted with numerous *Fortune* 500 organizations. He was a line manager for 10 years and training director for six years in a *Fortune* 100 company. For several years he was vice president at Development Dimensions International. He has a master's degree in genetics from the University of Wisconsin and a second master's degree in adult education from Syracuse University.

Jim and Dana Robinson co-authored the books *Training for Impact: How to Link Training to Business Needs and Measure the Results* (1989) and *Performance Consulting: Moving Beyond Training* (1995). The Robinsons co-edited a third book *Moving From Training to Performance: A Practical Guidebook,* which contains the contributions of more than 15 authors who share information regarding their own experience in transitioning to a performance focus. A fourth book, *Zap the Gaps! Target Higher Performance and Achieve It*, co-authored with Ken Blanchard, is to be published in 2002. In May 1999, ASTD presented Jim and Dana Robinson with the 1998 Distinguished Contribution Award for Workplace Learning and Performance.

The Robinsons can be reached at 2547 Washington Road, Suite 720, Pittsburgh, PA, 15241-2557; phone: 412.854.5750; fax: 412.854.5801; email: jrobinson@partners-in-change.com or drobinson@partners-in-change.com; Website: www.partners-in-change.com.

Consulting in State Government by State Government

Management Advisory Services in the Texas State Auditor's Office

Deborah L. Kerr and Thomas J. Shindell

Creating a consulting practice that serves the public sector may not be unusual; creating one that is a public sector organization is quite unusual. That is just what the Texas State Auditor's Office (SAO) did when, in August 1998, it originated a consulting practice to serve the more than 200 Texas state agencies. Management Advisory Services (MAS) in SAO provides state government clients with assistance and information to help develop solutions that improve their organizations and to help identify weaknesses that threaten their effectiveness. The key issues explored in this case include beginning this consulting practice and consulting within state government to state government.

Creating the Business

The Texas State Auditor's Office (SAO) is a legislative agency providing audit and assurance services to the Texas state legislature. Our mission is "To actively provide useful information to government leaders that improves accountability." With a $16 million budget, SAO identifies and audits high-risk areas in the state of Texas. In other words, SAO is the "PricewaterhouseCoopers" or "Deloitte" of Texas government.

SAO has long been nationally and internationally recognized as a leader in innovation. Over the past decade, SAO has been highlighted in numerous private and public sector publications as it pushed the envelope in public sector management, auditing, performance measurement, and performance-based budgeting. Its management systems have been studied by public organizations around the world. Most

This case was prepared to serve as a basis for discussion rather than to illustrate either effective or ineffective administrative and management practices.

recently, SAO was named one of four national "best practice" implementations of the balanced scorecard by the Society for Human Resource Management (Pike, 2001). So when SAO's 1998 strategic planning process indicated a need for SAO to address risk in state government in new and creative ways, it was not unusual for SAO to respond to the need for a different kind of service to the state—a consulting and advisory service to help agencies provide their services more efficiently and effectively. This is especially desirable considering the size of Texas state government.

Texas is big business. In fact, it would rank around number 16 of the *Fortune 50* if it were a private business, generating annual revenues of about $49 billion in fiscal year 2000, slightly lower revenues than Texaco and slightly more revenue than Duke Energy. In fiscal year 2000 the state employed some 272,000 employees—more than twice the number of Exxon Mobil, 100,000 more than either Ford or FedEx, and five times the number of PepsiCo. Obviously, the need for effective management is as important in this public sector context as in any private sector operation.

There were three major drivers to starting the consulting practice. First, the need for services to help state agencies correct problems became clear during SAO's strategic planning process when it viewed risk in the state from these strategic directions:
• identification of risks and problems
• support of risk reduction and solution generation
• education of state employees to avoid future problems.

That meant that the practice would fulfill one strategic direction for SAO as well as help reduce risk in the state management systems. Second, a statewide risk assessment process conducted annually by SAO's Assurance Services division indicated that ineffective management systems and practices were high-risk areas in state government. Third, audit reports contained enough repeat findings to indicate some agencies could use help to take corrective actions to address long-standing organizational problems. Based on this analysis, SAO planned to achieve its mission by:
• identifying risks and problems in its Assurance Services (audit) strategy
• supporting risk reduction and solution generation through the new Management Advisory Services (MAS) strategy
• educating state employees to avoid future problems through the new External Education Services strategy
• overseeing and helping agencies implement Texas's classification and compensation systems through the State Classification Office.

The market niche for MAS was clear:

- As a state organization working for state agencies, MAS would bring an in-depth knowledge of government policies, procedures, and practices (which government agencies themselves have to follow).
- MAS could use tools that were designed specifically to meet public sector challenges.
- State-of-the-art technology and software tools and knowledge were available through SAO for MAS to use with clients.
- MAS could customize information and assistance to meet specific government client needs.
- MAS's billing rates could be significantly lower than those of private sector firms because fees were set to recover the costs of providing services, as required by law.

At the same time, MAS would be a small enough service within a state with an annual budget of about $50 billion that it does not compete with private sector firms that still have plenty of opportunity to generate business.

Making the Transition

The fledgling MAS strategy faced several major internal challenges during startup: credibility, integration, and human capital. While SAO's Assurance Services staff enjoyed a national reputation for excellence, the MAS strategy was new and unknown. Research turned up no models for providing consulting services to the public sector by the public sector, so there was no external referent to provide some implied credibility to the service. The practice was made up from scratch with credibility built from the ground up. And the construction was slow.

At first, the Assurance Services staff questioned the wisdom of offering an organizational "help desk" to state agencies. There was concern about overlap, customer response, independence, credibility, turf, and reputation. One stark indicator of the lack of internal credibility was most evident during SAO's monthly "Achievement of Our Mission" meeting—a 90-minute knowledge-sharing opportunity attended by senior staff and managers and facilitated by the state auditor, Lawrence F. Alwin. At these meetings, there are presentations of new techniques, new work tools, and recent staff successes. The presentations often generate questions and lively discussion, but when MAS made its presentations, there was only polite silence.

To help promote credibility, the MAS manager attended numerous internal team meetings with audit managers and staff. The presentations at these meetings were designed to use the language of auditing and to refer to risk management as the core of the MAS business.

This carefully crafted communication approach helped the highly skilled yet skeptical audit staff understand the connection between its work and the work of MAS.

Credibility grew slowly during the first 18 months as MAS began to collect data that indicated high levels of customer satisfaction and as MAS identified fiscal impact and potential cost savings to agencies. In addition to the information sharing and data collection, MAS staff began to change the way they presented their information. They told stories about their engagements, stories that illustrated how MAS work addressed the risks identified in audits and how clients had found value in the work.

After the seeds of credibility had been successfully sown and cultivated, Assurance Services managers and staff slowly began to refer their audit clients to the MAS team for assistance. MAS project managers began to collaborate with Assurance Services managers by routinely sharing information about contracts and seeking advice from this group of agency experts that could be used in refining the scope of the engagements. And as auditors began to see MAS consulting as a partner in addressing agency problems, the integration of MAS into the day-to-day business of the agency began to solidify.

The integration was furthered when information about engagements began to be reported in the state auditor's monthly letter to the Texas legislature's Legislative Audit Committee and when MAS data from completed projects was internally shared with audit staff in monthly updates. That meant that MAS knowledge of risk in specific agencies became part of the larger office documentation and management of risk in the state.

The third challenge, that of human capital, was evident from the start. The founding MAS manager had extensive consulting experience in the private sector and he understood the skill set needed in a startup—and that skill set differed from that required for an auditor. He addressed the challenge in several ways. First, he hired another experienced consultant from outside state government to help him design and launch the practice. With this base of experience, the team hired a talented Assurance Services auditor who had shown not only interest in MAS, but also had already demonstrated some of the more important consulting skills in her audit projects.

Having secured several contracts, the team expanded with the hiring of another experienced consultant who had been working in another agency and a second SAO auditor with a strong financial and technical background. As business picked up (six contracts by August 2000), the professional staff expanded to six consultants supported by one administrative assistant. With no real marketing effort, the consulting service exceeded its revenue projections in its second year of operations. That was due to the development of loyal customers, repeat engagements, as well as business expansion through word of mouth.

Developing a Strategy

One of the main purposes of the Texas State Auditor's Office is to identify, minimize, and eliminate risk in state government. "Risk" is defined by SAO as the chance that something will happen that will have an adverse impact on the success of achieving expected results. Risk may be indicated by such factors as instability in the agency's management environment or changed customer expectations, ineffective or inefficient controls over significant resources, significant gaps between expected and actual results, large commitments of state dollars or other resources, or significant impact on citizens' quality of life. SAO does this through a three-pronged approach mirrored in the three business strategies of the office: 1) assurance services (conducting audits and reviews to detect risk to the state); 2) education services (teaching agencies how to avoid potential risks to the state); and 3) management advisory services (consulting with state agencies to address clearly identified risks to the state). (See figure 1.)

By working collaboratively with state agencies, SAO is able to move beyond the roles of identifier of current risks and educator to prevent risks to one of partner to eliminate or resolve risks. MAS helps agencies resolve problems in three areas of risk: 1) financial risk (addressing issues around "How was the money spent?"); 2) service risk

Figure 1. Three-pronged approach to risk.

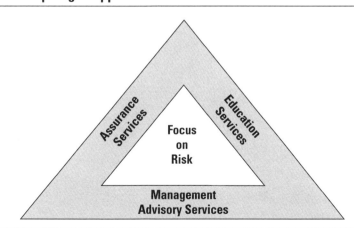

(addressing issues about "What services did citizens get for the money?"); and 3) business risk (addressing issues about "How does the agency conduct business?"). (See figure 2.)

Using a consulting strategy helps SAO move beyond the outdated paradigm of the "adversarial" auditor/auditee relationship to the more progressive partner/collaborator relationship of consultant/client. While this has been occurring in the private sector, this is new and progressive for state government. Using MAS allows SAO to be on the

Figure 2. Risk categories.

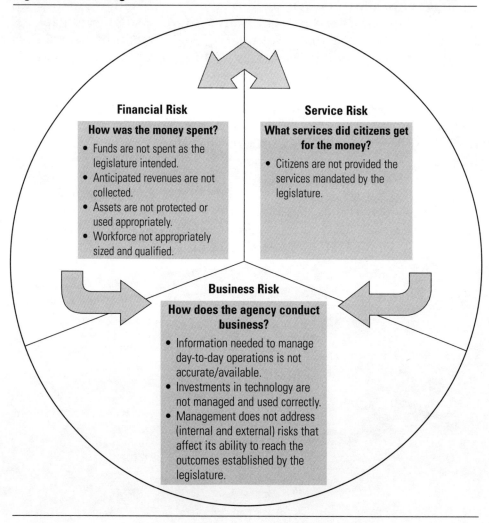

cutting edge of state government auditing while at the same time minimizing its financial exposure because of the cost recovery nature of the enterprise.

Structuring the Business

MAS was created as one of three major strategies in SAO. Its work helps drive the organization's results toward mission achievement. For SAO, its mission is to "actively provide government leaders with useful information that improves accountability." For MAS, its mission is "to provide state government clients with assistance and information to identify weaknesses and develop solutions to improve their organizations."

MAS is staffed by a manager, five organization improvement specialists, and one support staff member. (See figure 3.) MAS is fortunate because it already has access to many services that private sector firms would have to staff or outsource. For example, MAS uses the legal services of SAO to review and approve contracts. MAS also uses the business services section of SAO for billing, accounts

Figure 3. Texas state auditor's office.

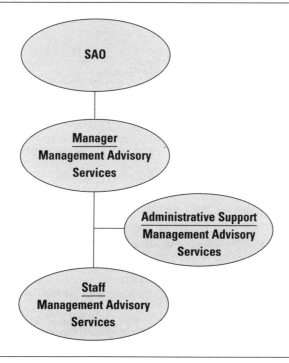

receivable, purchasing, and payroll. While these costs are calculated into the MAS billing rate and are cost recovered, not having to staff or perform these functions directly provided a competitive advantage for MAS.

MAS generates revenue by offering the following services:
- organizational design and structure analysis
- performance management (including balanced scorecard)
- process analysis
- organizational development
- financial management and analysis
- leadership development
- strategic planning and performance-based budgeting
- benchmarking
- change facilitation
- human resources management
- performance measure development
- information systems strategy and architecture.

Managing the Business

MAS is managed using a balanced scorecard that is based on the research of Harvard's Robert Kaplan and David Norton (1996). (See figure 4.)

Like all public sector organizations, MAS was not designed to make a profit. It was designed to provide services that ultimately benefit the citizens of Texas through agencies that are better managed (and thus less costly to run) and services that are more efficient and effective. MAS is designed, however, to recover the costs of providing its services to agencies. Rather than controlling costs to ensure a profit, MAS controls costs to ensure that the state is receiving a high value/high return on its expenditures for MAS consulting services. The "profit" is generated when value is created for the state.

There are two major measures of value creation. First, the overall profit is measured as the cumulative fiscal or economic impact identified. The target for that measure is greater than or equal to 200 percent of the total annual MAS costs.

A second measure that substitutes for the profit measure is fiscal impact as compared to actual job cost, where actual cost is defined as number of hours spent on the project times the billing rate. For each project, the result answers the question: "What value/financial impact has MAS reported for the funds expended or the resources used?" The target for this measure is greater than or equal to 175 percent of the costs of a project.

Figure 4. Management advisory services scorecard.

Perspective	Objective	Measure
Mission	• Help improve service delivery • Help maximize utilization of resources • Help prevent problems/eliminate problems • Identify and correct inefficiency • Recovers costs/revenue generation	• Fiscal Impact • Fiscal Impact to Actual Job Cost • Impact Rating • Total Revenue Target
Customer Focus	• Delivery of value • Proven credibility • Quick response • Recognized expertise • Tailored projects and deliverables (customization) • Trust (confidentiality)	• Percent of On-Time Delivery
Internal Processes	• Defining the project • Packaging deliverables • Process controls/project management • Project acceptance process (intake process)—assessment of project desirability • Technology	• Percent of Active Projects On-Target • Hours—Actual per Project
Learning and Knowledge	• Customer communication skills (ability to articulate customer needs) • Positive employee climate • Subject matter/technical skills	• Employee Feedback Rating • Skill Capacity of MAS Staff
Financial	• Budget allocation (size of efforts) • Revenue generation targets	• Budgeted Revenue • Cost Recovery Rate • Hours—Billed

Measuring Business Success

The success of MAS is measured and reported monthly on SAO's balanced scorecard, which is a subunit of SAO's scorecard. From the beginning, MAS was designed to be a "strategy-focused" operation. In other words, MAS was created to help SAO achieve its mission and its strategic goal more effectively and efficiently.

The MAS scorecard is built using five perspectives, an adaptation of the Kaplan & Norton private sector. The performance information is reported using pbviews©, a performance management software package designed to extract data from SAO's management information system and organize it within an easy-to-use "dashboard" format. (See figure 5.)

Each month, measure data is collected and reported electronically. Commentary that explains variances from targets and as action plans for addressing problem areas also is entered into the report by the measure "owner." The strategic implications of the performance results are discussed at a monthly meeting of MAS staff as well as at the monthly meeting of the entire SAO executive team. MAS's performance goal in

Figure 5. MAS balanced scorecard dashboard.

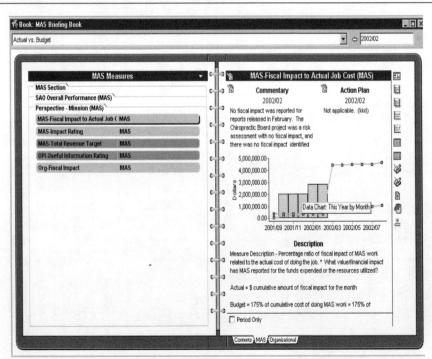

its first full year of operation was to recover 60 percent of its total costs. MAS exceeded that goal. In the second full year of operation, the bar was raised: MAS was expected to recover 70 percent of its total costs while using a billing rate derived from the budget and expenses approved for the fiscal year. As MAS enters its third year of operations, the cost recovery goal has now been set at 100 percent.

Coping with Growing Pains

MAS encountered several growing pains in its first 12 months in the areas of staff selection, physical location, training and software, working with internal service providers, changes in managers, and "scope creep."

MAS initially began with three organization improvement specialists, one manager, and one administrative assistant. After the first three months, it became clear that there was a difference between the work MAS planned to do and the skill set of a staff member. It took several months to get this issue resolved, which placed tremendous stress on the MAS team and its manager.

Physical location was another growing pain MAS faced. Initially, the manager and the administrative assistant were on one floor while the organization improvement specialists were housed in two offices on another floor. It took a year, including a move of the entire SAO to a new building, before MAS staff was in one location.

Appropriate training and software are keys to the success of any new consulting practice. Initially, software was selected for preparing flowcharts for clients. While one member of the MAS team was well versed in the software, none of the other MAS staff could master the program. Moreover, no training in the software program was available. SAO's production services staff was reluctant to support the software because it was not used by the entire SAO. After much frustration, another flowcharting software was selected.

MAS was also challenged by the use of PricewaterhouseCoopers' TeamMate audit management software. SAO uses TeamMate to manage audit projects and to provide a mechanism for documenting work for quality control review. While a very useful program, TeamMate had to be modified several times to meet the needs of MAS and its various consulting projects. Training the MAS staff in the use of Team-Mate has been an additional task.

Working with internal service providers at the SAO (for example, human resources, business services, legal, and production services) also was a challenge. The primary challenge MAS faced in this area involved production services. Initially, production services agreed to support MAS projects and its timelines, which were much tighter than those for most audit projects. However, after conflicts, missing deliverable deadlines, and stressed relationships between MAS and production services staff, the production of MAS deliverables has been moved to MAS.

An additional challenge came from the SAO legal department's review of MAS contracts. The challenge was twofold. First, MAS experienced the normal challenge expected in trying to reach agreement about consistent contract format and language. The second challenge, however, was addressing the perception of MAS that SAO's legal staff would suggest one approach, agree to it, and then later suggest a contradictory approach. Those perceived changes in approach caused consternation on the part of MAS staff.

MAS also experienced the growing pains when changes were made in management of the strategy. Initially, Pat Keith was the manager of MAS from its formalization as a strategy until May 2000. Then Tom Shindell served as the acting manager of MAS until September 2000, when Frank Vito was named manager of MAS and led the team until May 2001. Currently, Deborah Kerr is the manager of MAS. When a new consulting entity is being created, such rapid turnover in management places a strain not only on the employees but also on the concern itself as it continues to adapt to its own emerging identity and to the changing visions and expectations of various managers.

The final growing pain MAS experienced was "scope creep." In trying to please initial clients and have satisfied customers to serve as marketing references, MAS often agreed to provide services and products not specified in contracts. While scope creep did not affect revenue projection targets, it did have a significant impact on the timeframes to complete projects (generally, they took longer) and on the number of hours required to complete the projects. MAS literally had to expand its staff hour budget to accommodate the scope creep encountered.

Facing Barriers and Fears

MAS faced several barriers and fears. The barriers MAS faced included developing a consulting infrastructure from scratch, determining the best way to accommodate and fit into an audit organization, and developing mechanisms to provide consulting services while also operating in a public organization. Fears MAS faced included attracting clients, "meshing" with SAO, running a business inside a larger organization, and having to go through some of the protocols of "audit work" rather than "consulting work."

Resolving Ethical Issues

There were several ethical issues MAS had to cope with in its formation. The first issue was how to protect the "independence" of the state auditor—the ability of the audit staff to conduct audits in agencies where MAS assistance work had been performed. The crux of the issue was providing assistance that did not compromise or potentially compromise the work of the Assurance Services staff in the performance of its duties. Several fears were raised by audit staff such as, "If you make a recommendation we don't agree with, how can we audit it?" or "What happens if you are doing assistance work and we want to do an audit?" or "What happens if you find fraud?" and so forth. Several drafts of guidelines were developed and circulated before a policy was adopted, which basically included several procedures about notification and a separation of time between audit and consulting work. What stood out most in the development of the guidelines for independence was the skeptical attitude of audit staff toward MAS staff. It really felt like a "we/they" dynamic until the independence issue was resolved and a more collegial relationship between audit and MAS developed.

Since drafting this chapter in the fall of 2001, an important event occurred that affects consulting in state government. The issues about the energy company Enron and its consulting and auditing relationship with Andersen have raised professional ethical concerns about a single organization providing both auditing and consulting services. The auditing profession has updated its guidelines governing these relationships. The Texas State Auditor's Office and MAS comply with these revised professional guidelines. Compliance occurs as a result of high levels of horizontal communication between audit and MAS about projects, which ensures that independence is maintained. This relationship is documented in the office's policies and procedures.

The second ethical issue MAS faced was assuring clients' confidentiality. Working in a state agency for other state agencies requires operating in a very open and public environment. That can be challenging when clients request assistance about sensitive matters that they would not want to be made public. On the other hand, because everything an agency does is subject to an "open records request," which forces the agency to supply requested information, the challenge of providing confidential assistance can be great. The solution was to state that work in progress is to be considered "working papers" of SAO. This allows MAS to provide confidential services. Of course, all final reports and final deliverables, which MAS clients have reviewed and agreed to, are public documents that are subject to open records requests.

The third ethical issue MAS faced was determining the appropriate level of quality control review and the associated standards. Auditors working in Assurance Services have very specific guidelines and standards they are required to follow. The level of "proof" for assertions or statements made in audit reports is equivalent to what would be supportable in a court of law. However, there are no comparable, widely accepted standards for consultants. While no one in MAS would ever do sloppy work, how could the work be evaluated? According to what standards? Eventually, the following position was adopted so that all clients received the same level of work and so that work can be reviewed the same way:

> In performing its consulting services, MAS will ensure sufficient and relevant data is gathered and used as a basis for any conclusions or recommendations. The data used by MAS may be either qualitative or quantitative in nature. Analyses and assertions of issue, fact finding, conclusion, or recommendations by MAS will be documented in working papers and presented in a manner that would lead an objective third party to reach the same or similar conclusions and recommendations (*MAS Guidelines*, p. 15).

The fourth ethical issue MAS faced was how to consult in a public setting. Considering the normal standards of restraint and conservatism associated with state government, and especially state auditors, beginning a small consulting business was considered avant-garde. Even though the idea was accepted, implementing a small business that corresponded with the operations of state government proved to be full of ethical issues, which included the following:

- creating a fair and equitable billing rate that does not create a "profit" and at the same time allows MAS to recover a percentage of operating costs
- marketing in a way that is tasteful and comparable to private sector consultants
- maintaining the privacy of clients while also being accountable to the state legislature
- selecting work that not only assists the client but also benefits the state.

Attracting and Keeping Clients

MAS is in a unique position when it comes to attracting and retaining clients. Initially, as the strategy was being defined and its infrastructure was being established, there were no advertising or marketing efforts made. As the structure was further defined and approved, clients conveniently appeared, either through referrals from the audit staff (analogous to a "built-in salesforce" for MAS) or from connections made during other SAO activities. While an initial advertising brochure was developed, it was never widely distributed because the business grew at a rate that kept pace with MAS's ability to deliver services. That is no longer the case. Nationally, state governments have realized a reduction in revenues because of the current economic downturn. The Texas governor recently requested a voluntary budget reduction from all state agencies in anticipation of a statewide budget shortfall. These are some of the factors that have led to a decline in clients for MAS.

MAS has, however, developed the following mechanisms to attract clients:

- a brochure listing MAS's vision, mission, purpose, and services
- a Website located within SAO's Website
- a quarterly newsletter
- a listing of past clients who are willing to serve a business references.

Other strategies have emerged to attract clients—especially repeat customers. One strategy has been MAS's conscious effort not only to meet, but also to exceed, customer expectations. For example, MAS has

- provided a larger scope of work than originally contracted
- provided "extra" information or analysis to benefit the client
- provided extra deliverables such as information on CDs in addition to written reports.

That effort has proven effective for several clients who have either entered into second contracts with MAS or who have amended current contracts to expand the scope of paid work. Of course, there has been some scope creep in order to preserve goodwill with clients and to build MAS's reputation. While that has increased costs, it has been a worthwhile investment. MAS also obtains clients through referrals from the legislature.

Identifying the Keys to Success

There are at least three major keys to the initial success MAS experienced. The first was having a secure financial base from the beginning and having the resources of an existing organization from which to draw. Having to worry about making payroll, paying expenses, and so forth was a major barrier that did not have to be confronted. Further, the nature of the business is cost recovery (as opposed to profit making), which creates a different set of financial expectations. Having to recover one's costs is much easier than having to make a profit.

The second key to success was the strong skill sets of experience and expertise that was present from the beginning. Initial staff had served as successful consultants in their own businesses, in other consulting firms, and in state government before coming to SAO. Having staff who knew the ropes and knew what was needed (and what to avoid) to create and support a new consulting operation was critical to MAS's success. The critical skills MAS staff possessed were

- developing a workable consulting infrastructure
- consulting engagement and contract negotiation
- managing projects and contracts
- creating credibility and projecting expertise
- thinking systemically and long-term
- dealing with ambiguity effectively
- coping with constant change, both internally at SAO and externally with clients
- using internal and external resources creatively to further the development of MAS
- communicating effectively both internally at SAO and externally with clients and potential clients.

The third key to success was MAS's ability to overcome obstacles—both internal and external. Internal obstacles included preserving the "independence" of the Texas state auditor (ensuring that MAS's consulting work did not interfere with other Texas state auditor agency staff's ability to conduct audits by creating conflicts of professional judgment) and adapting to an audit environment in which the identification and mitigation of risk are the primary objectives of the larger organization. The support of the Texas state auditor, Lawrence F. Alwin, was critical to the development and success of MAS.

The external obstacles included getting clients to accept MAS as true consultants and not as an arm of the state auditor or in some other way secretly checking up on them. MAS also needed to build credibility with the Texas state legislature's Legislative Audit Committee, which the agency is accountable to by providing it with a synopsis of completed MAS projects.

Falling Short of the Mark

While MAS does not really consider any of its activities to date a failure, there have been several hurdles. Among these were staffing issues, organizational "fit" and "acceptance" issues, and project management issues. The first hurdle to overcome was staffing issues. MAS not only had to justify additional staff from a business perspective (how the extra staff would allow MAS to complete more work, meet its commitments, and recover the additional expense), but also had to recognize and deal with poor performance. With such a small staff, having a member of the team who does not contribute to the work or who creates tension and stress has a significant impact.

MAS has experienced a reduction in staff. Two staff members left for other opportunities (both promotions—one inside and one outside SAO) and have not been replaced because of the drop in business. MAS is currently implementing a marketing plan to increase business with new clients. As business increases, staff will be added as needed.

The second hurdle was creating a good fit and gaining acceptance within SAO. Initially, other SAO staff were skeptical about the creation of MAS. MAS made deliberate attempts to build bridges to the audit staff, including providing updates on MAS activities, distributing MAS's guidelines, and even hosting an officewide "beach party" to invite other staff to learn more about MAS. As a result, there is increasing acceptance and recognition of the work MAS does and its contribution to SAO. The third hurdle has been project management—scope creep, as discussed above.

Pinpointing the Lessons Learned

The major lessons learned about creating a public consulting firm fall into four categories: 1) organizational structure; 2) management; 3) staff; and 4) clients. From an organizational structure perspective, it is best to set up as much structure as possible as early as possible. That includes thinking through policies, procedures, and process, getting as many relevant stakeholders involved as early as possible, and building bridges as early as possible. It also is critical to be properly capitalized. MAS was fortunate to be in a unique position of not needing to worry about income and cash flow, although it did have to worry about cost recovery. Taking these steps could help minimize the need to sell yourself internally at a later date and minimize internal barriers to acceptance.

From a management perspective, it is preferable to ensure stable management. While a little more than three years old, MAS has had four different managers. Each manager stressed different issues, had a slightly different vision for the practice, and steered MAS on a slightly different course. The turnover in management has been a challenge for the staff to work through. It is also critical that there is proper support for the manager of the practice. If the manager is not well supported, then the acceptance of the practice as a whole can be jeopardized.

From a staffing perspective, it is critical that staff be chosen cautiously and carefully. Review applicant qualifications thoroughly and, if possible, try to simulate some of the tasks they will be performing to be able to assess performance during the selection process. For example, MAS asks applicants to evaluate the hiring process in a writing sample applicants prepare at the end of their interview process. That activity mimics the type of analysis they would do with clients. The other lesson learned about staffing is to deal with poor performance as quickly and directly as possible. MAS, being in the public eye, cannot always act as fast as its private sector counterparts. However, staffing problems in a small start-up consulting practice can stress the staff to the limits of its ability to function effectively. Avoid that situation at all costs.

It is important for a practice in the start-up mode to deliver more than clients expect. Providing more analysis, and more deliverables, adds value and surprise and helps ensure client satisfaction. It also is important to meet specified deadlines—even finishing work early, if possible. Being willing to do "pro bono" work also helps boost the firm's visibility. Finally, the practice must keep all stakeholders in mind. In MAS's case, the list of stakeholders went beyond clients to include the Texas state auditor, the Texas state legislative audit committee, and the legislature—not to mention the citizens of the state of Texas. Being a public entity requires a level of operational "transparency" that private sector firms avoid. Thinking about all of the stakeholders is always a good yardstick by which to measure the actions taken to develop your practice.

Questions for Discussion

1. What barriers do you think government entities in your state would face if they attempted to begin a similar practice? Would the barriers be different at the federal/state/county/local level? If so, how?
2. If you were a government decision maker, how would you respond to such a consulting practice? If you were an elected official, how would you respond to such a consulting practice?
3. If you were a private consultant, how would you view such a practice? As competition? As a potential employer? As a resource?

4. What challenges does a government entity face as it begins a consulting practice? How are these alike and different from starting a private practice?

5. What specific challenges do you see when government acts as a consultant to itself? What are the benefits? Are there any drawbacks?

6. What extra challenges do consultants face when they work with or for auditors? What are the special issues to be addressed?

The Authors

Deborah L. Kerr is chief strategy officer at the Texas State Auditor's Office and a visiting lecturer at the George Bush School of Government and Public Service at Texas A&M University where she teaches policy formation and advanced public management in the graduate school. As a member of the state auditor's executive team, she helps define the strategic direction and management systems for the office. For more than 20 years, Kerr has worked both in the private and public sectors, helping organizations increase efficiency and effectiveness through improved management systems. Her design of performance appraisal systems for the public sector was cited as one of four outstanding national public sector management initiatives by *Financial World* magazine in its May 1993 review of 50 states' management practices. Kerr also served on the national advisory panel to develop public sector performance measures for the "Grading Government" series published in *Governing* magazine. While working in the public sector, she has successfully introduced and adapted traditionally private sector strategies, including leading the design and implementation of one of the first public sector balanced scorecards in the nation. That project recently was recognized as one of the four most successful balanced scorecard implementations in the country by the Society for Human Resource Management. Kerr is often asked to speak on management and human performance issues at regional, state, and national conferences. She can be reached at the Texas State Auditor's Office, 1501 Robert E. Johnson Building, 4.224, Austin, TX 78701; phone: 512.936.9500; email: dkerr@sao.state.tx.us.

Thomas J. Shindell is the team leader of management advisory services for the Texas State Auditor's Office. A former assistant professor in human resource development at Northeastern Illinois University and former adjunct faculty for the Open University of Tamaulipas, Shindell received his Ph.D. in human resource development and adult education from the University of Texas at Austin.

He has worked in state government, private corporations, and higher education. Shindell has been both the assistant executive director and executive director for the Academy of Human Resource Development, and has served as an external consultant for more than 10 years with various clients. He has published articles in numerous publications and is a reviewer for HRDQ and CHOICE. Shindell serves on the ASTD Research to Practice Committee.

Acknowledgment Note by Authors

The authors wish to thank Mary Avila and Judy Valando for their technical assistance and expertise in the preparation of this case.

References

Kaplan, R.S., and D.P. Norton. (1996). *Translating Strategy into Action: The Balanced Scorecard.* Boston: Harvard Business School Press.

Texas State Auditor's Office Management Advisory Services Group. (2000). *Management Advisory Services (MAS) Helping Agencies Improve Texas: A Guide to Implementing MAS at the State Auditor's Office.* Texas State Auditor's Office, Austin. Photocopy.

Pike, Valerie E. (Spring 2001). *Balanced Scorecard Basics on Implementation.* http://my.shrm.org/whitepapers/default.asp?page=manage.htm. Society for Human Resource Management.

Becoming a One-Person Consulting Firm

McCoy Training and Development Resources

Carol P. McCoy

McCoy Training and Development Resources (MTDR) was founded as a sole-proprietorship two and a half years ago by Carol P. McCoy who took an early retirement package from her previous employee. The company provides training, consulting, and HRD tools to organizations and individuals in New England and throughout the United States. McCoy had already gained experience as a one-person training department inside a company. The new challenge was learning to use these same skills to serve customers as a one-person external consulting firm. The business has enabled her to earn a living in HRD while still having enough time to pursue her love of genealogy.

The Practice

Two and a half years ago, I took advantage of an early retirement program to obtain a small pension and health benefits package after more than 25 years in corporate life and academia to start my own consulting business. I founded McCoy Training and Development Resources, a sole-proprietorship that operates from my home in Falmouth, Maine. MTDR is dedicated to helping organizations and individuals achieve their goals by providing HRD and training solutions, which increase their effectiveness and resilience in a constantly changing world. The business generated a profit within the first year.

This case was prepared to serve as a basis for discussion rather than to illustrate either effective or ineffective administrative and management practices.

MTDR serves both profit and nonprofit organizations, as well as individuals, located in the northeast United States, primarily Maine. Products and services include:

- design and delivery of customized training and educational programs
- delivery of standardized training programs offered by large training companies
- books and articles to help trainers and managers
- motivational talks and keynote addresses
- team building and facilitation of meetings
- development of competency models and tools
- development of performance management tools
- coaching
- Myers-Briggs Type Indicator®
- genealogical research for individuals.

The primary business segment is delivery of customized training and educational programs and externally certified programs. The next segments are design and team building, followed by consulting. The company also receives income from writing articles, book royalties, and manuscript reviews.

I began the business on July 15, 1999, with one for-profit consulting client and a nonprofit team building client. In 1999 MTDR launched a personally managed Website that described services and credentials, promoted my books, and offered free articles and tools on training. The Website started out promisingly but then crashed on leap day February 29, 2000. After the crash, I hired a Web master and had a professionally managed and improved Website up and running by March.

Since 1994 I have taught managing training and development at the Center for Continuing Education of the University of Southern Maine (USM). I used my book *Managing a Small HRD Department* (1993) as the textbook for that course. I now teach a shorter introduction to training and development in the university's trainer certificate program. MTDR typically offers about six to 10 complimentary workshops and speeches as marketing events per year. In spring 2000 I was invited to submit articles on human resources and management to an online newspaper. These articles have provided publicity and have served as tools to reinforce concepts taught in my workshops.

In June 2000 I chaired the two-day Maine ASTD Conference, where Jack Phillips was the keynote speaker. As chairperson, I had an opportunity to work closely with Phillips, who has been a mentor and a source of inspiration to me. This prestigious event provided tremendous learning and publicity but it required a year of planning and relentless follow-up.

By the summer of 2000 I had facilitated some train-the-trainer sessions for a large bank and also led some change leadership workshops for several bank locations. In fall 2000 the bank's training director decided to purchase a leadership program from a large vendor. The director offered to certify me to teach those leadership workshops. The certification process entailed attending a one-week train-the-trainer program. That process not only enabled me to instruct leadership programs for the bank, but it also provided an opportunity to meet other training managers. Consequently, another participant in the certification invited me to develop a workshop on handling challenging customers for a client in Massachusetts.

Also in the fall of 2000, my previous employer hired me to do a consulting project and then certified me to instruct a different leadership program, which I facilitated throughout that year. In January 2001 I offered a coaching workshop for a college in Maine. That initial contact led to repeat business with one of the directors who attended the workshop. MTDR now has a core of regular clients who require consulting and training at various points throughout the year.

Recently I have become a contributing editor for *IOMA's Report on Training Programs* published by the Institute of Management & Administration. I have also begun to offer genealogical research services for individuals. Genealogy has been my passion for more than 20 years, and I intend to supplement my primary HRD work by teaching workshops on genealogy and helping people to trace their family roots.

Making the Transition

Starting my own HRD business was not something that I had always dreamed of doing, but was an idea that blossomed when my employer merged with another company and offered a generous early retirement package. I jumped at the opportunity to take early retirement, but wasn't sure what to do next. I went to the company's career development center and participated in an outside seminar, where I discovered that my top values are freedom, creative self-expression, and personal development. After only one session with my career counselor, I decided to go out on my own. The only way to be free to express myself and learn what I wanted was to be my own boss.

I was confident that I had the right skills and background. I had written books on human resource development, taught psychology and training in a college setting, had designed and delivered training programs for a money center bank and for a leading disability insurer, had been an internal performance consultant, and had managed two small training departments. As a result, I already knew challenges facing my target audience and had a working knowledge of business strategy, budgeting, and business dynamics. I expected to focus my practice on small training departments and on financial services companies. Finally, writing books had helped me to clarify my philosophy, to create some useful learning tools, and to start building my credibility.

I began my journey by meeting with other consultants who gave me great advice and occasionally referred business to me. I also took workshops through SCORE (Service Corps of Retired Executives), which helped inspire me to write my mission statement and my business plan. Having a clear and focused mission and plan are essential for launching a successful business. I also saw my accountant and found a lawyer, who both advised me to set up a sole proprietorship.

In transitioning from a corporate employee to a self-employed contractor, it helps to have tangible signs of your new business identity. I worked with an artist friend to design a logo and a business card. I felt such pride and satisfaction when I saw my name and logo on my card and my new stationery. Finally with the help of a colleague from my former employer, I created a simple Website on a free host. Those steps helped me to focus and to make my new business more real to me.

Strategy

My business plan identified types of services, areas of expertise, types of clients, geographic area of concentration, and approach to marketing. I also developed short- and long-term financial, marketing, and developmental goals.

Services and Areas of Expertise

My services focus on five primary areas:
1. train-the-trainer, including needs assessment, design, delivery and facilitation skills, and managing the HRD function
2. leadership and management skills, such as performance management, coaching, and feedback
3. leading change and dealing with change
4. communication and conflict resolution
5. achieving service excellence and dealing with challenging customers.

An important strategy has been finding a balance between consulting, writing articles and books, designing, teaching, and delivering training. Initially I expected to deliver workshops that I designed personally. But I have learned that delivering standardized programs offered by large training companies can be profitable and satisfying. My primary strategy is to offer some standardized programs on training and facilitation skills, management, dealing with change, service, and communication, which can be customized to fit the needs of particular customers. For example, I designed a performance management program, which is offered as part of a university sponsored supervisory certificate program, and which I offer as a stand-alone workshop. Also, I created a framework for needs assessment, described in McCoy (1993). Based on that, I teach needs assessment as a two-hour stand-alone workshop as part of a managing training and development college course, as a customized half-day workshop for a key client, and as a module in the New Hampshire ASTD Trainer Certificate program.

In the future, I would like to derive more income from consulting and genealogy and less income from delivering workshops. I like the challenge of helping clients to solve important problems, and I want to avoid burning out from teaching the same programs repeatedly. Also, I plan to create tools such as videos or workbooks, which provide some passive income.

Market

Because my goal was to increase freedom to do what I love, my core strategy has been to serve local clients who live primarily in New England. To keep costs and travel time to a minimum, I aim to do 80 percent of my work within driving distance. Given the current fear of air travel, this also suits my personal needs. A second aspect has been to identify five to 10 core clients with whom I would do repeat business versus trying to do work with many clients whom I don't know well. Also, I have a balance of for profit and nonprofit clients, with whom I work at a discounted rate.

Financial Strategy

My overall financial goal is to make enough money so that I can retire within 10 years and transition to full-time genealogy. To keep start-up costs low and to achieve a profit, I decided to work out of my home. Having a small pension and subsidized health, dental, and life insurance helps. Without any secondary income, I would have been reluctant to start my own business. (See table 1 on start-up costs.)

While I have a monthly income target, my income varies greatly from month to month. Expense management is critical because of the ups and downs of the annual training cycle. I try to maximize work during busy months and take advantage of down times in the Maine economy to do enriching activities, such as genealogy and gardening.

Table 1. MTDR business start-up costs.

Categories	Considerations	Costs
Office	• Work out of my home	0
Computer—Desktop	• Already had a good computer	0
Computer—Laptop	• Did not purchase a laptop	0
Fax Machine	• Fax machine and set up charges	$485
Training Equipment	• Flipchart stand; projector	$350
Training Supplies	• Overhead transparencies and covers, flipchart paper	$350
Health & Life Insurance	• Subsidized by previous employer	$2,640
Business Insurance	• Commercial insurance	$300
Telephone	• Use home phone for business	$360
	• No listing in Yellow Pages	0
Cell Phone	• Purchased a cell phone for car	$360
Fax	• Charges for separate fax line	$360
Logo Design	• Friend designed logo	$100
Business Cards and	• 500 cards	$250
Stationery	• 500 letterhead, envelopes	$300
Business Labels	• 500 mailing labels with logo	$330
Business Flier	• 500 fliers	$225
Website Management	• Domain name, site creation, and annual hosting charges	$1,000
Internet Access	• Use "Road Runner" to avoid tying up the phone line	$504
	• Keep AOL account	$120
Business Account	• Business checks and tracking book	$113
Total Annual Expenses First Year of Operation*	• Based on monthly average	$8,147

*Approximate MTDR start-up costs based on monthly averages and annual expenditures in major expense categories for the first year of operation.

Structure of the Practice

McCoy Training and Development Resources is a sole proprietorship. I decided not to incorporate to save money and to simplify the structure. At times I subcontract work with colleagues. My accountant has worked with me for 10 years, and the company that sold me my computer helps me resolve technological problems.

Attracting and Keeping Clients

I market MTDR primarily through networking with business contacts, a Website, courses offered at USM, conference presentations, newspaper and Web articles, and mailing of fliers and articles to prospects and clients. A key to success is building positive relationships with several core clients, regular marketing, finding new income streams, and maintaining the relevance of my Website.

Fortunately before leaving my old company, I had written two books and also delivered workshops for several local organizations, including the Maine Chapter of the American Society for Training & Development. In addition, I had taught training courses for USM since 1994. As a result, training and human resource managers of several companies already knew me. (See table 2 on marketing approaches.)

The next step was letting people know that I was out on my own. I developed a prospective client list of people with whom I had worked, contacts made when giving presentations, and others who were recommended by colleagues. I called people and asked to meet with them to find out what their needs were. I explained that my goal was to identify a handful of key clients that I would get to know well and be able to service on a personal level. I also referred people to my Website in order to supplement information that I provided through meetings and phone calls.

Generally I follow the model of interview questions recommended by Robinson and Robinson (1996). I ask about the organization's goals and problems and opportunities facing its departments and try to identify any performance improvement needs. If it looks like there is a match of need and skills, I suggest possible solutions. If they seem interested, I write a brief proposal and follow-up to answer questions.

Initially when meeting with prospective clients, I brought along a one-page description of my business mission, services, and personal credentials. Over time as I gained clients and successful experiences, I revised my description. I created a tri-fold flier that had more white space, pictures, a client list, and testimonials. That flier is easier to read and can be mailed without an envelope. Periodically, I send it to clients and prospects, along with articles that I've written.

Table 2. Pros and cons of marketing approaches.

Marketing Activities	Benefits	Concerns	Typical Outcomes
Networking meetings	• Personal impression • Demonstrates your approach to problems • Able to uncover needs • Find new leads	• Takes time and energy • Need a referral versus a cold call • Travel time and cost	• Is the best way to generate business and to build relationships. • Can lead to proposals.
Writing articles for newspapers or free Websites	• Gain credibility • Good exposure • Can use in programs • Use in mailings • Clarifies my thoughts	• Need discipline to do it regularly	• Generates publicity and goodwill with current and future clients. • May trigger a call from a client.
Delivering free workshops or speeches	• Live work sample • Able to reach new audience face-to-face • Can customize later • Can show or leave work samples, fliers, and books	• Time and work • May require travel • Nonreimbursable expenses • Venue constraints can limit effectiveness	• Is excellent way to generate positive interest in establishing a working relationship.
Website with biography, services, tools, articles, links	• Professional impression • Provides useful tools • Generates goodwill • Faster than mailing • Lets clients get to know you before they meet you	• Time and energy • Hire a professional Web master • Need to think through goals • Regular updates • Need a backup system	• Has provided extremely positive feedback. • Helps to crystallize my image. • Provides tools that are useful to reinforce concepts. • Has generated a few leads. • Has generated interest in working for my company.
Mailing flier (with sample articles)	• Reach large audience • Cheaper than travel • Can reinforce teachings • Helps you focus your business • Reminds people that you exist	• Must keep up the mailing list • Need to design a professional flier that will last • Lack of face-to-face connection • People may throw it out as "junk mail"	• Generates more positive feedback than business leads.

Table 2. Pros and cons of marketing approaches (continued).

Marketing Activities	Benefits	Concerns	Typical Outcomes
Writing books for sale on Web or face-to-face	• Gain credibility • Some profit • Educate customers • Satisfaction and contribution • Express your philosophy	• Time-consuming and labor intensive to write a book • Comes across as hard sell when done face-to-face • Books can become outdated • Publishers focus on high-profile authors	• Garners some royalties. • Offers more "psychic" than financial income. • Is excellent publicity and credibility builder. • Works well as a textbook in my courses.
Teaching at local college	• Meet local training and HR managers • Demonstrate competence and services • Keep in touch with what is happening • Able to use my book as a text	• Does not pay well • Can be exhausting to teach during night hours	• Has led to some new business with clients that I've met in other venues.

This represents a sample of activities that I have pursued at various times.

To gain some publicity on a timely topic, I wrote an article on dealing with change for the *Portland Press Herald*. After I was confident that the business would succeed, I wrote a press release announcing my new business and sent it to local papers. Several newspapers published a brief description of MTDR at no cost. That news release resulted in two new clients who hired me for projects.

Keeping clients has a lot to do with delivering what you have promised on time and with quality. After doing work for my first client, I asked if I could use them for a testimonial. When I asked them what I'd done that pleased them, they said "Even though you knew nothing about our business at first, you learned our business really quickly. After two weeks, it was as if you knew this business for years. You told us what you would do and you did it!" Getting to know the business meant doing some research on the company, having a knowledge of business dynamics, asking good questions, listening, observing, and summarizing observations and issues for the client.

Another strategy in keeping clients is following up after providing a service to see whether clients are satisfied and whether you can provide additional services to reinforce the value of the original work. A good example of this is Bates College where someone I knew through the local ASTD chapter invited me to do a two-hour workshop on coaching for several directors. At the session, Laurie Henderson, a department director, expressed interest in talking with me about doing some team building with her staff. She had two highly skilled staff members who resented each other and did not consistently share information that the other needed. The director felt as if she had tried everything, but nothing had improved the situation.

I suggested that I conduct some needs assessment interviews and then do two team building sessions with her and the two staff members. After interviewing her staff, I learned that one person felt overworked and the other felt underworked! The solution was obvious but couldn't be implemented until the two people were able to build a more trusting working relationship. The assessment interviews enabled me to do coaching with the team prior to the team building sessions. The team made great progress after two sessions, which focused on clarifying team members' needs and concerns, learning to give feedback, and identifying ways to improve work distribution.

After two meetings, team resentment subsided, they began to divide work more equitably, and productivity and communication improved. By the second meeting, communication had improved so much that the discussion focused entirely on dividing the work versus giving each other feedback. The team decided that having a clear mission would help in focusing on priorities and in assigning tasks more sensibly.

After completing this initial team building contract, I offered to facilitate a session on creating a mission. As a result, the director invited me to lead a workshop to create a mission for the broader team of nine people. Since then, I've facilitated a retreat for this same group and observed the continuing positive behaviors of the initial group. I've also been invited to conduct a workshop on "Improving Your Attitude" for the rest of this director's staff. Following up with the director not only allowed me to reinforce the work and coach her to increase her effectiveness as a leader, but it also resulted in additional paid work!

Managing the Business

Keeping on top of the financial picture and maintaining momentum are crucial. I use Excel™ and Quicken for Home and Business™ as management tools to help create and manage a budget. Also, I set up a separate business checking account. Because I work from home, I need to allocate some expenses to business and some to myself. I use Quicken™ to generate invoices and to apportion business and personal expenses. I have found it challenging to keep all of my accounts in order.

Managing cash flow as a sole proprietor is a constant challenge. Large companies may delay paying vendors in order to manage cash float. To ensure timely payments I charge half my fee up front and the other half upon completing the project. I send an invoice via fax as soon as a letter of agreement is signed, and follow up to ensure it has been received. I also follow up by email or phone to ensure that the check is being processed in a timely way. Generally I am paid on time.

I keep a journal to learn from experience, to debrief what has happened, and to maintain a record of activities. I track marketing activities, requests for proposals, reactions to workshops, and projects. Once a project is completed, I record what went well and what I have learned. For the first year, I actually had monthly goals in key results areas, just I had done when I was employed by a corporation.

In the past I used to rigorously review what I had done and re-typed my revised goals. Key areas included new business, design, delivery, marketing, and personal development. Eventually I realized that this was more time-consuming than necessary. I now have annual and quarterly goals and am less rigid about the process.

What is it like to manage this business? Much of the challenge lies in overcoming fears and ineffective work habits. Several years ago I had ruled out becoming a consultant because of the plusses of corporate life—a steady paycheck, helpful colleagues, and a technology help desk. I was worried about making enough money, having enough social contact, and managing my own technology. How have I done in managing these concerns?

Everyone told me to expect ups and downs and be prepared for lean times, especially in the first year. I can't emphasize that enough. As a first step, I made sure that I saved enough money to cover expenses on low-income months. Because I started marketing before I left my old employer, I had business right away—giving me the false impression that I might be able to have constant business throughout the year—an unrealistic dream! While I thought I had enough saved, the lack of business and income can get depressing and worrisome.

To cover expenses it helped to have a line of credit—besides credit cards—to fall back on and to adjust my spending habits. But the real solution is finding steady income. A challenge has been finding new projects while working on a current project. You can never do too much marketing—people need to know you are in business and what you have to offer. The constant need to find new business can be a strain.

What about the isolation? Surprisingly, that hasn't been much of an issue for me. Being chairperson of a conference gave me some regular social contact with a group of wonderful, hard-working people. I liked having someplace to go and a reason to talk with people besides marketing calls. My many networking meetings with colleagues and clients and teaching also keep me in touch with the outside world.

Now for the last concern, being my own technology department. My computer's memory shriveled to nothing as I added more documents, yet I waited to update it. A colleague ensured that my computer was ready for Y2K and helped me set up a Website on a free host. I enjoyed setting up the site and watching it grow, like a rambling New England barn. Sometimes my colleague updated the site and sometimes I did it myself. Everything was fine and I survived January 1, 2000.

But life changed dramatically on February 29, 2000. When I made a minor change to my index (home) page and pressed "save," the page went totally blank. To make matters worse, I had not saved a backup copy. My Web host did not recognize "leap day" as a real date, and then took two weeks to respond to my plea for help by sending me a note saying, "Thanks for your feedback"!

After much anxiety and struggle, I managed to reenter a new abbreviated homepage. I got some great learning, however. Now I pay for someone to host my site. I have a dot.com address, a site that is easier to navigate, and backup. I also bought a faster computer with enough memory. This is all money well spent.

Measuring Success

Since I founded MTDR primarily to enhance my personal satisfaction versus to enhance my income, I have developed the following criteria for determining the success of my venture:
1. Have I met my monthly income target? Can I pay my bills and taxes without having to borrow money? Have I contributed target amounts to retirement?
2. Have I fulfilled my contracts in a timely way according to my clients' and my own quality standards? Do clients use processes and tools that I develop? I assess those things through interviews, observations, and personal reflection.

3. Am I maintaining, developing, and building good business relationships with present and future clients? I assess those things through the quality of my discussions with clients and the amount of client activity.

4. Am I enjoying my work and learning from my experiences as a consultant? I take a pulse check after every assignment and assess my learning through journaling.

5. Am I developing my skills and knowledge to prepare me to work as a genealogist and family historian? How am I spending my free time? Have I made progress in learning about genealogy or in tracking ancestors?

6. Am I maintaining my health and a sane schedule of travel? Do I go for regular walks and work out at the gym?

A Successful Intervention

Currently I measure the success of consulting interventions by clarifying expectations and then following up with a client to see how well they have been met. For example, more than a year ago I met with Dom Restuccia, chief financial officer, and Jacquie Lynds, manager of human resources, for Medical Mutual Insurance Company of Maine (MMIC). Lynds was a former student who had recently attended my presentation on performance management at the Human Resource Association of Southern Maine. Restuccia and Lynds invited me to do a similar workshop at MMIC. I arranged to meet with them and identified the problems that they wished to overcome by offering the workshop.

The project changed from offering a workshop to helping them redesign their performance appraisal tool to focus on key results versus vague qualities. I explained to them the benefit of identifying broad company goals and creating key results areas for each of the main departments. I met with the senior management team to help them identify company goals and then with department heads to help explain the process and address their concerns. As department heads identified essential work, they changed the performance appraisal tool as well as job descriptions to reflect what people needed to do for the company to succeed. Once the tool and job descriptions were revamped, I facilitated a half-day workshop on performance management.

Key objectives of the project were to have performance discussions and reviews focus on important work and to encourage people to give timely meaningful feedback to address problems. To measure success, I kept in contact with both Restuccia and Lynds to assess their satisfaction with the project. One year later, I interviewed Lynds to see how performance management had changed. She told me that the performance tool and performance discussions now focus on key areas, and some managers now provide timely feedback to problem employees. For example, one manager had felt discouraged by an employee's negativity that was affecting department morale and productivity, but had not known what to say to the employee. As a result of the new focus on key results and her enhanced skill, the manager confronted this employee who has become more positive and productive. The client achieved its goals, and I enjoyed the experience and made a profit as well.

Learning From Failure

A key measure of success is that clients use processes and tools that you have helped to create. For this to happen tools must match the organization's experience and culture. I learned a lot about this from one of my first clients. My previous employer had supported development of sophisticated tools to help manage and develop employees. I had gained expertise in developing these tools and was anxious to apply my learning to new clients. My first client was a small family business of about 80 employees that sold construction equipment throughout New England. The culture was highly results-focused, top-down, and generally nonempowering. There was little time for coaching and personal development. The immediate problem was to replace an ineffective store manager and the longer term goal was to provide a process to help all the store managers attain both a profit and a positive work environment.

I worked with the vice president of marketing and sales and other key managers to help the business develop several tools designed to focus store managers on key activities, to create consistent standards across locations, and to build essential management competencies. After interviewing managers, I identified core competencies and standards to help select and develop store managers. All the managers reviewed tools created to ensure that they focused on essential results and competencies. The VP was impressed with the process and tools, nevertheless, he was still reluctant to coach his staff and to put "teeth" into new procedures. In retrospect, I believe that the tools and process we created were too formal and complicated given the newness of the process. I was trying to inspire a large change versus taking small steps in the right direction. In essence, I should have created a simpler process for that customer.

Another consulting experience provided me with valuable insight into the importance of personal satisfaction as a success criterion. Some clients take a toll psychologically when the project is a no-win situation. For example, I took on a team building client who was president of a small business. I discovered early on that the client had some personal challenges that prevented her from focusing on the work and made her resistant to looking at how she contributed to the problem. As a result, even though the data clearly showed how the manager created the negative climate, she was unable to reflect on her role and make needed changes in her own and her co-leader's behaviors. The project was very frustrating and drained me of my energy and confidence. I persisted in trying to get through to a client who didn't want to look at her employees' point of view. I should have let this client go earlier. Now, I listen to my inner voice when a client is resistant to looking at what is needed to improve a situation and sometimes forgo working with a client.

Measuring Personal Satisfaction

Having my own practice has been a great move for me. I love my freedom and enjoy jumping from task to task. Now I can create a program, write an article, mow the lawn, go for a walk, or search for ancestors whenever I like. I enjoy being my own boss and directing my future. I love the constant learning, getting to know my clients, and having variety. If something doesn't work out, I have other clients. I like working on a project basis—instead of getting a steady paycheck regardless of what I do, I know I'm *earning* my living. What I like best is doing what I enjoy and what I'm good at for clients who really want my services.

Keys to Success

1. *Have a focused mission and plan.* Be clear about what your strengths are and what you enjoy doing. Describe what you do on paper and in person. Set realistic goals for income and expenses. Don't make optional purchases during low-income months. Follow up and adjust your plan to ensure it continues to work for you.
2. *Get your name out there.* Continuously market through a variety of media. Write articles, do volunteer talks, write a flier/newsletter/brochure, write a book, and call or email people. It probably takes three contacts to really make an impact.
3. *Develop long-term relationships with clients.* Build long-term relationships with people so you really understand their needs and can cut

through a lot of red tape. When clients know you, they often don't expect you to write a full-blown proposal. Often you can write a simple letter of agreement or even just an email note.

4. *Be persistent.* A key to success is following up with a client who decides to cancel a training program because of low enrollment. In several instances I convinced a client, who had let marketing run on autopilot, to market the program to a broader audience. Enrollment increased so drastically that the client called me to ask about the limit on class size!

5. *Take advantage of your personal freedom.* As a one-person business, I have complete freedom over how I spend my time. Originally, I tried to develop business during dead times or I worried about financial survival. Now I know to save enough reserve funds to cover these down times and to enjoy working at activities that replenish me—gardening, exercising in a gym, and exploring genealogy.

Lessons Learned

What do I wish I had done differently from the beginning? If nothing else, starting your own consulting business produces many lessons learned.

- **Maintain a professional Website.** Get a dot.com address and hire a professional Web master. A professionally managed site is easier to find and navigate, looks more professional, gets more hits, eliminates illegal programming, and provides responsive service and backup in case of problems.

- **Choose your business wisely.** Identify and get rid of "bad business" early on. Listen to your inner wisdom. Pay attention to your measures of success and don't take on clients who take too much of a toll psychologically or who require more work than they are worth.

- **Manage your time.** Avoid being overcommitted to time-consuming volunteer activities when you need to get your business off the ground. Avoid being both a conference chairperson and a presenter. Consider being a committee member rather than being chairperson.

- **Customize your products to your clients.** Make sure that your tools fit your clients and focus on the client's situation versus your previous experience.

- **Keep marketing.** Keep your name in front of people. Over time I found that I could directly impact new business by making calls and sending emails to people.

Questions for Discussion

1. What do you have a passion for doing? Can you make money doing it?
2. What are you likely to spend too much time doing and too little time doing? How can you build in safeguards to ensure you focus on what you should?
3. How are you going to market your services? What logo best reflects who you are? What are the primary goals of your Website?
4. What target audience best fits your goals and expertise? Which types of clients do you want—geographic area, nature of business, profit versus nonprofit?
5. What system will you use to budget and track expenses? How will you ensure that you save enough money to cover expenses during down business times?
6. How will you create a backup system and find reliable technology resources to help you with computer problems?

The Author

Carol P. McCoy is the president of McCoy Training and Development Resources, a consulting firm in Falmouth, Maine. MTDR's mission is to provide HRD solutions that help organizations and individuals succeed in a constantly changing world. She also provides genealogical research for individuals who wish to trace their family history. She serves customers throughout the United States, primarily in New England and the New York area. Prior to starting MTDR, McCoy had more than 25 years HRD experience with Chase Manhattan Bank and Unum Life Insurance Company of America and in higher education. A frequent conference presenter, McCoy has written articles and a book, *Managing a Small HRD Department*. She as also edited *In Action: Managing the Small Training Staff* (1998). She is co-editor of IOMA's new newsletter *IOMA's Report on Training Programs*. She earned her B.A. in psychology from Connecticut College and her M.S. and Ph.D. in psychology from Rutgers University. She can be reached at McCoy Training and Development Resources, 11 Johnson Road, Falmouth, ME 04105; phone: 207.781.7515; email: cmccoy3333@aol.com; Website: mccoytraining.com.

References

McCoy, C.P. (1993). *Managing a Small HRD Department: You Can Do More Than You Think*. San Francisco: Jossey-Bass, Inc.

Robinson, D.G., and J.C. Robinson. (1996). *Performance Consulting: Moving Beyond Training*. San Francisco: Berrett-Koehler.

Further Resources

McCoy, C.P. (1998). *In Action: Managing the Small Training Staff.* Alexandria, VA: ASTD.

Patterson, S., and C.P. McCoy. (Eds.). (2002). *IOMA's Report on Training Programs.* New York, NY: Institute of Management & Administration.

Establishing a World-Renowned Consulting Business

Linneman Associates

Margot B. Weinstein

This case describes the successful consulting practice of Peter Linneman, principal of Linneman Associates. Linneman has established a world-renown consulting business with leading U.S. and international companies, as well as universities. For more than 20 years, Linneman's unique background in academia at Wharton, University of Pennsylvania, combined with his active involvement in business has enabled him to develop expertise in several areas. His advice is sought after by leaders in organizations and universities. This case provides an in-depth examination of his practice and an analysis and discussion of the elements necessary to build a successful consulting business.

Introduction

Consultants have long been essential to the success of top businesses world wide. It is estimated that companies spend billions of dollars per year on consultants (O'Shea and Madigan, 1998; Rasiel and Friga, 2001). Challenging business environments, amplified legal and ethical concerns, and technological advances have increased the need for companies to hire consultants to find creative solutions to business problems. This case study describes the successful practice of world-renown consultant Peter Linneman.

Linneman, an economist, is the principal of Linneman Associates, located in Philadelphia, Pennsylvania. Linneman is widely recognized as a strategic thinker and innovator who provides advice to leading U.S. and international corporations and universities. Linneman's

This case was prepared to serve as a basis for discussion rather than to illustrate either effective or ineffective administrative or management practices.

background as a professor at the Wharton School, University of Pennsylvania, combined with his active involvement in corporate governance, strategy, and operation has allowed him to develop expertise that is sought after by leaders in business and universities.

Linneman formed Linneman Associates in 1978 and has been a consultant in all areas of business on topics such as real estate finance and investments, human strategy, general business strategy, and financial analysis. He has also advised many universities on how to develop successful programs with concentrations in real estate; in this capacity, he provides advice on all aspects of the programs, including designing curriculum, hiring staff, marketing programs, and attracting and retaining students. The author gathered the information for this qualitative case study through formal and informal communications with Linneman in person, by telephone, fax, and email; it is presented here with his permission. The information was also confirmed through a review of business documents, interviews with other professionals, and a review of literature in the field. This case provides an in-depth examination of his practice and an analysis and discussion of the elements necessary to build a successful consulting business.

Linneman's Background

Peter Linneman holds both a master's and doctorate degree in economics from the University of Chicago. In 1977, Linneman was a post doctoral fellow in economics at the Center for the Study of the Economy and the State at the University of Chicago. In 1978, he became the assistant professor of business economics at the Graduate School of Business at the University of Chicago. From 1979 through 1984, he was the assistant professor of finance and public policy at Wharton. In 1984, Linneman became an associate professor of finance and public policy at Wharton, and in 1988, he was appointed professor of finance and public policy at Wharton.

Linneman is the Albert Sussman professor of real estate, professor of finance and public policy and management at the Samuel Zell and Robert Lurie Real Estate Center at Wharton, where he was the director of the center from 1985 through 1997. The Wharton program has been identified as the top MBA program in real estate for the past nine years by *U.S. News and World Report,* and Linneman is credited as a major contributor to the program's success. He continues to teach at Wharton, and he is the editor of the *Wharton Real Estate Review.* He has published more than 50 articles, and he regularly serves as a keynote speaker for leading corporations and professional associations around the world.

In addition to Linneman's academic background, he has been actively involved in corporate governance, strategy, and operation. Among his business accomplishments, Linneman served as senior managing director of Equity International Properties, a global real estate investment firm. Linneman served as chairman of the board of Rockefeller Center Properties, the public real estate investment trust that until 1996 held the debt on New York City's Rockefeller Center. In this capacity, he was involved in foreclosing on its Japanese owners and the successful sale of Rockefeller Center. He has also served on the board of directors of five New York Stock Exchange firms and one Tel Aviv Exchange company. He has served on the boards of numerous private companies. He is the chairman of Resolution Capital, a real estate technology investment fund.

Linneman's clients have included Lubert-Adler Investments, Equity International Properties, Sunbelt Management, General Electric Capital Corporation, GMAC, IBM, Michelin Tire Company, Scott Paper Company, Merrill Lynch, Baring Brothers, AT&T, Chubb & Sons, CIGNA, the Federal Trade Commission, Federal Express, Eastdil Realty, International Realty Investors, the Paramount Group, Microsoft, Commerzbank, the Equity Group, the Trammell Crow Company, University of Colorado, John Hopkins University, and Roosevelt University.

The Practice

After Linneman completed his Ph.D. in 1977, he started doing research and teaching at the University of Chicago in its economics and business school, and, almost immediately through recommendations, he began consulting as a sideline for Michelin Tire Company and Scott Paper Company. When asked about his expertise with his first clients, Linneman says, "I knew a great deal of relevant theory and I had complete confidence in my ability to deliver valuable information to clients. However, like anything else in life, when people first come to you, you pretend you are experienced in what you are doing, and you wing it as you go. In retrospect, I was able to frame their problems in the context of theory, devise practical ways to research their position, and explain what it would mean to their organization. It was fun and they must have been satisfied, because they came back again."

Linneman says he became a consultant because he understood that he had enough energy and the personality to blend the life of a university professor with business consulting. University life offered stability and loftiness, and business consulting offered immediacy, rapidity, and energy.

Because Linneman continues to work full time as a university professor at Wharton, he can be selective of the clients that he chooses to work with in his practice.

Linneman's market niche is top management. He has a very high level clientele of CEOs, CFOs, presidents, and principals, for whom he serves as counselor and advisor, generally one-on-one and more often through discussion than through written reports. He has written very few reports over the years; most people want to talk with him and hear what he is thinking. Linneman has a relatively unique combination of theory and practice: "I have much more practice than most theoreticians, and more theory than most practitioners, and I also have a blend of finance, economics, and real estate. The best definition of what I do is: I do theory better than any practitioner and I do practice better than any theoretician."

Making the Transition

Linneman realized early in his career in academia that consulting in his field would be financially and personally rewarding.

Key Drivers

When Linneman began his college education, he played football. He still enjoys team sports, and he is an avid basketball player. According to Linneman, consulting provides many opportunities for collaboration and working with teams, and he learns effective teamwork through sports. Linneman says that one of the great frustrations about being an academic is that it does not value teamwork much, and he enjoys the freedom of consulting and the collaboration. Although he says that being a consultant often means being on your own a lot, you are always working with a team.

Linneman's role as a consultant is to act as an agent, an advisor, or as a counselor. He tells clients what he thinks, along with the reasons why he might be right or wrong in a way that is meaningful to others, and he is known for being exceptional in his communication skills. He understands that the job of a principal is to take the gathered information and make a decision, and he realizes that there is a big difference between providing information and making a decision. Figure 1 shows the five steps in the consulting process.

Linneman has both the technical skills that a modern economist has and a old-time feel for business activity. He says that most academics and consultants come into their career and think that their skill is technical or some niche or field of expertise they possess. He has learned that his greatest skill is his ability to learn and keep adapting

Figure 1. Steps in the role of consultant process.

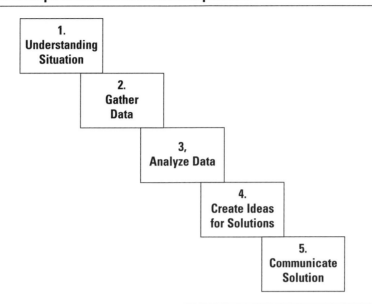

and changing. When he started out, he was a skilled economist doing antitrust work. Later, he consulted on mergers and acquisitions. Now, he largely does real estate consulting on a wide-range of activities.

Linneman decided early in his career that he did not want to create or run a large employee-based consulting firm such as Arthur Andersen Consulting or McKinsey and Company. Linneman's practice consists of himself, a full-time assistant, a few students who work part-time, and two young partners who work with him on special projects. Linneman has never had to fund much overhead. He considers his office space, a full-time assistant, a phone, and a computer as trivial business costs. From the beginning, Linneman decided that what he was going to sell was himself and his advice, rather than a label like McKinsey, because he didn't want to develop a large corporation. Five or six times during his consulting career, he has revisited that direction and each time he has made the same decision. Linneman says that what is important to him is the freedom and flexibility to change what he does and to be who he wants to be.

Attracting and Keeping Clients

Linneman says that he has never needed to have a specific marketing strategy to attract and retain clients. His name has been connected with the top consultants in the field, and he believes that clients come to him because they learn of his reputation in the business. Over the years, his name has become ubiquitous in consulting.

Linneman's success is partly due to his ability to build successful client relationships and client loyalty. He uses the following example to explain this process: After completing several projects for the Paramount Group, the CEO called him about 10 years ago wanting a recommendation of someone who could help analyze the company. He asked Linneman to talk with him about it and from that situation Linneman formed a non-retainer-based relationship that has been beneficial for both of them over the years, and they have become close personal friends as well as business colleagues.

Managing the Business

The six key components Linneman uses to manage his practice follow. (See summary in table 1.)

1. *Ensuring profits.* Linneman says that his business has been profitable from the beginning. He attributes his financial success to keeping a low overhead, and he has been fortunate to have a continuous flow of quality clients.

2. *Handling growing pains.* Linneman continued to work for his first clients, Michelin Tire Company and Scott Paper Company, on several matters for many years. From those first clients, his business just grew. He never advertised, but people continued to call him through word of mouth and recommendation. When he began, he first consulted on antitrust matters, and by the mid-1980s his consulting was increasingly becoming mergers and acquisitions and corporate work for generally small and midsize companies. As he became involved in consulting, he found other aspects of mergers interesting, including the strategic, the operational, the economic, and the financial aspects. And as he continued, people began calling to ask his advice on other matters. Now, he consults on all areas of business and university activities.

Linneman has dealt with growing pains by actively refusing to grow. He has always understood that his niche is building one-on-one relationships, therefore, his key relationship with the principal is critical. He says, "In order to do great work, I need to be involved in the relationship. When I work with a company, I earn a reputation for doing good work and not conning them into doing more than they asked. The loyalty comes from not doing more than I could or should do in giving them my insights, ideas, and reactions. When it is clear to me that I am not the right guy to do it, I tell the clients why and help

Table 1. Components for building Linneman's consulting practice.

Component	Method
1. Ensures profits	By attracting and retaining clients and low overhead.
2. Handles growing pains	Planned for size and structure and areas of his expertise.
3. Manages crises	When clients are in financial trouble, he renegotiated his fees.
4. Controls challenges	Found it difficult to work with difficult clients. He only selects clients with whom he can build relationships.
5. Deals with ethical issues	When clients compete for advice, he is honest and forthright about the situation.
6. Measures success	Both through financial and nonfinancial measures: money; continued relationship and referral of clients; client satisfaction; quality of life.

them find someone who is appropriate. People hate to turn away business in that regard, but it is better than poisoning your reputation."

3. *Managing crises.* The only crisis that Linneman has encountered was in 1991. He had several clients who owed him 20 percent of his billings for the year, and they were in a difficult financial situation. He had to negotiate down his fee and analyze if it was better to get 50 cents on the dollar.

4. *Controlling challenges.* The biggest challenge that Linneman has encountered in the consulting business was working for a difficult client. Although he found the work to be interesting and challenging, he learned from that experience that he would only choose to work for clients with whom he could build relationships and friendships that were mutually satisfying.

5. *Dealing with ethical issues.* Linneman believes that he does not have to deal with the ethical issues that many consulting practices encounter in the business because he only employs a few people. The major ethical concern that he has faced a few times in his career is when clients become involved in competing situations. He tries not to work for clients who are likely to be involved in the same arena. However, when there is a conflict of interests, Linneman believes that the best policy is to be honest and forthright with the clients.

Linneman says his most unique situation arose when he was chairman of the board of Rockefeller Center Properties and he was heading the sale of Rockefeller Center. Even though he had an ongoing relationship with clients on other matters, he was honest about what he was involved with. According to Linneman, for most clients, timing is crucial. Therefore, he had to tell them that although he is their friend and he has given them advice in the past, as chairman of the board of a public company, he could not give them any advice on that transaction because his total loyalty and involvement could only be for the public company. Linneman believes that clients thought that he did a good job because they claimed that he treated everyone the same.

6. *Measuring success.* Linneman measures success in the following ways:
- financially
- continued relationship with client base
- referrals from former clients
- continued growth of business through new clients
- quality of life, such as independence
- client satisfaction.

Linneman commands top fees for consulting in the real estate industry; his practice has been financially successful since he began consulting. In the past year, he has teamed up with two young partners to publish a quarterly research publication called *The Linneman Newsletter*. A subscription to the quarterly newsletter is $12,000 per year, and it does various types of economic analysis, real estate forecasting, and marketing analysis. Linneman has a number of individual companies, opportunity funds, and institutional investors who subscribe to it. Although the newsletter is a recent addition to his practice, the success of the publication is a way that he will be able to measure his success fairly tangibly; his goal is to double the number of subscribers during the next year.

Of the six measures, Linneman cites independence and client satisfaction as the top reasons that he considers his practice a success.

Independence

Linneman's number one metric of success is his independence. A long time ago, he decided that he could make enough money to be comfortable. Therefore, his metric of success became independence and the control that he has while making money. As a result, 12 years ago, he decided to stop doing litigation support because he would have to be there when the lawyers wanted him, and vacations, trips, and classes would have to be canceled. He tries to have five to six key clients a year. About half of them have been with him for several years and the other half are short-term clients with a one-time challenge to solve.

Measuring Client Success

Linneman explains that his client satisfaction is actually more important than his client's success. The reason for that is because he understands the difference between a principal and an agent, and he wants his clients to be satisfied that he has given them his advice and that they feel that they have received more than their money's worth. Although he hopes that they do well, the part that he is involved in may only be a small part of a project. He believes that his relationship is akin to what a good doctor does: Although it's hard to measure, most of the time you know if you are satisfied with your doctor. Likewise, clients know when they are happy, and he receives a tremendous amount of repeat clients and recommendations. As long as people continue to request his services, he believes he is delivering value.

Keys to Success

Linneman's skills and abilities give him the following areas of expertise. (See summary in table 2.)

- *Ability to combine theory and practice*. Linneman draws from both his technical academic background and his practical business experience.
- *Ability to gather data and analyze problems*. Linneman has the ability to do extensive research, identify a problem, and find a solution using a wide variety of resources such as experts, mentors, and so forth.
- *Ability to see the big picture*. Linneman excels at analyzing situations and seeing the big picture. Using the impressionist artist's George Seurat's painting "In the Park," as an analogy, Linneman says consultants must be able to look at a problem from afar. He explains that if you look at Seurat's painting up close, you don't see a painting, you see the paint dots, but if you stand back, the dots combine to form a cohesive scene. Linneman has the skill for seeing the big picture. Many people only see the "dots" instead of the greater whole.
- *Excels at conveying ideas to others*. Linneman prides himself on saying things in way that people can understand. He attributes part of his success to both his knowledge of theory and practice and his ability to articulate information so that people can grasp and gain insight from the ideas.
- *Good communication skills*. Although Linneman believes that he is essentially a talker, he says he's also a pretty good listener—a skill essential in consulting.
- *Continued learning*. Linneman examines a tremendous amount of information each week, some of it seemingly different and often

Table 2. List of Linneman's key skills and abilities for success.

Key Skills	Method
1. Combination of theory and practice	Employs technical skills from academia and practical skills from business
2. Ability to gather data and analyze problem	Uses extensive research, analytical, and problem-solving abilities
3. Ability to see the big picture	Can synthesize information to see solution
4. Excels at conveying ideas to others	Can express ideas to clients to provide insight and understanding
5. Good communication skills	Possesses good speaking and listening skills
6. Loves to learn	Continues to learn; reads extensively from a wide range of materials and subjects
7. Practices professionalism	Acts with integrity and professionalism
8. Created a network	Values and works to build relationships
9. Ability to work in teams	Learns skill through team involvement in sports
10. Values use of mind	Uses mind over technology to solve problems; computer is a tool for specific procedures
11. Builds a healthy body	Exercises regularly: jogs, weight lifts, scuba dives, plays basketball
12. Mentors students	Has ongoing mentoring relationships through scuba diving trips that enrich the lives of all parties

conflicting. He talks with people continually, and he reads all types of literature such as business literature, practitioner articles, trade journals, economic academic material, nonacademic material, and popular press information. He observes that often people read only narrowly in their area of expertise—academics read academic literature; the "data people" read charts; most executives only read *Forbes*—but he reads it all. People often ask him if he is searching for an answer, but he says he's not looking for a particular answer; rather, he's looking for information that he can use to help him figure out how it all fits together. He possesses the skill for creating a mosaic that gives clients more insight into what is really going on in their business.

- *High level of integrity and professionalism.* Linneman learned the value of professionalism early in his career: "Lucille Ford, my undergraduate economics professor, was a brilliant and passionate teacher. She turned me on to economics and a hunger for learning, and she changed my life. She has become a dear friend, and I have attempted throughout my career to emulate her integrity, her quality, her selflessness, and her energy."

- *Create a network of people.* Linneman thinks that "Most people underestimate the value of having a diverse and high-level network; I have it, and I treasure it. I get real information from talking with people about how their business is doing, and over time the information becomes part of the information that I use. If all the information that I read is saying that everything is going great, and everybody that I am talking with says it is awful, than something is wrong. My network has played a key role in my consulting success over the years because I have people whom I deal with on an ongoing basis who can answer important questions."

- *Ability to work in teams.* Although Linneman is an independent person, he likes team and team involvement. He still plays basketball competitively with young people in leagues, largely because he enjoys teams. From sports, he has learned about the importance of being a great team member.

- *Use of mind over technology.* Linneman thinks that, while technology is obviously helpful, it is not a critical part of what he does as a consultant. He often jokes with others that he carries the most expensive computer he has—"his head." He believes that many younger consultants forget that personal contact, including face-to-face, is extremely valuable. Of course, he agrees that when doing statistical analysis, having good software and a fast computer is also helpful and saves time.

- *Healthy body is important for success.* The job of consultants usually requires traveling. Consultants need to be in good shape physically to meet the demands and challenges of the job. Linneman works out regularly because he realized long ago that people in their 40s who don't exercise don't have the energy to do what he does and wants to continue to do. They would become exhausted late in the afternoon and they couldn't travel overseas without resting or taking a day or two to catch up. He says staying in shape is a key part of his job—just as keeping a race car in performance condition is a key part of winning a race.

- *Mentors students.* Linneman says that one way he measures success is to keep in regular contact with former students, some of whom even come with him on scuba diving trips. He gets pleasure from helping young people with their careers. He believes that as we age, we forget how confusing things can be for young people. When he was very young, Lucille Ford, his mentor, took a tremendous interest in his life and his wife's life. He suggests that mentoring is a wonderful way to enrich the lives of all involved parties.

Lessons Learned

Following are Linneman's key lessons learned. (See summary in table 3.)

- *Know yourself, especially your personality.* Know your personality and how it can contribute to your success. Also, know your mission and goals for the practice.
- *Find a market niche, but don't be married to your niche.* Linneman advises that consultants should find their niche, but they shouldn't be married to it. They should be open for the changes that will happen over 20 to 40 years. Something that is important today will be an afterthought 15 or 20 years from now, and if consultants remain married to a narrow expertise, they will end up being an expert in something that nobody cares about, which is what happens to many academics. At age 27, they decide to be an expert in something and 40 years later they are the only person who still cares about their expertise.
- *Develop communication skills.* Communication skills are essential, especially listening skills.
- *Be a good team player.* Learn the skills for working well in teams.
- *Choose clients wisely.* Good work comes from building a relationship with your clients and people in organizations. Difficult clients can make the work arduous.
- *Value honesty, integrity, professionalism, and hard work.* Be upfront in addressing ethical issues with clients. When two companies collide or compete for your services, be forthright in discussing the situation with both.
- *Complete work on time.* The biggest challenge is to assess your time correctly to be able to complete work on time. Linneman shares that his biggest challenge was the misassessment of the time it would take to do the work when he became chairman of the board of the

Table 3: Strategies for building a successful practice.

Strategy	Method
1. Know yourself	Understand your personality, goals, and mission for your business.
2. Have a market niche	But do not be married to your niche.
3. Develop communication skills	Good communication skills, especially listening skills, are essential.
4. Be a team player	Learn how to work as a member of a team.
5. Choose clients wisely	Difficult clients can make work arduous.
6. Be a professional	Value honesty, integrity, hard work, ethics.
7. Complete work on time	Assess your time correctly to complete job.
8. Don't bill for extra work	Don't do extra work and bill your client.
9. Use technology	Technology is helpful and saves time.
10. Continue to learn	Read material from diverse subjects.
11. Build a network	Talk to people. People provide information.
12. Mentor people	Mentoring is productive and informative for both parties.
13. Embrace change	Change is a skill that allows you to stay current.
14. Remember people are people	Realize that some things never change.
15. Exercise regularly	A healthy body is important for the energy to do business.
16. Enjoy the journey	A good consulting practice takes time to build.

company that owned the loan on the Rockefeller Center. He thought the work would take five to eight days per year, and within eight months the situation had changed dramatically, and it suddenly took between 1,000 to 1,100 hours that year. The difficulty here was not the task, but the misassessment of the time that it was going to take to complete the job. Time management skills become critical to the success of a practice.

- *Don't do extra work and bill the organization.* Do a thorough job, but don't do more than clients request and bill them for extra services.
- *Use technology in consulting.* Technology is helpful and saves time, but people matter more than technology.
- *Continue to learn.* Continue learning through a wide range of sources.
- *Build a network.* Success in the consulting business is through word of mouth, recommendation, and referrals. You must have the ability to get and keep clients, and building relationships is key to success and satisfaction in the business.

- *Mentor others.* You learn through relationships. You help others with their careers and you gain as much as you give in a mentoring relationship.
- *Embrace change.* Linneman believes that most people hate change so if you can embrace change, you will be well positioned for success. He points out that there will be frustrating times when dealing with people who hate change, but if you can handle that, you will have a unique skill. He also finds it frustrating when the people he's consulting with don't like change; but on the other hand, he says, if everyone liked change as much as he did, he would be a lot less valuable.
- *Understand people are people.* As Linneman reflected over the past 25 years as a consultant, he says some things have not changed: "A consultant must remember that people are still people, and they have the same concerns. People want to make money. Although tax laws differ, the oil prices fluctuate, the 'enemy' changes—people are the same, and they want the same general things." Linneman believes that it is important in consulting to know the factors that will change from the ones that will remain the same. He advises that if you decide to consult on the strategic and the judgment levels, as he does, that will greatly impact your career.
- *Exercise regularly.* A healthy body makes for a healthy mind. Staying in shape is essential to have the ability to do the job as one gets older.
- *Enjoy the journey.* Linneman believes passionately that building a successful consulting practice should be a "journey not a destination." He tells the following story to illustrate this idea: "Students always want their career success to happen overnight, and a good consulting practice is more about the journey and building relationships. Samuel Zell, chairman of nine leading U.S. and international corporations— and, if it wasn't Zell, it was someone as bright as him—had a student walk up to him on campus in front of me and say 'I want to be just like you in five years.' To which Zell responded, 'Why do you think it will take you only five years, when it took me 40?'

   "That is a very interesting point. When you are young and a student, you want success to happen fast, and I spend a lot of time counseling students and former students. There is a phrase in sports, 'Let the game come to you.' In other words, when you run too fast, you trip over your feet. When you are young, bright, and energetic, you are excited about being successful. Sometimes you just have to step back and let it come to you; patience is a virtue; know where the stops are in your career, but enjoy the journey!"

Questions for Discussion

1. What are the factors that contributed to the longevity and success of Linneman's consulting practice?
2. What methods, both financial and nonfinancial, were used to measure the success of the practice?
3. What are the critical skills and strategies Linneman attributes to the success of his practice?
4. What conclusions and recommendations were learned from this practice?
5. How could these strategies be applied to developing your consulting practice?

The Author

Margot B. Weinstein is vice president of Kingston Group Inc., a commercial real estate company based in Illinois since 1978. She received her doctoral degree in education from Northern Illinois University and she is member of the Kappa Delta PI International Honor Society in education. She has two master's degrees from National-Louis University, one in psychology and one in adult education. She earned the Certified International Property Specialist Designation in 2001 and is a member of the International Real Estate Federation. She is a professional advisor for DePaul University. She has published on a wide range of topics in business and education but her expertise is real estate. She can be reached at: 491 Lake Cook Road, Deerfield, IL 60015; phone: 773.549.9861; fax: 773.549.9863; email: MWeinstein@aol.com.

References

O'Shea, J., and Madigan, C. (1998). *Dangerous Company: Management Consultants and the Businesses They Save and Ruin.* New York: Penguin Books.

Rasiel, E.M., and Friga, P.N. (2001). *The McKinsey Mind: Understanding and Implementing the Problem-Solving Tools and Management Techniques of the World's Top Strategic Consulting Firm.* New York: McGraw-Hill.

Building a Performance Improvement Consulting Practice

Stractics Group, Inc.

Pierre Mourier

This case study tells the story of a performance improvement consulting practice focused on process optimization and change management that grew from one employee to 15 employees with projects on four continents and more than $1.5 million revenue in under four years.

The Practice

Stractics Group, Inc., was founded in 1997 by Pierre Mourier to help clients design and implement results-producing organizational change. The practice is focused on three primary areas of activity: 1) business process optimization, 2) change management, and 3) performance measurement and management. A key differentiator between Stractics Group and other organizations in this field is that it offers clients a results guarantee. Provided that a client agrees to structure the performance improvement project in a certain way, Stractics Group will guarantee measurable performance improvements equaling a minimum of three times the client's investment in the project within a one-year period from completion of the project.

Additionally, the firm guarantees clients that engage the firm in a situational analysis that Stractics Group, Inc., will uncover and quantify an improvement potential of a minimum of $200,000 per 100 employees or the analysis is conducted for no professional fee.

The firm started with the commitment from one client for a small engagement that generated enough cash flow to engage the founder

This case was prepared to serve as a basis for discussion rather than to illustrate either effective of ineffective administrative and management practices.

but no one else (if he took no salary) and that would begin to provide some capital for developing the firm's branding. Now, not even five years later, the firm employs 15 consultants and has engaged in projects in North America, Europe, and Asia and has broken through the million dollar revenue level.

In the early days, the firm's focus was to establish its reputation within its chosen niche through a combination of marketing-related branding activities as well as active society memberships and the development of speaking and writing opportunities across the United States. A key ingredient for the firm's success was establishing lasting relationships with key clients through personalized service and an emphasis on flexibility. It quickly became apparent that once the firm got a new client it was likely that it would get more business from that same client, simply because of the relationships and results that were being developed. Almost 90 percent of the firm's clients to date have given Stractics Group more business. So the focus became how to get new clients.

Getting new clients during the early days was largely a case of trial and error. The firm tried cold calling, using references and referrals, writing articles, attending conferences, putting on seminars, and even hiring someone to conduct telesales on behalf of the firm. In retrospect, it appeared that there was no right or wrong way to generate new business—the key was to continue exploring all avenues, measuring results, and continuing to explore the avenues that seemed to work. What also became apparent was that the more systematic and rigorous the sales effort, the more success the firm experienced. Many reject the notion that sales is a numbers game. But it was apparent again and again that the harder the principals worked at sales and the more systematically they tried to get new business, the more successful they were.

A significant investment in branding the firm was made early on. The branding included creating a corporate brochure, a Website (www .stractics.com), as well as other collateral material. Also early on, the firm developed a relationship with a talented graphic designer, someone who had experience working with large multinational organizations, but who was willing to work within a limited budget. That enabled Stractics Group to "look big" from the beginning while not having to spend what large organizations do.

In the early days when the founder was the only employee in the firm, it became evident that it would be important to have a sounding board for ideas and concepts. The founder contacted a couple of people that he had worked with in the past, and they were willing to engage in a series of informal conversations and acted as the founder's support group. The impact of this group cannot be understated particularly if you are starting a consulting venture on your own. This informal group met regularly both in person and via telephone conferencing and provided an opportunity to share ideas and exchange information about ways to generate new business. The group let the members feel that they were a part of something bigger. The two original members of the group were Pat Murphy and Martin Smith. Murphy became a partner in the firm, and Smith co-authored with Mourier the first book written by members of the organization: *Conquering Organizational Change: How to Succeed Where Most Organizations Fail* published by CEP Press in 2001.

Making the Transition

The founder started the firm after working as a consultant for various consulting firms since the mid-1980s. As happens with many consultants, he became fed up with working for others, feeling undervalued, underpaid, and not in control of his future. As is so often the case, wanting to break free collides with an event that finally makes the idea of becoming an entrepreneur a reality.

In the case of Stractics Group, Inc., the final straw was working for someone that the founder did not respect professionally, combined with a lack of any perceptible career path and an unbelievably slow and arrogant payment of his expenses, which created the opportunity to break away. When he left the building, a few doors were slammed, so to speak, and, in retrospect, he realizes that leaving without a safety net contributed to Stractics's success. Because there was no going back, it made it even more important to succeed.

An important note here is that the founder realizes that many consultants share his dream to become independent, so the trick now is for Stractics to create an environment where consultants who work with the firm can flourish so they do not have a need to start their own organizations. Factors that encourage this longevity with Stractics are providing a visible opportunity for growth within the organization, sharing profits, and paying people fairly for their work and on time.

Strategy

The firm's initial strategy was to broaden the scope of services offered (in comparison with the employer that Mourier had recently left). That strategy turned out to be a mistake. As time went by, it became more apparent that what was needed was a clear focus for the firm, and the ability to articulate a unique selling proposition or competitive advantage. How could Stractics be differentiated from its competitors? To be frank, in the beginning, the founder didn't really know, but as time went on, it became clearer that the firm was in business to help clients improve their performance measurably and significantly through design and implementation of process-related organizational change as well as change management. That realization led to establishing a results guarantee. The firm now guarantees clients a certain return-on-investment (ROI) on specific engagements or the difference will be paid back to the client. That has become a powerful selling tool.

Structure of the Practice

While the firm's main offices are located in New York City, the employees are located all over the United States, including New York City, Boston, Sarasota, Albuquerque, Hilton Head, Atlanta, Las Vegas, and Minneapolis.

During the early days everyone did everything— business development, project consulting, research and development, writing, and so forth. Now, the various roles tend to be split. The president focuses most of his attention on developing and maintaining the company's image, which includes marketing activities, writing books and articles, speaking engagements, client liaison, and administrative duties. Murphy is now mostly focused on operations, which includes managing project staff, projects, and project staff development. The third original participant, Smith, is now mostly focused on research and development activities, including specific research, methodology development, and writing and publishing. The split of activities plays to each person's strengths.

Attracting and Keeping Clients

Over time, the way the firm generates new business has changed significantly. Initially clients were developed purely through referrals or, perhaps even more, through work extensions with existing clients. Stractics's partners have always had an aversion to cold calling and have chosen to rely on softer sales techniques such as writing articles and books and participating in conferences and speaking engagements as a way to obtain new business. But you never know where the next piece of business is going to come from. And therefore the firm has established the following mantra: "In this business you start from scratch and you have to keep scratching." The fact is that you have to try a lot of avenues for business development. Stractics even once hired a telesales person with less than optimal results.

Lately the firm is finding that workshops and seminars are generating a lot of leads for new business. The firm has had some success offering workshops in public forums around the world. And while the workshop success rate in the firm's early days was low, a constant effort has increased this over time. The workshops were originally designed to generate new consulting business, but they are generating revenue in and of themselves.

The firm has now realized that a formalized sales organization is needed to take the organization to the next level. Subsequently the firm has recently added two full-time outside sales professionals supported by internal sales and telemarketing. But there are also some risks associated with growing too quickly that must be considered. One word of caution: If you are serious about building a significant consulting business, and if you, like most consultants, have an aversion against or simply are not good at selling, align yourself with someone who possesses those skills; that person can make the difference between success or failure.

Managing the Business
Finance

Two examples will illustrate what can be the challenges of cash flow: It is early winter and the company's founder is driving around town with his wife looking for a restaurant. Generally they are particular about the cuisine they eat and the type of restaurant they go to and that is the case on this particular evening. They are also looking for a restaurant that accepts the one credit card they have that is not "maxed-out." The problem is that very few restaurants accept that particular credit card, so they return home to eat leftovers. At the same time, the other main partner of Stractics is putting an additional $10,000 on his home line of credit, fielding "why-do-you-keep-thinking-that-this-Stractics-thing-will-pay-off-for-you" comments from friends and associates. One of the main reasons for the cash flow problem in these instances was the failure of a major client to pay its bills on time.

Frankly, the financial management of the firm is one of the areas that has received the least attention, until recently. And it is an area that will undergo a significant amount of additional scrutiny if the firm is to continue to flourish. After struggling through financial issues like receivables, payables, taxes, social security, and the like, the firm decided to employ the services of an accountant to manage these aspects of the business.

The firm currently uses various formalized management routines that concentrate on managing project costs. Professional fees are generally quoted as fixed, and this causes the firm to focus particularly on estimating the right costs for the project as well as on achieving those costs.

Staffing and Development

Another management aspect that is beginning to receive more attention is recruiting and developing project staff. As the company grows, it is becoming increasingly difficult to hire project staff capable of performing at the required standards. The partners seem to have settled on a rule of thumb that it takes interviewing eight or nine consultants to find a really good one. For that reason, they have kept in contact with a number of former colleagues whom they know are capable of performing when needed. Additionally, the firm is working with industry headhunters who have been able to introduce appropriate new players into the business. Sometimes, however, it has been hit or miss. On one occasion, a project director had to ask someone who had been hired through a headhunter to leave a project after only two days on the job.

Stractics has developed a methodology that is offered to clients as workshops. New consultants, irrespective of prior knowledge or experience, are taken through a more comprehensive version of these workshops prior to being hired to work on projects. These training sessions last a week and include not only the methodology but also training on the firm's image, branding, and values. Additionally, consultants start their first project under the direct tutelage of one of the firm's partners, and the amount of slack they are given is proportionate to their experience. Partners frequently follow up with clients about how the new consultant is being received in the client environment.

Client Management

Another key aspect of managing the business is managing the relationship with the firm's clients. Stractics quickly found that the key to a steady growth of the business is how well the relationship with current clients is managed and maintained. The firm's relationship with its clients can be summarized as: 1) always stay two steps ahead of a client's needs and respond immediately; and 2) do not be afraid to tell a client exactly how you feel, even if you think it might cause you to lose the client.

As an example of when the firm kept ahead of the client was the time it determined after two days that one of the firm's consultants would be a wrong fit for that client. The consultant was taken off the project immediately, and the client was told that the action had been taken before they found out for themselves that there was a problem. That event caused the client to respect and trust the actions of the firm.

As an example of when the firm told a client something that they knew the client would not like to hear, was the time the client had engaged in a project with the firm but had certain opinions about how the project should be done, particularly relating to what the firm knew were critical issues for the success of the project. The project manager told the client that the firm would disengage from the project unless the client agreed to certain things. The client had never worked with a consulting company that was willing to forgo billing as opposed to not achieving promised deliverables, and was impressed with the firm's stance. That relationship has now turned into a long-term one based on trust and mutual respect.

Many consulting firms find themselves caught in a balancing act between making money and providing honest advice. Stractics chose to focus on providing good advice.

Measuring Success

Table 1 shows some measures for determining the success achieved by Stractics thus far.

Stractics Group, Inc., thinks the following are the top critical factors that can ensure success when building a new consulting practice:
- Provide excellent service in your chosen niche, and manage your client relationships.
- Focus the firm on doing what you are good at.
- Publish and speak.

Table 1. Measurements of success.

Measure	1997	2001	Goal 2002
Revenue	$40,000	$1,600,000	$4,000,000
Consultants	1	15	25
Number of clients served	1	6	10
Number of continents served	1	3	3
Number of projects completed	2	10	15
Percentage of clients with repeat business	100	90	90

- Try all possible selling avenues—something *will* work.
- Hire people who are smarter than you are.
- Create superior branding.
- Do not give up.

   Among these, not giving up is, by far, the most critical success factor.

Lessons Learned

- *Don't become isolated.* Maintain a network of colleagues to discuss ideas, provide advice, and offer candid encouragement or constructive criticism.
- *Play to your strengths.* Don't try to do everything yourself—share the workload. Do what you do well and assign other accountabilities to your associates who are better suited to accomplish those tasks.
- *Keep trying.* You never know where the next project will come from. It might be right around the next corner.
- *Treat your people well.* With a young company this lesson is sometimes easier said than done, particularly during times when the company is facing cash flow issues. However, show that you are making every effort.
- *Create a common vision and a set of values.* With a new firm, you have a golden opportunity to create an operation that functions exactly the way you, as the founder, want it to function. Create a set of common values and communicate these values to those involved in your new organization as often as possible.
- *Systematically create and actively defend your branding.* If you want to create an organization that is going to compete with big consulting firms, look the part. That means spending what it takes to look as if you are successful right from the start. Take time to develop your logo, letterheads, and business cards. Carry the design over to your Website and to other materials such as the MS PowerPoint™ presentations you make.

Questions for Discussion

1. Discuss the advantages and disadvantages of offering a limited scope of services to clients.

2. What are some means a consultant can use to establish a solid financial base for the firm?

3. Do you think offering clients a guaranteed result is an effective way to obtain clients?

4. What are some things a consultant can do to establish a brand for his or her firm?
5. Discuss ways to market the firm.

The Author

Pierre Mourier is the founder and president of Stractics Group, Inc., a management consulting firm dedicated to helping clients achieve results-driven organizational change. Since becoming a consultant in 1985, he has helped organizations on four continents solve process improvement problems and has been involved directly or indirectly in the redesign of more than 250 processes worldwide. Mourier is a regular speaker at the International Society for Performance Improvement (ISPI) and at other conferences and societies around the globe; in May 2002, he conducted a two-day seminar at the Singapore Institute of Management on organizational change. He has been on the program at the annual meeting of ISPI for the past four years. He has published 10 times in the past three years in various industry and society publications. He can be reached at Stractics Group, Inc., 245 Park Avenue, 24th Floor, New York, New York 10167; phone: 212.278.0730; email: Pierre.Mourier@Stractics.com.

When in Doubt— Say "Yes!"

Neil Cerbone Associates, Inc.

Neil Cerbone and Eileen Claman

This case study will follow the evolution of Neil Cerbone Associates, Inc., (NCA) from its conception as a twinkle in the eye of a 25-year-old song-and-dance man through the major developmental milestones that have marked its evolution into a global professional services consulting firm. NCA specializes in the implementation and delivery of strategic organizational development initiatives and the learning experiences that provide the tactics to support them. Currently, NCA bills more than three million dollars annually to a client base of more than 50 Fortune 500 companies around the world. NCA's history is one of organic growth that has been driven by the passion and pioneering spirit of its clients.

Background

The quickest way to take a snapshot of Neil Cerbone Associates, Inc., is to examine the promises it makes:

To our clients: We are passionately committed to increasing *your profit* by constantly challenging the status quo that exists between business acumen and human insight.

To the men and women who work for our clients: We are passionately committed to impacting *your lives* by provoking you to challenge your fears, extend your reach, and more fully realize the value and power of your individual and collective contributions to the world around you.

This case was prepared to serve as a basis for discussion rather than to illustrate either effective or ineffective administrative and management practices.

To our employees: We are completely committed to fulfilling our promise to the men and women of our client companies by harnessing *your passion* in a way that embraces the rhythm of your individual drum.

Based on these commitments, NCA has evolved over the past 20 years into its role of provocateur and catalyst to select organizations that are seeking mechanisms to mobilize their human resources. Almost every NCA proposal ends with this ultimate commitment, "We are dedicated to the pioneers."

For those who are compelled to categorize it more traditionally, one would probably look under organization development in the library.

The evolution of Neil Cerbone as a sole practitioner into Neil Cerbone Associates, Inc., was driven by 10 critical lessons learned along the way. These lessons were taught by clients, friends, and colleagues, most of whom were not in the consulting world. Although their names are not famous, the lessons they taught remain inestimably valuable.

Ten Critical Lessons Learned

1. When you repeatedly accomplish what many people are telling you is impossible, you begin to see all things as possible. (Learned from Gary Cohen, Cerbone's first business partner in professional theater.)
2. The best way to overcome your own doubt is to sell the solution to someone else's. (Learned from Tina Sokoloff, retailer, Cerbone's first boss.)
3. All the education in the world is no match for raw talent and nerve. (Learned from Barbara Hahn, client and senior vice president, human resources, of a global investment firm.)
4. All the talent in the world is not a substitute for due diligence. (Learned from Fran Riemer, client turned colleague and friend, vice president of strategy integration for a large financial services firm.)
5. Your grasp can absolutely exceed your reach. (Learned from Roger Goldman, client, senior executive vice president of a major financial services institution.)
6. If you want to get big, think big. (Learned from John Higgins, client and friend, chief learning officer of a global consulting firm.)
7. Success is reached incrementally, not by winning the lottery. (Learned from Bob Jud, Cerbone's second boss and first true mentor.)
8. Ethics are neither flexible nor expendable. (Learned from John Majeski, client turned colleague and friend.)

9. If you don't perceive rejection, then you never have to overcome it. (Learned from Eileen Claman, managing director of NCA and close friend.)

10. Just because 80 percent of your effort will dazzle most of the world, it takes 100 percent to make a difference in it. (Learned from Thomas Devaney, significant other.)

Those lessons were neither taught nor learned in any traditional format. They are the result of *paying strict attention* to the people in one's life. Paying attention and extrapolating that which is observed into lessons learned is extremely valuable on two fronts:

1. There is so much to learn from the behavior of others.

2. The act of learning through observation is completely analogous to the consulting process.

NCA's rise from its first-year revenues of $35,000 to its current yearly revenue of more than $3 million is based largely on those lessons.

The NCA Niche

NCA has created its niche by integrating the core operating methodologies of the performing arts into the fundamentals of classic organizational development and training and development methodologies. In essence, it is the integration of the visceral and the cerebral. All engagements are approached from the human perspective. It is not enough to address the mind alone, emotions must be affected as well. In order to operate successfully within this framework, all efforts must be evenly balanced. Too much of one side and not enough of the other, undermines both.

Products and Services

NCA has developed a branded methodology in its approach to human development called Emotional Ergonomics™. The standards of Emotional Ergonomics™ ensure the comfort and viability of the learning process by creating *learning sanctuaries* where people are free to experiment with complex skills and behaviors critical to their professional success. (See figure 1.)

Although much of the work that NCA does is specifically focused on the individual needs of its clients, over the years much of this work has coalesced into a cadre of defined products and services that are accessible to a broader range of potential users. All of these products were developed using the standards of Emotional Ergonomics™.

Figure 1. The benchmarks of Emotional Ergonomics™.

1. Specify and align all technical language and content.
2. Conduct cultural research necessary to articulate the organizational climate at the time of delivery.
3. Conduct the program in the vernacular of the learners.
4. Assess how the new information will most likely be received by the learning population.
5. Present the results of that assessment openly in the learning environment and test the supposition(s).
6. Embrace the cynics as the "voice of the people." Address their issues in program design, development, and delivery.
7. Clarify senior leadership's endorsement of the learning content; don't proceed without it.
8. Provide clear, measurable, first-person experiential learning opportunities throughout the program.
9. Offer honest, direct, responsive, and, most of all, *provocative* facilitation.
10. Discourage passive learning at all costs.
11. Acknowledge and embrace all learning styles.
12. Acknowledge and embrace all personal Priority Systems™ at all times.
13. Create all curriculums to be flexible and address the evolving needs of the learners.
14. Promote every learning experience as a teambuilding experience—it creates the sanctuary.
15. If it ain't broken, don't fix it.
16. Keep breathing.

PrioSys®

PrioSys® is an original interpersonal communications tool that succeeds because:

- It can be taught in one hour.
- It is an active field tool rather than an academic construct.
- It is based on business rather than psychological techniques.
- Its use requires observation and logic alone.
- It can be delivered in electronic, classroom, and large event formats.
- It has been field tested by more than 75,000 people in *Fortune* 500 companies over the past decade.

Total Immersion Simulation™

Total Immersion Simulation™ (TIS) is a blended learning construct that immerses learners into a virtual reality offering plausible real life circumstances without real life consequences. Every Total Immersion Simulation™ has the same overall objective: to provide a series of opportunities for learners to embrace and exercise the requisite skills, attitudes, and behaviors they will need to be successful in their real life environment. TIS attracts organizations that share the belief that their people are the key to their success and, moreover, that the stakes are high enough to warrant investing in those people.

Customer Centricity Programs

NCA's Customer Centricity programs are based on its Customer Centricity Triad©. The Triad provides a graphic realization of Customer Centricity as an overarching operating strategy incorporating interpersonal, structural, and technological components. NCA provides core curriculums designed to behavioralize these components throughout all levels of its client organizations.

Contract Trainers

NCA's Contract Trainer team brings the 10 NCA Attributes (described later in the chapter) to all of the clients it supports. The ability to provide high levels of program design and delivery competency at a fraction of the cost of internal design and delivery resources ensures that NCA Contract Trainers are equally at home with NCA material and any other curriculum its clients require.

Transactional Simulations

Transactional Simulations are exactly like TIS only with a narrower objective. They are applied when a transaction is limited in scope yet critical to the health of a business. Typical applications include: bank tellers, telephone reps, customer complaints professionals, compliance professionals, help desk staff, concierges, retail sales associations, recruiters, interviewers, and so forth.

Case Study Development

NCA case studies are developed and used in process training environments. In order to create a level learning environment, they are never just ripped from the client's reality nor are they academic constructs. They are, instead, a careful blend of fact and fiction that results in a product that is provocative and plausible but not "second guessable."

In Addition...

NCA provides comprehensive video production services and large learning event strategic planning to be able to provide 360-degree support to its clients.

Figure 2 shows major NCA milestones and figure 3 shows where NCA is now.

Key Decision Makers: A Triumvirate to Reckon With

Currently, NCA is driven by Cerbone, president and CEO; Eileen Claman, managing director; and Julie Lyons, comptroller. Cerbone is responsible for providing client solutions, Claman is responsible for delivering those solutions in the most efficient and timely manner possible, and Lyons is responsible for keeping track of every dollar that comes in and goes out of the business.

Figure 2. NCA milestones: Charting the journey.

Year	Milestone
1980	Cerbone joins Jud as administrative assistant/apprentice.
1981	Jud creates Robert A. Jud Associates, Inc., and Cerbone becomes a training consultant.
1983	Cerbone secures his first client as an independent consultant; NCA is born.
1991	Claman, current managing director, joins NCA to market, sell, and deliver products and services.
1992	Lyons, current comptroller, joins NCA to handle business support.
1992	NCA team of contract design and delivery associates is established.
1993	NCA annual revenue exceeds $1 million.
1995	NCA loses its biggest client. Revenue plummets and rebuilding begins.
1996	Key strategic alliances are established.
1998	NCA develops "e" solutions. Resource expansion begins. Annual revenue exceeds $2 million.
1999	NCA opens its first official headquarters.
2000	The NCA team totals eight full-time and 40 contract team members. Annual revenue exceeds $3 million.
2001	NCA launches a global products and services campaign.

Figure 3. NCA today: Evolving at the speed of change.

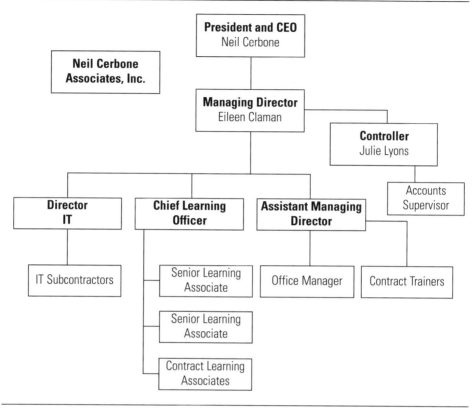

Cerbone and Claman share all marketing and sales responsibilities. The three principals are responsible for all major organizational growth expenditures. Technology development, facility improvement, compensation packages, and even employee bonuses are the product of their joint decision. All engagement letters of agreement, the pricing structure, and profit margins are configured collectively, as well.

If there is a secret to the success of this triumvirate it is this: Cerbone is fearless; Claman is relentless; Lyons is meticulous. And they all respect those attributes in each other.

Strategy

NCA was not born out of some great strategic plan. In fact, NCA was not born at all. It evolved. The day Cerbone met Bob Jud, senior training and development consultant, in the offices of William Mercer, Inc., and accepted a job as his administrative assistant, the seed of NCA's evolution was planted. Jud already had more than 15 years' experience in training and development and was looking for someone who could not only be his administrative assistant but could also be developed as an apprentice for the consulting practice he was building. Cerbone already had a great deal of teaching experience in his role of theatrical producer, director, and choreographer. Like many theater people of his generation, he also typed more than 130 wpm. Oprah Winfrey defines luck as "the result of preparation meeting opportunity." That meeting was one of those moments.

Within 10 months of that meeting, Jud began his own training and development firm, Robert A. Jud Associates, Inc. Cerbone joined Jud's new consulting practice and began to add program delivery to his administrative duties. It was during this period of due diligence that Cerbone envisioned a training and development consulting practice of his own. He shared his vision with Jud who agreed that Cerbone had an entrepreneurial spirit and would most likely do well on his own. Jud then expanded the range of the mentor/apprentice relationship and began to introduce Cerbone to client marketing techniques, proposal writing, and many of the other components such a business requires. Jud also introduced Cerbone to several prospects who were "always looking for talented trainers." Six months later, Cerbone was operating independently. Jud Associates and Neil Cerbone Associates became strategic allies. Jud Associates specialized in packaged programs while Cerbone Associates specialized in customized programs. There were several factors that made this sequence of events so successful.

1. The subject matter was extremely compelling to Cerbone. The impulse to work in training and development was not driven by dollars but by an intense desire to help others. He was aware that that field could also be lucrative, but that was not the force behind his action.

2. The due diligence process led by Jud was action oriented. There was a great deal of opportunity to practice and demonstrate the requisite consulting skills.

3. Jud was a mentor with great confidence and tremendous knowledge. He never saw Cerbone's progress as threatening. In fact, he was (and remains) proud of Cerbone's relatively quick success.

4. It was not necessary to invest any money into the business other than stationery, business cards, and a typewriter. The business ran successfully for more than a decade out of Cerbone's house. There was never a need to find investors. There were never partners that could obstruct the forward momentum of NCA.

5. As part of his due diligence under the mentoring of Jud, Cerbone had already established several sustainable client relationships by the time he began to operate as NCA. That meant that, from the onset, there was little to no scrambling to make ends meet.

Although at the time, it did not feel like a plan, the following five factors came together in a way that may shed light on starting a consulting firm:

1. Do something you love, the dollars will follow.
2. Garner as much experience as you can, however you can.
3. Don't go it alone, find a mentor.
4. Do not begin by investing any money—your own or someone else's.
5. Develop clients while you are gainfully employed somewhere else.

Methodology—Looking for Ways to Say "Yes!"

The core methodology behind the evolution of Cerbone into NCA is based, primarily, on a simple principle that Claman brought to the business in 1990. Her approach was to eliminate every roadblock that stood between NCA and its potential clients. Any requests, no matter how "unnerving," were met with a resounding "Yes!" At the precise moment of the "Yes!" it was not always clear exactly how the work would proceed, but once the commitment was made, there was no going back and in one way or another the promise was delivered. That may, at first, seem reckless, but in the 11 years since the "Say Yes!" approach began, there has never been a single occasion where NCA has not come through. That is not because of any extraordinary abilities unique to the NCA team, but rather a reflection of human nature and the power of optimism and commitment. If you believe that you can "figure it out," you will. Oftentimes that quality alone is what differentiates a successful consultant from the rest of the pack.

Saying "Yes!" is not about taking an order from a client and doing whatever he or she may ask. Every client request must be assessed to be sure that the client is indeed asking for something that will actually be of benefit. There are many examples when this is not the case. Clients will often request products and services that will not deliver the outcome they desire because they have inaccurately assessed their own problem. These are not times to just "Say Yes!" These are the opportunities to begin illustrating your value by redirecting the assignment so that it becomes in the client's best interest. Once you are sure that the client's request would indeed help the client, the "Say Yes!" methodology begins.

Saying "Yes!" is also at the core of most every successful customer centricity strategy. Long-term client relationships are predicated on clients feeling trusted, welcome, important, special, and pleased. The surest way to make that happen is to "Say Yes!"

The rationale for saying "Yes!" is based on three basic assumptions:

1. **Most roadblocks seem more prodigious than they actually are.** More often than not, roadblocks solve themselves. The circumstances inevitably change. The scope shifts. The timeframe shifts. The people move on. What was once overwhelming, simply isn't any more.

2. **It is unnecessary to "add it all up" in advance.** Oftentimes when a client approaches with an enormous assignment, the temptation is to try to swallow it whole. Once one starts down that road, it is often littered with enough obstacles to make almost any engagement seem impossible. Let's face it, if you had enough resources lying around dormant *before* the engagement surfaced, chances are you were overstaffed—never a good idea.

3. **It is OK to proceed without knowing exactly where you are going.** Being a consultant requires a certainty that if you don't know how to deliver every component of what is needed, you can learn or find someone who can.

Using these three assumptions as fundamental guidelines ensures that saying "Yes!" is less reckless than it may at first appear. It has been an extremely powerful operating methodology for NCA.

Ten NCA Attributes

Another fundamental methodology that drives the NCA consulting organization are "The 10 Attributes." This methodology originated as a result of a critical self-assessment during which Cerbone took stock of his own strengths and weaknesses. Because NCA was going to rest squarely on his shoulders, Cerbone believed that he needed to capitalize on his strengths as differentiating qualities for which people would be willing to pay. He believed that if he leveraged his strengths well enough, it might compensate for his weaknesses, at least until he could afford to hire people who could counterbalance them altogether. In essence he was counting on his individual strengths to get him through until he could be joined by Claman and Lyons and, ultimately, what is today's NCA team. Following are the 10 NCA Attributes:

1. Agile. The ability to be completely responsive to the mercurial needs of a client at all times, to zig and then zag with grace.

2. Provocative. The ability to challenge the status quo in the name of achieving a client's objectives.

3. Resourceful. The ability to create a solution *without* the obvious resources.
4. Optimistic. The ability to see the opportunity and value in whatever has just transpired.
5. Engaging. The ability to capture the imaginations of everyone in the client's environment.
6. Unflappable. The ability to "keep on keeping on."
7. Collaborative. The ability to integrate the contributions of others without losing ownership.
8. Savvy. The ability to harness all of one's *collective* knowledge and to discern which is relevant and which is not.
9. Courageous. The ability to withstand being targeted and unpopular with those people in the client organizations who would rather *not* see the solution implemented.
10. Smart. The ability to integrate new information quickly and proceed effectively.

Those attributes were powerful enough to drive Cerbone's one-man band along for several years. In 1990, Cerbone added Claman to NCA. She added her "Say Yes!" methodology to the mix, and NCA grew into a consulting firm using more than a dozen full-time consultants and a cadre of more than 60 contract contributors.

NCA has never relied on formal academic constructs or models as many other successful consulting practices do. In fact, it operates with a strong bias against "ivory tower education." The strength of its two driving methodologies is found in the humanity at the core of each of them. *All* of NCA's people are always accessible to *all* of its clients at *all* levels of their organizations *all* of the time.

Strategic Alliances

NCA's first strategic alliance began early with Jud Associates, Inc. It became the model on which it has carefully established other such alliances. NCA invested significant energy into developing several alliances with other firms whose work complemented its own. Joining forces with these firms allowed each to broaden their delivery capabilities by capitalizing on each other's strengths and competencies.

NCA understood from the start that any firm that it introduced to its client became NCA to that client. As a result, NCA turned away from many partnering opportunities based on a lack of confidence that a particular firm would appropriately reflect "The 10 NCA Attributes" and "Say Yes!" methodologies.

The vast majority of the firms with whom NCA did establish partnerships in the mid-1990s are still partnering together now. They provide each other with extended client bases as well as built-in marketing opportunities.

Growing the Business
1983 to 1990: Stage One—Individual Growth

The first seven years of NCA were really all about "NC." There were no associates. The "Say Yes!" methodology had not yet appeared. Cerbone was a "gun for hire." He had identified his 10 attributes and he leveraged them for all he was worth. It was an intuitive process in those years. Most leads came from word-of-mouth referrals. Cerbone realized from the start that he had to generate those referrals by his performance. If there was one overriding strategy on which he relied, it was "one good job is *not* enough." His objective was always to knock it out of the ballpark again and again. If the client asked for two options, he gave three. If the client said Wednesday would be all right, he submitted the project on Monday. If the client cancelled unexpectedly, he refused cancellation fees. If clients were down, he cheered them up. He remembered birthdays and anniversaries. He never encumbered them with policies. He never let price be the deciding factor. If a prospect wanted to engage him, he found a way to alter the fee or the scope of the project to make it happen. He did everything he could to always be their first choice. NCA still maintains close relationships with many of the clients Cerbone supported during those first seven years.

1991 to 1995: Stage Two—Real Associates

After seven years of organic growth that centered on Cerbone as the single creative contributor and driven strictly by referral and client need, he came to a critical juncture in his career. He began to recognize that he was not an infinite resource that could be tapped at any time into eternity. It was time to either curtail the growth of the business by limiting the amount of work that he would accept— or, to go all out and see just how large it could grow. The decision was intuitive. Stage Two began with the decision to expand the gene pool both creatively as well as operationally. It was time for Neil Cerbone Associates to have real Associates! Thus entered Claman, Lyons, and a cadre of individual contract contributors. Supported by these talented people, NCA was able to provide greater reach and depth of service to its increasing client base.

Although Stage Two brought the ability to do multiple concurrent engagements, it also required close resource management.

NCA was not in a place where its ongoing operating expenses could ever exceed its revenue streams. It was a hand-to-mouth existence, there was no cushion to bridge any gaps in cash flow. Aside from Lyons and Claman, who joined Cerbone in full-time capacities, NCA relied heavily on contract resources. That was a prudent strategy in that these contributions were almost always 100 percent billable. Contractors were only engaged when there was work suitable for them. This was a double-edged sword given the high standards that drove NCA throughout Stage One. Finding and developing contract resources that embodied the "10 NCA Attributes" was arduous.

There was constant pressure by the clients on two fronts. There were those who "wanted Neil, only Neil, no one but Neil," and there were those who pressed to "send someone, anyone." It required a great deal of restraint not to buckle under those pressures. It was critical that clients could accept NCA professionals other than Cerbone and begin to value them not as "Cerbone substitutes" but as significant contributors in their own right. It was also critical that clients understood "just anyone" was never a good solution.

This dynamic became further complicated by ever shifting client needs. A team of first-class contract contributors would be assembled and engaged. The project at hand would then change and the players would get displaced. They would find other opportunities and NCA would be left having to repeat the process when another engagement began.

Even with these challenges, that plan kept NCA in the black almost every year of its existence. Overhead was kept to an absolute minimum. There were no NCA offices and no employees other than Lyons and Claman. There was only that which was necessary to deliver quality products and services to the clients. (In later years, clients would joke that NCA had virtual offices before it had computers.) During this time, Claman coordinated all of the contractors in addition to developing and delivering products and services. Lyons handled all accounts payable and receivable and served as the administrative hub of the business. She was also the "Voice of NCA." When clients or prospects called, they always reached Lyons. This is an incredibly important function, as it often sets the tone of the entire client relationship. Lyons greeted every caller as if they were the happiest surprise of the day, no matter what. Having a person like this at the other end of the phone was extremely important to NCA's growth in two ways:

1. Credibility. Constantly leaving messages on voicemail ultimately erodes client confidence while increasing client frustration.

2. Responsiveness. NCA made its reputation on being completely responsive at all times. If Lyons received a call that required immediate

attention, she would track down the necessary party by any means necessary. Most problems were solved within 15 minutes. If for some reason, contact was impossible, Lyons would stay in constant touch with the client until resolution was achieved. She was eternally optimistic with all callers and that went a long way to keep them calm no matter what the circumstance.

This rather loose infrastructure marked Stage Two for NCA. During this time, the annual revenue rose above one million dollars. The client base expanded significantly as did penetration within existing client organizations. There were also some scary downtimes that also helped shape the company, such as the following:

1. The first year that NCA's revenues exceeded one million dollars was 1993. This happened as a result of a burgeoning relationship it had with one client, a midsized national retail bank. The atmosphere in that year was heady. Lots of work; lots of money. More and more resources were brought on board to accommodate the exciting projects that were coming rapidly one right after the other. Salaries for the principals expanded accordingly. It was "Camelot." And then in 1995 the bank was sold and in that moment it all ended. Not only were all the new resources released, but also the principals had to take sizable cuts in salary just to pay the bills. Camelot turned into "Death Valley." In many ways, that turn of events was exactly what NCA needed to correct its trajectory. In their naïveté, Cerbone and his team had failed to realize that:

- One behemoth client provides an artificial sense of success.
- When revenue spikes as a result of a single client, that is the time to "invest" in your own business by building up enough capital to operate the business during an unexpected downturn.
- It is important to periodically target your largest clients and then assess the state of the business in case any one of them disappeared tomorrow. If you discover that your business cannot survive without its largest client, you're in a heap o' trouble.

2. NCA attracted the attention of family and many friends. It looked like a fun place to work. Involving them seemed like a good idea. Because most of the work was contractual, which meant that by definition it had a predetermined end point, many friends and family members were hired. It seemed relatively safe, because all work assignments were finite. The result of these decisions was mixed. Absolutes like "don't ever work with family or friends" do not adequately address the issue. Cerbone and Lyons are brother and sister and their working relationship was and remains synchronous. Cerbone and Claman had been close friends for more than a decade before they began successfully

working together in 1991. Lyons and Claman were classmates throughout high school and they have always worked extremely well together. It would be too simple to merely advise "never work with family or friends." The real lessons were about how to make working with them fruitful. Consider the following:

- Be absolutely sure that the parameters of the work are clear before any professional relationship begins with family or friends.
- Create a work document that specifies what success will look like and what the consequences will be when and if that success is not achieved.
- Always begin with a substantial trial period where either party can "get out" unscathed.
- If your relationship with a friend or relative is too complex or fragile to withstand this level of specificity—don't do it!

Those lessons were learned the hard way. There were many circumstances where the employment parameters were based on good faith. But good faith is far too general in a business setting.

1995 to 1998: Stage Three—Rebounding

Stage Three is defined in NCA's history as the rebound stage. Having learned the painful lessons from Stage Two, it became obvious that NCA had to rethink several of its operating strategies. It was very difficult during those times to determine what should have/could have been done to better prepare for NCA losing its critical client. Everyone was feeling somewhat disillusioned. One could hear comments like, "What were we supposed to do, turn down the work?"

But the truth is that NCA interpreted its bonanza as an absolute sign that things would always be at least as good as they were. In this case, the optimism that had gotten them so far worked against them—coupled with the fact that too much of the money from Camelot was going into the pockets of the key contributors. These people worked like maniacs, they deserved to be rewarded. The impulse was generous. The forethought was nonexistent.

There were two key objectives to Stage Three:
1. Keep up the morale of the people who now were being asked to take pay cuts as they watched their contracted colleagues be terminated altogether.
2. Build back a more stable version of what was lost one step, one engagement at a time.

Those objectives could not be accomplished easily or quickly. The first thing Cerbone did after cutting his own pay by more than 50 percent and Claman's and Lyon's by more than 30 percent, was to go out and buy everyone tee shirts that read: "Be realistic, expect a miracle." He required that everyone wear the tee shirts to work *every day* as long as there was no client around to see them. He also bought river stones and had the word "Believe" carved into them and put them on everyone's desk. He also kept his personal feelings and frustrations on the turn of events to himself. He knew that tee shirts and river rocks would not be enough without his own optimism and passion being out there for all to see.

Building back the business was not quite so inspirational. Cerbone and Claman began a process of meticulous phone calling to all clients and prospects with whom NCA had previously had a relationship. The process was meticulous in that it often took more than 10 calls to actually reach one person. Once contact was made, even though the prospect was friendly and open to exploring new working options, there were innumerable obstacles that often stood in the way. People were inevitably on vacation or promoted to some new position that no longer worked with "firms like NCA." New management teams were dedicated to using their consultants. Budgets were cut. Technology and system implementations were being given priority over learning and development initiatives. Competitor firms, vying for the same piece of the pie, also managed to make the process incredibly arduous.

This is where Claman's relentlessness and optimism paid off big time. If she learned that another firm was employed to conduct an assignment that NCA could have done, she explored the possibility of partnering with that firm. If the client said there was no money, she would get permission to call them periodically until "just coincidentally" she would call on the day the new budget was approved. Because systems implementations were taking the spotlight, Claman would shine a piece of that light on the change management issues that always accompanied such implementations. No obstacle was ever interpreted as a roadblock. It was a painful process of meeting after meeting and proposal after proposal, all the while not allowing any feelings of desperation to ever coalesce. This was no time for desperation.

1998 to 2001: Stage Four—Organizational Growth

By 1998, NCA had fully rebounded from the devastating blow it had taken in 1995. Salaries were back to 100 percent, the client base was now divided more evenly (not evenly enough, but more evenly), and many of the contract contributors who were let go in 1995 were put back to work.

NCA was at another critical juncture. It was time to reassess its marketing strategy. It should be noted that many marketing professionals had examined NCA's marketing efforts and literally laughed at the audacity it took to consider its energies in that area as a marketing strategy at all. NCA did not use any of the traditional marketing tactics including mass mailings, press releases, promotional activities, and the like.

Up until 1998, NCA relied entirely on the marketing process that had gotten it back on its feet after rebounding from the loss of its largest client. Although it was an extremely successful approach in that stage of development, it would not be enough if NCA was going to reach out into the great unknown global marketplace. In 1998 that felt like a big "if."

There were many factors to consider before jumping into that great big pond.

1. The biggest question to be answered was: Were we up to the physical, mental, and emotional challenges that would be required of us in order to succeed on a global landscape?

2. How would we capitalize our expansion?

3. It was during this period of time that e-learning, distance learning, and so many Web-based products were eclipsing other delivery systems. NCA previewed many of the electronic products that focused on communication skills that were on the market. They were and remain wholly unimpressive. They completely lacked visceral impact and were not much better intellectually. Given the appetite of the marketplace to love everything "e," NCA had its work cut out for it. If NCA was going to play in this arena, it was going to have to figure out how to make sense out of that which it found mostly nonsensical.

4. What were the alternatives? Was it possible to stay the same size company operating in the way that it had for the past 17 years?

It was the answer to the fourth question that helped NCA answer the first three. It was fanciful to consider staying the same as an option, given the speed of change, the power and impact of the Web, and the increasing competition in a truly global market. NCA had to answer questions one through three immediately.

Being nothing if not practical people, the three principals and the other members of the slowly expanding NCA team realized that they *had* to be up to the challenges. All alternatives seemed bleak.

As for funding, this time NCA was ready with some stored capital to begin the process of investing in itself.

Finding the right technology partners to support their "e" development efforts became and remains a primary operating objective.

As that search began, NCA examined the many products and services that were designed as part of its client solutions packages. Those products and services were field tested and ready to be packaged, marketed, and sold to a more universal market. While the search for the right technology partner continued, the NCA organization needed to be restructured in order to be able to reach out into the "e" marketplace.

That restructuring required three key elements:
1. NCA needed to implement an organizational infrastructure as well as operational standards and processes to manage incremental growth.
2. NCA needed to hire full-time professional contributors in order to package, market, and deliver its products.
3. NCA needed a headquarters in which to house the new team.

Process and Infrastructure

During the early stages of NCA when Cerbone was a sole practitioner, he relied on intuition and client focus in lieu of structure and process. Even when he was joined by Claman, Lyons, and a handful of others, things worked well without standardization and formal accountabilities. There was a synchronicity borne of an implicit understanding of how things needed to be done. There were certain processes in place but they were intrinsic and intuitive to the people who were involved. As the next generation of employees was hired, NCA proceeded on that same road and was met with a string of disturbing "wake-up calls."

The new additions to the staff, while extraordinarily talented and capable, were not able to simply intuit what the "NCA way" actually was. Upon reflection, it should have come as no surprise, but hindsight is, as they say, 20/20. Suddenly, performance issues were cropping up. Over time, the principals came to understand that those issues were a result of a lack of clarity around expectations. If certain standards, processes, and checkpoints weren't established, the company's growth would soon be stunted. NCA was no longer a one-, two-, or five-person operation. It couldn't expect others to be effective without the clarity that uniform processes provide.

Throughout 1999, NCA installed a reporting structure and performance management system. It also developed service providers' agreements for all engagement participants and activity reports to capture work hours. A formal new hire orientation program was developed as well.

Not all members of the NCA team embraced these changes. For the first time in its history, NCA had to take a stand that resulted in several of its employees leaving. The new structure was too confining to some who had been with the firm in its earlier days. They were unable to make the necessary adjustments. Ironically, these adjustments were difficult for everyone, including the principals. The difference was that only some people could place the growth of the firm above their immediate comfort. It was a difficult time for all concerned. NCA was a family and, right or wrong, it had lost some of its key members. Cerbone, Claman, and Lyons believed that NCA's new structure was imperative to its further growth even if it meant losing some valuable resources. That belief did not come out of some arbitrary need to "corporatize." It was rooted in the certainty that a lack of an adequate infrastructure would limit the development of a larger employee base.

In addition to adding structure to the internal operation, NCA also had to implement several client-focused standards in order to pave the road ahead. After several experiences with clients changing the scope of an engagement without warning, or postponing and canceling dates, NCA began preparing letters of agreement for every engagement it undertook. Those documents clearly stated the parameters of each project—how many consultants would be involved, dates, fees, and all other important information. It also contained cancellation and date change fee schedules. That was difficult for some of NCA's early clients to accept. They were quite used to doing business on a handshake. The principals took a great deal of effort to make these clients as comfortable as possible. There were times when they waived certain fees. The key here was that, now, there were established fees to be waived. That is very different from the freewheeling, anything goes tactics that Cerbone relied on in the early days. After a short time, clients stopped looking to waive fees. They began to see NCA in a new light. Everyone at NCA took great delight in sharing with those early clients that because of their continued support, NCA had reached a new level of professionalism. It gave the clients a stake in NCA's success. Instead of quibbling over fees, they were proud of what they had helped to create.

Hiring and Housing

The hiring process continues as it began. Hire one person at a time. Take the time to provide the new team member with a rich orientation of the "NCA way." Expose that person to the wide assortment of client engagement activity and seek to discover his or her hidden talents that can add value to the firm. Share NCA's history with that new employee. Introduce him or her to NCA's products. Immerse him or her in the early documents that helped to build NCA. Take that person on sales calls and co-author proposals with him or her. As soon as that process feels complete, hire another person and begin again.

In August 1999, NCA found an old apartment on the second floor of some retail space in the middle of a small town in New Jersey. It was very cheap, it had parking, and it was 23 minutes direct to midtown Manhattan where many of NCA's clients resided. More important, this access opened the hiring pool to include the New York workforce.

It was tempting that summer to seek more luxurious digs for NCA to call home. Instead, NCA depended on friends to "fix'r up," and the offices became an eclectic, almost bohemian, enclave with purple and silver walls and "interesting" artwork done by a talented friend of the firm. The office was embraced by NCA's clients and prospects. They saw it as a metaphor of the firm itself—creative and intriguing. It was clear that only a small percentage of the fees the clients paid were going to overhead. They liked that. Clients that never wanted to leave their office for any reason (including lunch) were asking to have meetings at NCA's offices. They said things about the comfortable and creative atmosphere being conducive to solid solutions.

By the summer of 2000 NCA had its own Website and eight full-time employees. They all were multitalented and wore many hats. The plan to bring NCA products and services to the global market was losing focus, however. Clients were demanding more and more and NCA was delivering more and more. This took all of the new manpower that was supposed to be working toward aspirational objectives and put them on client delivery teams. That is a dilemma that confounds NCA to this day. On the one hand, the ability to expand the work with any given client is a key objective for all consulting firms; on the other hand, as manpower is sucked into this vortex, new initiatives can lose momentum.

Looking Ahead

As NCA moves into 2002, it is once again faced with new challenges. The global products and services campaign is still in a holding pattern as NCA continues to deliver products and services to meet escalating client needs. The eclectic bohemian enclave is becoming claustrophobic and larger quarters are necessary. In looking for new quarters, NCA will continue to resist the allure of luxury. Perhaps just a larger eclectic and bohemian enclave—the clients seem to enjoy it so.

The hiring process that began in 1998 will, for the first time, begin to focus on specialists rather than the multi-hat professionals on which NCA has relied in the past. The need for professionals who have specific skills and experience to develop truly innovative e-learning programs and bring them to market remains high. Perhaps these professionals will come with the appropriate technology partner in tow, as this is a strategic alliance still waiting to happen. This new work team will drive a campaign that is dedicated to that endeavor.

NCA faces these challenges with enough capital to invest in their successful outcomes. It will take an estimated 24 months to begin to realize any return-on-investment from the 2002 initiatives that it is undertaking. It is the first time that NCA has taken on that level of risk. Armed with more "Expect a Miracle" tee shirts; more "Believe" river stones; and enough optimism, passion, and commitment to spare, NCA is looking forward to whatever is next.

Questions for Discussion

1. How would the development of NCA have differed if Cerbone did not have a Claman and a Lyons with whom to partner? Do you believe that a consulting practice like the one described here requires a single creative driver like Cerbone to get off the ground? Why, why not?
2. Given that many consulting firms must go through a "rebound stage," what things would you do differently than Cerbone and Claman did? Why?
3. How is building a consulting business different from building another kind of business? How is it the same?
4. NCA spent a great deal of time building clients for life. Which of their tactics do you support? Which do you not support? Why? Given what you have read about NCA, do you see other tactics that might have served it well?
5. What factors need to be considered before a sole practitioner can successfully launch a consulting firm?
6. The triumvirate that drives NCA is described as "fearless . . . relentless . . . meticulous." How important are these attributes to a successful consulting practice? Are there other attributes that are just as or more important?

The Authors

Neil Cerbone is the founder and CEO of Neil Cerbone Associates, Inc. He began NCA in 1981 and, since then, has devoted all of his professional energies to the clients that it supports. Those clients include J. P. Morgan Chase; Fleet Bank; Prudential; KPMG Consulting, Inc.; KPMG LLP; Motorola; J&J; and many other *Fortune* 500 companies. Cerbone's early life and education are in the theater. He has integrated the core communication principles of the theater into virtually all of the products and services that NCA provides. He is currently writing a book on human priority systems. He can be reached at Neil Cerbone Associates, Inc., 25W South Orange Ave, 2d floor, South Orange, NJ 07079; phone: 973.761.7722; email: ThePioneers @cerbonegroup.com.

Eileen Claman is the managing director for NCA. In this capacity, she supports the company's client base and manages professionals' resources and strategic alliances. Claman joined NCA in 1991 and continues to function as senior facilitator and simulation specialist delivering workshops focused on service, sales, coaching, and consulting skills. She received a bachelor of fine arts from Rutgers University in 1982 and is an active member of ASTD, the Women's Financial Association, and the Women's Campaign Fund.

You Are Known
by the Company You Keep

Lovoy's Team Works, Inc.

Sharon W. Lovoy

This study describes the development of a sole-practitioner consulting services business. Included in this study is the transition from working for a corporation to being self-employed. The study describes how client relationships are initiated and maintained when successful. It also documents the separation process when the relationships are not productive. Lessons learned provide valuable insight as to how knowledge, skills, and personality are tightly connected. It gives an overview of what is required to be a successful consultant and how that success can be measured in many different ways.

The Practice

Lovoy's Team Works, Inc., is a sole-practitioner organization owned by Sharon W. Lovoy, senior professional in human resources. It began in December 1991 and is still thriving. Before beginning the consulting firm, I was employed by a savings and loan bank as the vice president of training, after having been recruited away as chief of human resources with a high-profile government agency, where I worked for 15 years.

On November 29, 1991, representatives of the Office of Thrift Supervision, the government agency whose responsibility it is to oversee all savings and loan banks, visited the bank and informed top management that for the organization to stay in business under new federal requirements, the bank had to lay off 50 positions, including mine. So, on December 2, 1991, I was laid off from my job. Because I had

---

This case was prepared to serve as the basis for discussion rather than to illustrate either effective or ineffective administrative and management practices.

been thinking about owning my own consulting practice, Lovoy's Team Works, Inc. was born.

The practice provides training for groups and individuals in the following specialties: team building, time management, and leadership skills. All coaching and training is targeted toward developing specific competencies. The practice's other specialty is conflict resolution and mediation services for individuals, teams, groups, management, unions, and other sectors embroiled in conflicts that have resulted in damage to individuals or the organization. That does not include intervention in labor contracts but, instead, addresses the human side of conflict.

Success in this endeavor has resulted from developing long-term relationships with clients so as to become intimately aware of their problems and concerns. This approach requires that the principal maintain status in two camps: 1) as an objective outsider who can provide tough advice and counsel and 2) as an insider who is genuinely and deeply concerned about the personal and professional success of both the individual employees and the company. The ability to maintain both neutrality and to gain and keep confidences and trust has been absolutely crucial. Demonstrating respect for each person in the organization regardless of his or her position is also crucial.

Making the Transition

As a result of the layoff, I came to a fork in the road and the choices were obvious: seek other employment or start my own consulting practice. Word spread quickly among my colleagues at the American Society for Training & Development (ASTD) and the Society for Human Resource Management (SHRM) that I was out of a job. The first phone call of condolence and concern was from Bill Rush, who was, at that time, head of human resources for the JVC Magnetics Disc and Tape plants in Tuscaloosa, Alabama. I had worked with Rush for years on the state council for SHRM and on the annual Human Resource Management Conference at the University of Alabama. Rush called to let me know that he had heard the news and asked what I was doing now. I almost choked when I said the word "consulting." I cringed, waiting for his negative reaction and rejection. For me, the word consultant conjured unfair visions of all the people who had constantly visited me when I was an HR manager, peddling their wares, and nagging me with unceasing phone calls. Instead, he reacted with interest and asked, "Doing what?" I replied, "training," even though, truthfully, I hadn't figured that part out yet. At that point, I had no idea what specific services my company would offer. His response was, "Great! We need training! Come to see me!" We made an appointment for January 1992.

Then I received what I thought at the time was good news. A booking! The wife of a friend called in January 1992. She owned an advertising specialty company and wanted me to do a Myers-Briggs Type Indicator® (MBTI) workshop for her group on January 18. We arranged to meet at her company and travel together, as the session location was about 80 miles south of Birmingham, where we both lived. The morning of the workshop, I awoke to predictions of snow, a dire prediction in the sunny South. Few Alabama drivers have any experience driving in snow and the accompanying ice, no one has snow tires, and sand trucks are as rare as snow. I contacted the client who said that the workshop had not been cancelled and indicated she would look unfavorably on my decision to cancel. She intimated that she would also tell others that I was unreliable if I cancelled.

I conducted the fastest MBTI workshop in history as I anxiously watched the snow begin to fall. Our return trip came to an abrupt end when we crashed into a wrecker, which was across our lane trying to pull out a car that had gone over a cliff beside the road. I had on my seat belt but hit the right side of my face on the window, which caused severe and painful injuries. As a result of the accident, my dreams and plans for a practice were put on an extended hold.

Starting Over (Again)

After the wreck, a friend I had met through ASTD, Victoria Baxter, contacted me and practically commanded me to come to her house for an important meeting. With my damaged spirit and body, I met with her. In an extraordinary act of generosity, she took an entire day of her always-packed schedule to explain how to find clients, how to set up a business, and how to develop materials. We decided never to compete, but to always collaborate. I never failed to send her clients while she still had her practice, as a small repayment for the thousands of ways she is the embodiment of friendship.

Managing Time

A constant battle that I still fight is not allowing work to overcome my personal life. I was definitely sleep deprived for many years. I have a home office and there was a blurring of the lines between home and work. Until I learned to value my rest as an asset for my sanity and creativity, I spent the first eight years "running on empty."

I often suffered respiratory illnesses during most of those years and worked while under the influence of influenza. To maintain credibility, a class, with half of the participants traveling long distances to a training site, cannot be cancelled due to illness unless you are hospitalized or have a written excuse from the coroner. I will never forget the time I had a fever of 102 degrees and showed up to teach a class. When I turned to write on the flipchart, the class began laughing. It seems that in my feverish fog, I had forgotten to zip the back of my skirt and showed more of my assets than is appropriate!

The open door to my office still beckons me at odd hours because my creativity has the annoying habit of occurring at unusual times. But I now resist the urge to check email late at night because, for my time management training, I researched the value of sleep and found that looking at a computer screen confuses the body's circadian rhythms and makes going to sleep difficult.

The other issue I faced, because of sleep and rest deprivation, was driving an enormous amount of miles annually while not fully alert. I was such a phony for many years: I was admonishing others in time management workshops for not getting enough rest, but I was just as guilty. I still advise people to get adequate sleep, but now I am a member of the reformed believers!

In starting a consulting practice it is important to do extensive research and design so as to have enough tools when a client calls. Fortunately, I did not have to start from scratch. I had built a library of reference books and materials over the years I worked in human resources. No one should even consider becoming a private consultant without proper tools. Even with this head start, it took years to amass a wide enough inventory so that a call from a client didn't require hours and hours of preparation and research.

Strategy

In the beginning there wasn't a strategy—or it could be called, "be all things to all people." Say "yes" to everything that is legal and ethical. As a result, I found myself on a roller coaster due to lack of planning on my part. I said "yes" to projects that I should never have taken on. For example, I wanted Southern Company as a client (this organization is part of the Alabama Power and Georgia Power network and is considered to be one of the best performing organizations in the country). My husband is also employed by this organization. One of the members of the Southern Company College had heard that I did customer service training. He came to one of my classes and liked what he saw. He asked me to write a course that would be delivered by the college instructor cadre. For three solid weeks, I began each day trying to put the material together and ended each day with zero progress. I then had a meeting with myself to figure out the source of my writer's block. I realized that while I was an expert at developing and delivering my own material, I did not possess the patience (nor desire) to develop detailed materials for others to teach. Humiliated, I returned the project to Southern Company with my confession to the staff that I should have never have gotten involved in the project from the beginning. The happy ending to that story is that the staff remembered it, and I was selected later to work with several other groups in the company where I was successful.

I also learned the hard way that I am not good at anything to do with total quality management (TQM) or career counseling after failed attempts in these areas. In other words, I began with the strategy "I will do anything half way" and finally ended with "I will do some things well." I continued to look for the areas around which I could find joy, passion, and satisfaction.

I discovered that I had a talent for teaching prevention of sexual harassment training. I figured out how to make the class enjoyable even though, in most cases, my classes were part of a court-ordered remedy and attendance was mandatory and participants often came in slamming down their pens and being resigned to the forced attendance. My greatest compliments were "That wasn't so bad!" at the end of the class. And the participants would tell others and my practice grew in that area. I aligned myself with several top-notch labor attorneys and we did joint presentations around the United States.

I also keep files on other consultants. When a client contacts me and asks me about a service that I do not provide, I go straight to that file and provide a client with all the necessary information about the potential consultant. I then call the consultant and tell him or her to expect a call from the client. In each case, this process cultivates good will with other consultants and lets my clients know that I am not threatened by their hiring others. My clients remain loyal.

A concept shared with me by Jim Rowell, my best friend and colleague in the business, is the notion that there is no such thing as "home is home and work is work and the two things don't touch each other." Discussing that concept during a prevention of sexual harassment session enables participants to understand that everything they do impacts their whole lives, not just professional or personal. That is an excellent source of motivation because while individuals may not care about legalities, they do care whether or not their families, friends, and perhaps fellow church, temple, or mosque members discover their behavior. When they realize they could lose their family or livelihood and damage their reputation, if, for example, they sexually or racially harass others in the workplace, their attitude changes drastically.

Additionally, Rowell taught me to become more focused in my training classes. I had a tendency to have too much information and to lack logical structure. He showed me that all training is based on three components: awareness, accountability, and action. I further developed the concept of action and tied it to the choices that individuals make. I promote the ideas of dispelling "victimhood" and replacing it with accountability. Each course is designed around those elements and ends with participants having to teach each other what new choices they will make as a result of the training. Commitments are publicly made, which increases the likelihood that they will be kept. The commitment process also gives people an opportunity to tie their new knowledge to their previous experience. I am often taught by the words of wisdom that come from my participants at the end of a course. I have found that my clients are attracted to the idea that employees and management must be a part of the solutions for the workplace.

My normal approach to consulting services is to meet with a client and ask a lot of questions. Nosiness is a definite asset because I am not afraid of even the most sensitive subjects. I also request meetings with employees if they are part of the process. After attending a mediation training class, I was frustrated when I emerged with a jumble of information, but no logical way to implement what I had learned. After much thought and study, I developed a five-step process that I use for all consulting projects. I take my clients through these areas:

- information
- issues
- interests
- ideas
- implementation.

Information is related to the "who, what, where, and when" type of data, including timelines. Issues are the major categories of the problems and challenges facing a client. Interests are the fears, concerns, motivation, thoughts, or feelings that drive each person connected to the situation. Ideas are always jointly developed to ensure buy-in and must undergo the test of impact on others and systems, as well as the "logical consequence" of the ideas to make sure that the situation is not improved at the expense of making other things worse. Tailored solutions are the centerpiece of my services.

Structure of Practice

I began with no legal structure, but after a year and on the advice of my attorney husband, I incorporated. Lovoy's Team Works, Inc., is structured as a small business corporation (subchapter S corporation), which provides me and my family with personal immunity from any liability the company might incur.

I have been approached by several individuals who have asked to join my practice, but I have resisted all offers.

I have no legal ties to any other partners, but instead am bound by tight friendships that are both strategic and personal. For example, Rowell was the head of training for the University of Alabama. He attended my Myers-Briggs Type Indicator® workshop at the HRM conference. He later told me that he liked the workshop so much that he left and found a colleague who he convinced to attend the workshop. He later hired me to do consulting work for the university.

Eventually, Rowell became the head of the training department for Gulf States Paper Corporation (the inventors of the paper grocery bag). That corporation eventually became one of my major clients. Rowell left Gulf States to begin his own consulting business, HRD Associates, located in Tuscaloosa, Alabama. I send him all of my overflow business and he reciprocates. The relationship has evolved into one in which we co-present, and share lesson plans and handouts. He entered into a formal consulting contract with Gulf States Paper Corporation to provide a major portion of its training program. I am recognized by company officials as the silent partner in that venture and attend most planning meetings.

In the beginning years, I closely held all financial information. Consequently, I found myself teaching all day and invoicing clients at three in the morning. Then I found Mary Anne Parks Antonio, who used to be my sister's manager at a television station. She now has her own consulting business. I tentatively gave her a few duties to handle. As our trust foundation grew, I eventually turned over all billing, negotiations with clients for dates and rates, and collections. I contract out all of my financial matters to my accountant and Antonio.

Additionally, I have strategic alliances with four corporations (one major and three smaller). I am certified in several courses taught by those organizations and am bound by contractual obligations that determine for whom I may provide these services, as well as how I am compensated.

I initiate no contracts or requests for proposals unless specifically asked to do so. Most work is done simply by verbal agreement with an emailed or faxed confirmation of dates and financial penalty if the class or consulting event is cancelled within a specified period of time. I pay myself a base salary and rent for the home office space and receive periodic distributions.

Attracting and Keeping Clients

My marketing strategy consists of building on relationships that existed before I became a consultant. Prior to beginning the business, I had 15 years of ASTD and SHRM leadership and committee positions. I had also paid civic rent (doing things for others for no pay) by doing free workshops during the 15-year span when I worked for other organizations. I wish I could say it was due to altruism. It was altruistic in part—but I also conducted the workshops because my day-to-day corporate duties became boring and I liked meeting and visiting with people in other businesses. Little did I realize at the time that these people with whom I worked would become the foundation for my paying clients.

My second client came from a chance meeting while doing volunteer work. Because I was laid off at Christmas time, I was feeling sorry for myself and was engaged in a long pity party. My church was going to Vrendenburg, Alabama, where residents endure almost Third World poverty conditions. I decided to take my four-year-old daughter and show her and myself that we were better off than it seemed. While visiting the poor families, I ran into a friend from grammar school who is now an executive for a large insurance company. He asked me the typical "How are you doing?" question and I told him what had recently occurred. He said "Great! We need training at our company! Would you call us next week?" I made the call and it led to a relationship with that organization that continues now—10 years later.

Each client led to another and then to another. For example, Mercedes Benz (MBUSI) was building a new plant in the nearby area of Tuscaloosa/Vance. Several of my consultant colleagues said they were "... going to go after Mercedes for business." I deliberately decided not to be part of the pack of consultants.

The previous year a friend called who worked for a large corporation in Tuscaloosa. She had an employee who was enrolled in college with a major paper due on preventing sexual harassment. His wife had been seriously injured in a car accident leaving him no time to do the critical research. Because that topic is one of my specialties, she contacted me and asked for help on his behalf on providing information. I immediately sent him all of my books. My friend and I continued our relationship and she later became a member of the human resources team at Mercedes Benz.

I also taught classes at the University of Alabama on the main campus in Tuscaloosa. I was teaching a management certificate course for participants from outside corporations in which we were laughing and having fun while learning. The individual who was using the room next door came over to see what we were doing. He teased me that we were, ". . . having way too much fun," and asked if he could be in my class instead. He introduced himself as a member of the Mercedes human resources team and asked for my card.

Two weeks later, the MBUSI human resources team was meeting and searching for a consultant to conduct team training. Two MBUSI human resources members nominated my name almost at the exact moment. The training representative called me up and related that story. He asked me if I would be interested in taking over the assignment. I calmly and with dignity replied, "Yes." (I screamed loudly after I hung up!) He later told me that they had been overwhelmed by consultants' marketing materials and wanted someone who had not done that. We are still engaged in a mutually beneficial partnership.

The word "partnership" is not lightly chosen. I purposely use this language from the onset to imply that we are in a win-win relationship and that we are there to help one another. That is an important concept in how I have framed my relationships with my clients. In one situation, a long-time client was attempting to get me to undersell my services and said in the negotiations that I needed them as a major portion of my business. It was implied that I would suffer financial damage as a result of losing their business. In my reply, I stated that I *chose* to work with them but if we could not come to an agreement, I would simply choose to work with others because I had more business than I could handle. I have made it a policy that if I don't feel valued by a client, I will walk away from the business and this policy has served me well.

It should be understood, however, that walking away is usually not easy. I have on occasion felt hurt and betrayed. For example, a client with whom I had become emotionally attached as a long-time friend was discharged by the organization. Not only was I wounded by the discharge but also I had difficulty connecting to the new management. I am not certain if part of that difficulty was rooted in my perception that the discharge was done unfairly. Additionally, the new management in a cost-cutting move wanted me to teach one of their employees how to teach my training classes. Truthfully, I initially perceived this as the final act of betrayal. I unwisely got upper management involved in examining the decision and overestimated my relationship with the organization. Management stood by the new methodology of delivering the training. I learned a painful lesson not to overstate my value to an organization and again had to face the fact that my services or presence are never indispensable.

I tend to stay with my clients for a long time even though I never set myself up as the only one who can fix certain problems. My goal is to give managers and employees "tools" to enable them to handle problems themselves. If an organization gives me a project twice, I force the issue as to why we are facing the situation again and to determine why the problem was not fixed or did not stay resolved. My longevity is not because I "camp out" and make myself the all-seeing/knowing guru. I keep my skills current and add to my repertoire as the field evolves, offering new services as needed.

I also deliberately make friends with employees and management at all levels of the organization. I realized a long time ago, that it was important to befriend:
• people who know things
• people who buy things
• people who fix things (and they might not be the top-ranking persons in a company).

Consequently, I like to spend time with secretaries, the purchasing staff, the information services employees, and as many others as possible during the time I am on site. I was raised by egalitarian parents who taught me status and position are meaningless and valueless. I have never limited myself to one contact in an organization because the players can change so quickly.

My secrets to keeping clients are the following:
1. Link everything (recommendations, training, consulting services) back to the organization's mission/values statement and use

that language when communicating how this will help its mission become a reality.

2. Never use OSFA (one size fits all) solutions. Everything is tailored. This includes no canned prescriptions. Solutions are only found after asking questions, questions, and more questions during numerous interviews. My training brochure and Website offer a complete blueprint of what training courses could look like. All the details are listed down to room arrangements and equipment needed. This blueprint enables a client to visualize a framework. I ascertain their specifications with careful questions and review of documents. Again, tailoring is emphasized.

3. Never say "Yes, but . . ." because that phrase kills what the client is telling you and substitutes your own opinion. "Yes, and . . ." is a much more effective phrase because it aligns you with a client instead of putting you on opposing sides.

4. Use a client's language in selling your services. I often say, "I have been thinking about your problem X and here's a way to approach it." Their own language is the way I give them hard solutions, especially if it is something they don't want to do, but have to do it (for legal, ethical, or moral reasons).

5. The hard sell approach can set you up for rejection. Before I leave a training session, I always plant the next step in the minds of the participants. For example, during a Myers-Briggs Type Indicator® class, I will say, "I cover that in Advanced Myers-Briggs® and maybe I will get a chance to do that for you one day." I never leave without giving a suggestion of what is next.

6. In some parts of the South, "Who's your mama?" takes on a whole new meaning and can be an important question. In other words, who do you know that would recommend you as a trustworthy, upstanding citizen? You usually need to be "six degrees" from someone in the organization to have credibility. I came from a large family who knows everyone who knows everyone else (you get the picture). Being an extravert who talks to people in the grocery store line and on the street as well as having the radar to know when not to bother people is an absolute asset.

7. I never make cold calls or do requests for proposals unless I am invited.

8. Never leave a trail of bodies behind you. Be nice to everyone no matter what his or her station currently is. The Better Business Bureau contacted me with a sales pitch that I should renew my dues

because they had gotten me clients during the previous year. I promptly challenged that statement because I knew the origin of every single one of my clients.

"Who's your mama?" takes on a whole new meaning! You can't build alliances if you only have selfish motives in mind. People resent those that take and never give. Friendships have lines that travel many different directions and are always two-way streets.

Finally, I keep adding tools to my "toolbox" by attending continuing professional education each year. Some classes that I have attended include dialogue training, mediation training (three courses thus far), legal updates of human resources laws, advanced Myers-Briggs Type Indicator® training, time management training from Franklin Covey, review courses for certification in human resources, ASTD and SHRM training classes, and organizational development training. As I gain expertise, I alert my client base about the new area.

Managing the Business

Lovoy's Team Works, Inc., immediately became profitable with the first consulting job I had because there were no expenses or assets. After 10 years, the only expenses are normal ones including contract assistance, business supplies and equipment, home office expenses, and continuing education.

One of the biggest challenges has been charging cancellation fees when the client forfeits a class too late for the time to be rescheduled. If it is a continuous client and we have an ongoing, mutually productive relationship, I rarely assess the charge, especially if the reason was out of anyone's control. If I am having trouble with clients not respecting my time with last minute, frivolous cancellations, I always charge the fees in order to make them take the appointments seriously. It is difficult for a client to understand that if a class or consulting service is cancelled at the last minute and rescheduled later, that the opportunity to provide a profitable service on that day is lost and cannot be replaced.

As mentioned earlier, letting go of the financial management of the business was difficult because of the confidential nature of the information. When I finally realized that I do not like billing, I do not like to do the detailed work necessary to do a good job in this area, and that Antonio would guard my finances better than I ever would, I let go. She and my accountant diligently keep up with expenses and make up for my lack of attention to details.

Antonio and I have had trouble collecting two large accounts. In both cases, it took numerous phone calls and elevation to higher authority before the bills were paid. In each case, I was careful to preserve the relationship with my client by explaining to the higher authority that my contact client had done everything possible and that he or she was being mistreated by the accounting process. In both cases, we were successful.

I was negotiating with an accounting function of a well-known organization that had approached me about working with it. The accounting employee strongly suggested that I reduce my quoted rate in order to secure them as a client. I responded that I was already giving them the same rate as my best client in the same geographical area who had been with me since the start of the business and that I would not undercut my loyal client. The potential client said they probably would not do business with me. I refused to buckle to the pressure (even though I really wanted this client!) and I ended the conversation. That same afternoon the training manager called me and apologized for the behavior of the accounting employee and said that they made a major misstep in trying to get me to lower my rates. He agreed that my rates were already reasonable and that the matter was resolved.

I have purposely narrowed the geographical scope of my business and normally have most work within a day's drive of my home and usually only one to two nights away a month. I have refused offers to take my work out of the local area and to be on the road nationwide.

Handling Ethical Issues

One example of an ethical dilemma occurred when I was asked by a friend who is a labor attorney to conduct a diversity training class for one of his clients. When I met with the client, it was clear that there were deeper issues and diversity training was not the solution. I requested permission to interview several employees and managers. After conducting fact finding, I recommended they not do the diversity training. I diplomatically informed them they could correct one of the problems by discontinuing the practice of supervisors yelling at employees in front of others. I also instructed them to reveal to potential hires that they would be required to work 80 hours a week. The client objected saying no one would come to work for them. I pointed out that that practice was not honest. After their refusal, I left the partnership and passed my recommendations onto my friend, with which he agreed. I could have made several thousand dollars in fees by simply conducting the workshop but it would not have made any difference in the organization and there was no management support for that initiative.

When I conduct focus interviews with a client and the employees, I state up front to everyone involved that the source of information will remain confidential, and a summary of the data will be presented to everyone who participates but no names will be included. Ethical issues occur when an employer demands that I reveal to him or her who said what during focus groups. I have always refused. I have never lost a client because of my refusal.

One problem I have encountered on at least four occasions occurred when internal trainers sat through my training classes and took copious notes. Next, my training classes were either cancelled or not scheduled again. Then I discovered that my handouts and material were used by the internal trainers to present my classes, despite copyright notices clearly present on the materials. I have never confronted the clients about the use of my materials because it would have implicated the employees who revealed those practices to me and possibly would have cost them their jobs. In two instances, the clients began using my services again. However, I am now well aware of this ruse and have managed to prevent it from happening again. And, as a result, I do not allow my sessions to be videotaped.

Measuring Success

Lovoy's Team Works, Inc., is successful in many arenas. The obvious measures are ability to get and keep so many clients with no advertising or cold calls. As previously noted, each client relationship resulted from a referral from someone else or from the client experiencing firsthand the effect of the training from personally attending a session. I currently have served 112 clients. I am able to work with all kinds of businesses from industrial plants to medical groups to governmental entities to service providers. Revenue has grown accordingly and my schedule is booked almost every working day. I am able to send overflow to my strategic partner, Rowell, and other consultants that I hold in high regard.

But counting clients and coins is not the measure of success to me. More important is the ability to having lasting relationships with clients that are not only financially successful, but provide satisfaction, enjoyment, and a sense of accomplishment in helping others to enjoy and be fulfilled by their time at work. I never take my clients for granted. I try to always tell them how much I appreciate each and every opportunity to come to their place of business and be given the privilege of making a difference. I use my gifts and abilities to show them how to make their mission statements a reality instead of mere platitudes.

My success has also been formally evaluated in the four following arenas:

1. I have an ongoing relationship with American Cast Iron Pipe Company. This organization was founded by John Eagan who had the insight, in the early 1900s, well before there was an Equal Employment Opportunity Act, to create an organization in which fairness for all races was the foundation. When he died, he and his wife left the company to the employees. This organization has a corporate training program entitled the "Eagan College." The organization uses targeted selection to hire its employees. They are screened to determine how well they match with certain performance requirements. They are then evaluated on these same requirements and all training is designed around them. As a trainer for the organization, I am charged with making certain that every course I teach both matches the Eagan philosophy and supports specified performance requirements. All training is subject to review by the Jack Phillips Center for Research. The purpose of this structured multilevel review is to determine if the training is achieving the objectives of the college and the participants. It measures both short-term and long-term impact.

2. The second arena is a form of evaluation I use from labor and plaintiff attorneys. I teach prevention of sexual harassment and diversity training. My materials have been reviewed by 18 different attorneys (representing both management *and* employees). I have received nothing but positive feedback, not only for sound information from a legal perspective but also for delivery. My approach is pragmatic and is taught with an appropriate level of humor designed to put the participants at ease. The purpose is to teach them new guidelines for working with each other that will bring a sense of peace to the workplace and restore relationships to a productive and comfortable level. It also emphasizes getting rid of the "victimhood" mentality and emphasizes using employee empowerment to resolve problems. My training was approved as the remedy for two court-ordered settlements and 4,090 employees attended the training. Further proof of effectiveness is that each organization has seen cases filed in this area diminish after the training. I also testified in a sexual harassment case on behalf of an organization in federal court and the organization won the case.

3. The third arena is one in which results are achieved that cannot be gauged simply by numbers. For example, I was contacted to work with an organization that was having serious problems between a manager who was a person of color and an employee group that was mixed. I was told that the employees said that if there were not an intervention, there would be workplace violence (this was not a threat, but an expression of fear). There were two employees who were convinced that the manager was the sole cause of the problem. I worked intermittently with the group for four months. At the end of that time, the two employees who blamed the manager came to the recognition that they themselves were strong contributors to the situation. They had, in turn, contaminated others in the workplace as a result of their toxic behaviors. The employees agreed to engage in positive behaviors. The manager, who was emotionally tone deaf to her employees, worked on honing her skills to better resolve the employee problems. Management, including the two top managers, was also contributing to the problems by making decisions that were making things worse. I taught the employees new ways of handling relationship issues. We also put into place a new system for mediating disputes that kept management from issuing edicts and put problem resolution back in the hands of the employees. We agreed that I would return in three months for a checkup. I contacted management three months later as agreed, and management told me no follow-up was needed because things had calmed down and employees were solving their own problems!

Finally, I was working with a conservative school that was interested in reaching out to the African American community with its services. After a long pause, I stood up and looked around the room and said, "As long as the entire staff is lily white, you can forget that." There was dead silence after I sat down. I was sure that I could kiss my relationship with that client goodbye after my remarks. The silence finally ended when one of the faculty members said they had done some traditional recruiting but that it had yielded no appropriate candidates. I reminded them that the system was man-made and that they had to prime the pump to get what they wanted. They began an intensive search and located a prominent African American minister who has been an excellent addition to the staff. We still have a productive partnership today and my classes have been made permanent parts of two curricula.

4. Another way in which I measure success is through regular postmortem meetings I engage in with my clients after an intervention. For example, I recently assisted a client in a reduction in force. I was

present to help comfort both the employees who were being let go, talk to the workforce who remained and assuage their "survivors' guilt," and assist managers with the difficult conversations. Because I had been in this situation before and I held this client in high regard, I rendered this service free of charge.

In the postmortem, management told me they had consulted with at least five different sources before coming to me. They said that I was the only one who suggested:

- getting boxes for the employees in which to pack their personal items
- providing an opportunity, through a company luncheon, for the employees to say their farewells
- offering additional assistance to the employees who were losing their jobs by engaging the entire firm's workforce in this process so the employees could return to work as quickly as possible
- suggesting holding a meeting so that the rest of the firm's employees could console one another and be assured their jobs were safe.

As a result, there was little damage to any of the parties and all of the employees who lost their jobs have now found employment. The rest of the firm has indicated that they feel secure and appreciated the respect shown to those who were leaving. We are now engaged in a process to strategically plan how to get more work for the firm—work for which I will be compensated.

In summary, my approach has been to help managers and employees solve their immediate problems and equip them with new skills that stop the old problems from reoccurring and teach them how to resolve future problems. I measure success by the interpersonal situations that stay resolved and how well employees are empowered to correct their situations without my assistance.

Keys To Success

The keys to success of this practice can be summarized as follows:
1. Use your failures to teach others. If you do not put yourself on a pedestal, you will not be an easy target (or a sitting duck). Your defects and lessons learned are some of the most valuable tools you can offer to others.
2. You cannot do it all; decide on a specialty.
3. Use your library card more than your charge card. Stay current with the information in your field or specialty. This includes remaining competent in expertise as well as emotional maturity.
4. Stay neutral. This is especially critical when dealing with family businesses. And, never, never try to play both sides. People talk!

5. Plant one foot in the present and one foot in the future. This means tending to your current clients as well as cultivating future business.
6. Help those who have lost their jobs or are calling upon you for advice. I often receive calls from others who want to enter the consulting business. I am careful to paint a realistic picture without being discouraging or destroying their dreams. I always give them a detailed plan to follow. In the case of HR professionals who have lost their jobs, I always take their resumes and pass them on to everyone I know. I critique their resumes for quality and give advice about how to sell themselves. I send them books and offer support through telephone calls as a morale check.
7. You are paid to say the hard stuff. For example, I was working with an employee group that was making management weary dealing with the constant bickering among the group's members. I talked with each person to define the problems. When we got together, the employees told me they got along just fine, were friends, and that I wasn't needed. There was a long silence. Then I said loudly, "So, calling each other 'white bitch' is OK here? That's an appropriate way to talk to each other? I don't know about you, but I never insult my friends that way, even in joking!" The group sat there stunned. After another long silence, someone spoke up in a small voice and said, "Well, maybe we do need some help after all, because I can't stand the way we treat each other." We finally got started with the intervention and had wonderful success. One toxic team member left the team and it was good.

Lessons Learned

1. If you do not like the client, walk away. I worked with an HR professional who was tense and uncaring about the personnel in her organization. No matter what recommendations I made, I was unsuccessful in persuading her to work with the employees in a different manner. I woke up one day and realized that I disliked her style intensely and felt that she was wrong for the job. I left the client and have never looked back. In another situation, I was meeting with the head of human resources who was inquiring about my business. He continued to use warlike terms and described the competition as a group that had to be killed and constantly said that, "It is a war out there. Everyone not in this organization is our enemy and deserves to be treated as such." Needless to say, I declined to join his "war."
2. Ego can be a roadblock to listening and being taught by others. The strongest reaction I get in training classes is when I relate per-

sonal stories of my own failures. For example, I tell a story about attending a mediation training class. In the first three days of the class, I breezed through the material and training because many things in that area come naturally. Then there was day four. On this day we were being taught how to co-mediate with a partner. After our classroom session, we broke into 10 groups with an individual coach and were given a practice scenario. After my partner went first, I enthusiastically took over (and I want you to read those words "I took over" literally). I successfully got the two persons to talk face-to-face about their problems and work out their situation. I was pretty excited about the results. Then it came time for feedback. My partner said, "Great job. You got the two people together and I have never seen anyone help others to resolve a situation as fast as you did. It was pretty amazing. But that was not the point of the exercise. The point of the exercise was for us to work together and you didn't do that. You ignored me after you got started." My coach followed him and gave essentially the same feedback. The next day I came to class and talked to my coach and my practice session partner and told them I checked my ego at the door and I was ready to learn from them. Since that day, when I teach with anyone else, we have a postmortem at the end of the session and ask questions like:

- Did I get in your way?
- Did I take your stories?
- Did I interrupt you at any time?
- Did I try to become the center of attention?
- Did I monopolize the time?

Another example of my ego getting in the way occurred when I was asked to attend a train-the-trainer class in order to be certified for a particular training class. I came to the class with the attitude: "I can't be taught—I already know how to teach training classes." I was also resentful about having to forfeit an entire week to attend the class. I wasn't a troublemaker in the class, but I was not the most enthusiastic participant. Within one day, Jerry Aull from Franklin Covey convinced me that there were things I could do to make my classes even better. He taught me two phrases that I have used again and again to obtain client agreement on a tough proposal: "There are many ways to be right," and "Can we agree . . . ?"

3. Find a mentor and a tormentor. You need people who will tell you the truth about your faults. I have been lucky enough to have people such as Mary Anne Parks Antonio, Jim Rowell, Stephanie

Dunleavy, Jack Phillips, and my old boss Fred Dissen, who have given me some tough feedback about the times that I was arrogant or thought I knew everything, or when I was afraid to face conflict.

4. Give cheerfully and without resentment. I often agree to do workshops for churches and schools but do not charge them. I may look like a wonderful person on the outside for doing this but often on the day of the event, I wake up and wonder, "Why did I agree to do this workshop?" and have internal resentment. One hundred percent of the time I enjoy the workshop and, interestingly enough, 100 percent of the time, I get a client out of the process. I am not proud of this internal negative monologue and continue to work on my attitude.

5. I have to be careful to not only give my time, but to guard my time. I say "yes" to too many things and then wear myself out physically. I feel like a phony when I talk about not serving your family the leftovers of your time and energy when I am guilty of that exact behavior. I would do well to heed my own advice.

6. Always overprepare. I was asked to attend a meeting with a large organization and was told that its purpose was to meet me and to discuss diversity. I took the potential client literally and thought the meeting was going to be a one-on-one chat. I did not expect an entire committee who wanted to see a PowerPoint™ presentation about my organization and how I could establish an entire diversity program for their company. I was seriously underprepared and found out that I had been recommended by several members of the committee who had attended my training classes. I left the meeting feeling as if I had let them down and did not meet their expectations.

7. Integrity is critical. I have a client who is also a friend. She has many consultants who work for her and we have an agreement that we will not discuss others. One day she and I were in a lengthy discussion. During this conversation, she began to discuss the substandard work of one of her consultants. I did not stop the discussion and, in fact, participated in it. I later thought about the conversation and realized with shame the part I had played. I contacted my friend and apologized for my behavior and failure to keep our agreement.

8. Cancellations or holes in the calendar are not always a bad thing. On three occasions, clients cancelled business at the last minute. The conversation I had with them (in my head) was not charitable or respectful. However, in all three situations, there was that mysterious hand again working its wonder. In each instance, during the time I would have been teaching, there was a death or serious illness in my family and because of the cancellations, I was able to be where I was needed (and where I wanted to be) the most.

In summary, one of my greatest lessons came from attending a conference to hear one of the top gurus in the organizational development field. I had great admiration for this person based solely on his book and was even lucky enough to be slotted to attend a private session with him in which only 20 persons were to be admitted. His book, which I used as the primary text for a class I was teaching, was a source of inspiration about empowering the workforce and serving others. In his keynote speech he said consultants were in the business only for themselves and possessed "delusions of grandeur." He went on further to demean the expertise and commitment of consultants and their value to organizations. In the private session, he was both arrogant and cynical. My dream of meeting the man behind the words that had inspired in me a sense of service as a consultant was crushed. However, his negativity inspired me. I decided that I never wanted to embrace his cynicism. I rather chose to see my profession as a calling, to do a high quality job no matter the reward, and to treat every person as special. I often close my sessions by asking everyone to shake each other's hand and ask, "Hello, how are you, and what can you do for me?" I then ask them to repeat the handshake and ask, "Hello, how are you, and what can I do for you?" I then ask, "Which one feels better?" Unanimously the answer is the second one. I point out that the first one is speed networking—in other words, meeting every person and taking from them everything for oneself. But the second one is "networthing," the power to add value to the life of everyone with whom you come in contact.

Questions for Discussion

1. How can a consultant continue to be relevant to issues confronting the workplace and retain ability to communicate with various age groups and educational levels?
2. Can a consultant be close friends with clients and yet remain objective (or be seen as neutral in a matter involving individuals in the business)?
3. How can a consultant simultaneously tend to current clients while pursuing future business?
4. What do I bring to the table that others will pay me to do?
5. What efforts do I need to make to volunteer for organizations such as ASTD and SHRM in order to prove my worth to others and add value to our profession?
6. Will I be happier working for myself and by myself with no contract and no net to catch me if times become rough financially?

The Author

Sharon W. Lovoy grew up in Birmingham, Alabama. She attended Auburn University where she was graduated with honors with degrees in secondary education, economics, and sociology. She financed her college education by working for a local hospital. She began her career working for the federal government where she entered into an accelerated development internship. As a result, she was able to work in several positions including labor relations, director of training, and director of human resources. She also had the opportunity to help develop a national governmental publication, *The Leader's Digest,* which focused on key leadership challenges and concerns. After her career with the federal government, she worked in the private sector as head of training for a savings and loan bank. Next, she began her consulting business, Lovoy's Team Works, Inc. Lovoy holds a senior professional certification in human resources and has attended mediation training through Harvard Law School Program of Instruction for Lawyers, CDR, and Mediation Training International. She is a member of the Management Certificate and Master Management Certificate faculties for the University of Alabama and holds professional instructor qualifications in the Myers-Briggs Type Indicator® and Franklin Time Management®. She can be reached at Lovoy's Team Works, Inc.; phone: 205.991.8626; email: swlovoy@ltwinc.com; Website: www.ltwinc.com.

Maintaining Life Balance

The Pyramid Resource Group, Inc.

Barry F. Mitsch

The Pyramid Resource Group, Inc., was founded in 1994 by the husband and wife team of Barry and DJ Mitsch. Since then, the company has evolved into one of the most successful corporate coaching companies, with a stellar track record of serving many large, multinational companies. The Mitsch's have learned many lessons in developing a "family-owned" coaching business that operates on a broad, international scale. They have designed the business around their family and have maintained a work-life balance that is a model that many can emulate as they develop their own consulting businesses.

The Beginnings

Why do people choose to start their own consulting business? There are myriad reasons, some deliberate and some resulting from circumstances of career transitions that may be brought on by mergers, acquisitions, or simply a need for a change in course. In our case, the decision to establish The Pyramid Resource Group can be summarized in one word—freedom! DJ Mitsch had just left a successful career in broadcasting, one she loved but in an industry rife with turmoil and uncertainty caused by federal deregulation. I was working for a small startup that was faced with all the familiar struggles of a new business, including unpredictable hours and general uncertainty. These situations led to the obvious question—why not start our own company? We had two small children (at the time, ages five and one), some space in our home that could serve as an office,

This case was prepared to serve as a basis for discussion rather than to illustrate either effective or ineffective administrative and management practices.

and plenty of existing contacts and ideas. So we did something we probably would not recommend to many people—we started a home-based business without any guaranteed income or even a sound business plan. It was the ultimate leap of faith!

The past seven years have brought many challenges, but the greatest reward has been the freedom we have had to raise two kids and spend quality time together watching them grow. We keep sane hours, travel strategically, and make sure the business does not keep us from the most important things in life. The most valuable resource we can provide to people considering a consulting business is to share our experiences regarding life balance and the actions we have taken to maintain this balance while growing a successful business.

The Foundation

While we did not have any long-term contracts when we christened the business, we did have some savings, lots of marketable experience, and a plethora of ideas. I had been conducting training seminars for more than seven years, and DJ had been a participant in many advanced leadership programs while also being responsible for hiring trainers and organizational development consultants for her companies. We had an established relationship with one multinational company, but because it was going through a merger, there was no guarantee that we would maintain a favorable position with the new regime.

The focus of the business was going to be on corporate training and consulting. We began to craft a business plan that to this day has never been completed. We have found our business to be so dynamic that business plans were obsolete by the time they were nearing completion. Instead, we began operating on the principle of "strategic intent"—declaring the intent of the business and keeping all actions in alignment with that intent. Our original strategic intent was to "pioneer new technologies that transform personal and corporate communication."

The most significant shift in the early stages of the business was our exposure to the emerging field of coaching. DJ had hired a coach while managing a radio station, and we worked with a coach in developing our own strategic intent. It was quickly apparent that coaching was DJ's natural gift and she became totally immersed in the profession and is one of the pioneers in the field. Within a year, the business focus shifted to corporate coaching, and this has been our primary field of emphasis since that time.

The Business Model

DJ is a self-proclaimed world-class shopper, so our business model is based on a shopping mall. Malls have anchor tenants that form that foundation of the business, and we strive to keep our anchor positions in our mall filled with selected corporations. We have developed a description of what we consider to be our ideal client and only pursue corporations that fit that description. Many consultants, particularly in the early stages of their business, take any opportunities that come their way in order to make ends meet. While not immune to that impulse, we have been very successful in attracting clients that meet our criteria. When we have strayed from our ideal client description, the results have been less than desirable and the lessons learned have reinforced the need to stay the course.

A description of the ideal client includes size, location, gross sales, corporate philosophy, position in their niche industry, commitment to personal and professional development, the presence of a "champion" for our work, and an infrastructure that enables the development of a true partnership with our company. Determination of ideal client status often takes time, including many conversations by phone or in person. We have walked away from business on more than one occasion when the client did not meet our standards and, in every case, a more aligned opportunity presented itself soon after.

Building Infrastructure

A major turning point in the evolution of our business was the decision to seek office space outside the home. Office space meant overhead, complexity, and a change in lifestyle. But it was probably the best decision we have made and greatly expanded the potential for the business. Most consultants operate from a home base, which keeps overhead low and the office conveniently located—often too convenient. Separating the business from the home is one of the most important lessons we learned in achieving a work/life balance. It is a great feeling to walk away from the office at night and physically move to a space that is a haven for balance—our home. There is no temptation to run to the phone, fax machine, and computer to interrupt the flow of the family. The intangible value more than covers the tangible cost of office overhead.

Infrastructure also includes support systems and people hired to make the business run. We constantly look for efficiencies that will make our lives simpler, give us more time to work on projects that produce income, and provide for sound management of the business.

Consider the following:

1. Hire a payroll service for payroll and tax reporting. This is a great time-saver and also helps with budgeting and projections. The cost is minimal but you have to make tax deposits regularly and, in some cases, ahead of schedule. Payroll services make their money off the "float," which keeps your cost low.

2. Hire a bookkeeper to keep your financials in order. We have a bookkeeper who works about three hours a week and is responsible for all check writing, accounts payable and receivable updates, book balancing, and pretax preparation. She is an expert on our software system and can perform tasks much faster that we can, and we don't have to waste time learning the details of a software system when we only need to know general functions. That is another time-saver that more than recovers the cost. As much as you may be tempted to keep your own books, consider taking this route as a way of freeing yourself for more important things. Keep control of the money by requesting regular reports on at least a weekly basis, review and sign all checks, and note all receivables when they arrive.

3. Secure the services of a reliable IT consultant. When the computers go down, you need them fixed immediately. There are many IT consultants available in today's market; find one that can respond to your needs within an hour.

4. Join a business dialogue group. Every business can use the advice of a board of directors. There are many venues for sharing ideas and gaining insight from other business owners and CEOs. Look for a business dialogue group through your local chamber of commerce or consider joining a TEC Group in your area. We have been part of a TEC group for more than a year and it has dramatically improved our operation. From crafting a disaster recovery plan to choosing a contact management system, the input of TEC members and the TEC chair have been valuable resources and an extension of our company.

5. Hire a coach. We have both used personal coaches to help us keep perspective and promote personal growth within and outside of the business.

6. Use virtual assistants. There are many virtual assistants who can help on a project basis or on a more permanent arrangement. A virtual assistant operates remotely using Internet and telephonic technology and can help you expand your staff as needed.

Taking Care of the Home Front

The most important factor in achieving balance is to take care of the home front. A family-owned business does not work if there is too much worry about needs at home. Here are some tips:

1. If you have kids, hire a nanny for the after-school hours. Local universities are great sources of nannies looking for part-time work. Once you find a good nanny, he or she will usually help you recruit a replacement when he or she graduates or moves into a professional job. Our nanny makes sure the kids are home safely, their homework is completed, and simple household chores are accomplished. A nanny can also help out in the office when tasks such as envelope stuffing and collating are needed. When both parents work in a business, a nanny is a necessity if you want to maintain a high level of productivity and preserve family time.

2. Stagger work hours if necessary to adjust for the kids. I am a morning person and like to get to work early, so I take the early shift and go home first. DJ comes to work later and works into the evening. We follow the natural flow of our personal high energy peaks this way.

3. Find services to take care of menial tasks. There are lots of services available to help you maximize time. For example, dry cleaners will pick up and deliver at your office. Even small companies can tap into valet services that are available in most communities.

Creating a Team

Another important decision we made was to grow our capabilities by creating a team of professionals who would associate with our company. The sense of community is often missing in a consulting business with many consultants being lone rangers. There are also limitations on the size of initiatives you can take on if you are a small organization. This can also lead to the "doom loop" of being too busy *doing* the work to have the time to continually develop new clients.

A critical factor in forming a team is determining when to develop formal relationships with key associates. Do you build the team first and then look for contracts, or get the contracts and then build a team? In our case, we were fortunate to have clients when the work gradually expanded. We were able to bring associates on board with work in hand rather than a promise of work. And we have been exceptionally fortunate in attracting an outstanding group of professionals who have developed loyalty to our company. In our seven-plus years in business, we have not had a single associate voluntarily leave the group.

A key to maintaining our core team has been the creation and preservation of a genuine professional community. We meet regularly by phone and try to gather in person at least two to three times per year. Our associate team is scattered across the country—and internationally—so it can often be challenging to maintain consistent contact. The team has helped create products and services and collectively has created an exceptional source of support, camaraderie, and creative inspiration.

Keeping contractors loyal to your company can be a challenge and we feel fortunate to have such a great group. Of course, the most important factor in maintaining a stellar team is choosing the right people in the first place. We have identified specific competencies for our associates and follow our guidelines very carefully when looking to add to the team. We have also established a mentoring program and systematic orientation to incorporate new members to the group. Our core team members are instrumental in recruiting, screening, and orienting new associates. And along with these efforts, we also strive to provide the best financial incentives possible. The percentage of revenue paid to our contractors is high relative to the industry in general and this helps keep quality professionals working for our company.

Our tips for working with contractors include:
1. Make sure you have contracts and legal protection, and be familiar with federal regulations that delineate employee versus contractor relationships.
2. Set criteria and competencies for your contractors and don't leave out important characteristics such as humor, flexibility, and enthusiasm.
3. Pay fairly and promptly and keep the percentage share in the upper range of your industry.
4. Develop a systematic plan for keeping in touch, developing community, and fostering cooperation.

Our contractor team brings many benefits to our company. But the greatest benefit is the ability to expand our work without creating more stress on the family. Without our team, travel would be greatly increased and our ability to service a more diverse group of clients would be diminished.

Operating Globally

Technology and the design of our business have enabled us to operate on a global scale. While there is and always will be great value in face-to-face contact, our coaching services can be delivered anywhere in the world using the most reliable technology available—the telephone. That allows great flexibility for us and our clients and also reinforces the theme of balance that we try to emulate in our work. The telephone also keeps us in touch with our team. We own a telephone bridge that is available for use internally and with clients and is another expense that greatly increases efficiency.

Lessons Learned

We have learned a lot of lessons since beginning our business. Some key lessons include:
1. Remember that your kids are much more important than the business.
2. Contractors are better than employees. A consulting business expands and contracts and it is much better to stay flexible in staffing the company.
3. Get it in writing. Have written contracts with contractors, clients, vendors, and any other entity where the exchange of money takes place.
4. Treat your contractors as well as your best customers; without them you cannot grow and maintain the business.
5. Only work with "ideal clients," and make sure you have a clear picture of what your ideal client looks like.
6. Develop a support group that can provide advice for the business.
7. Use professional coaches to help promote personal growth.

Discussion Questions

1. What life balance issues are most critical for people running their own consulting firm?
2. What support systems need to be in place to help you maintain life balance?
3. What are the dangers of not having an active business plan?
4. What are the benefits of technology in maintaining life balance? And what are the potential detriments?
5. What other tools are available for attracting and sustaining a team of contractors?

The Author

Barry F. Mitsch is vice president of The Pyramid Resource Group, Inc. A versatile professional, he has been involved in training and development activities for nearly 20 years. His background includes work in both technical and nontechnical training, and he has designed and delivered classroom, self-instructional, and distance learning programs.

He specializes in group and individual presentation skills training for technical professionals and is also responsible for managing infrastructure and marketing for The Pyramid Resource Group. He can be reached at The Pyramid Resource Group, Inc., 1919 Evans Road, CentreWest Commons, Cary, NC 27513; email: barry@pyramidresource.com.

About the Editor

Patricia Pulliam Phillips is chairman and CEO of the Chelsea Group, a research and consulting company focused on accountability issues in training, HR, and performance improvement. Phillips conducts research on accountability issues and works with clients to build accountability systems and processes in their organizations. She has helped organizations implement the return-on-investment (ROI) process, developed by Jack J. Phillips, in countries around the world including South Africa, Singapore, Japan, New Zealand, Australia, Italy, Turkey, France, Germany, Canada, and the United States. She has been involved in hundreds of ROI studies in a variety of industries.

Phillips has more than 13 years' experience in the electrical utility industry. As manager of a market planning and research organization, she was responsible for developing marketing programs for residential, commercial, and industrial customers. Those programs included such initiatives as the residential load control program, the energy services program, and the district sales initiative. As manager of market planning and research, Phillips also played an integral role in establishing Marketing University, a learning environment that supported the needs of new sales and marketing representatives.

Phillips has a master of arts degree in public and private management from Birmingham-Southern College. She is certified in ROI evaluation and serves as co-author on the subject in publications including *Corporate University Review; The Journal of Lending and Credit Risk Management; Training Journal; What Smart Trainers Know*, Loraine L. Ukens, ed. (Jossey-Bass/Pfeiffer, 2001); and *Evaluating Training Programs*, 2d edition, by Donald L. Kirkpatrick (San Francisco: Berrett-Koehler Publishers, 1998). She is a contributing author to *HRD Trends Worldwide* by Jack J. Phillips (Woburn, MA: Butterworth-Heinemann, 1999). Phillips has written and co-authored several issues of the American Society for Training & Development *Info-line* series including *Mastering ROI* (1998) and *Managing Evaluation Shortcuts* (2001). She served as issue editor for the ASTD *In Action* casebook, *Measuring Return on Investment,* volume 3 (2001) and *Measuring Return on Investment in the Public Sector* (2002). Phillips is also co-author of *The Human Resources Scorecard: Measuring Return on Investment* (Woburn, MA: Butterworth-Heinemann, 2001) and author of *The Bottom Line on ROI* (Center for Effective Performance, 2002). She can be reached at thechelseagroup@aol.com.

About the Series Editor

Jack J. Phillips is a world-renowned expert on measurement and evaluation and developer of return-on-investment (ROI), a revolutionary process that provides bottom-line figures and accountability for all types of training, performance improvement, human resources, and technology programs. He is the author or editor of more than 30 books—12 focused on measurement and evaluation—and more than 100 articles.

His expertise in measurement and evaluation is based on more than 27 years of corporate experience in five industries (aerospace, textiles, metals, construction materials, and banking). Phillips has served as training and development manager at two *Fortune* 500 firms, senior HR officer at two firms, president of a regional federal savings bank, and management professor at a major state university.

In 1992, Phillips founded Performance Resources Organization (PRO), an international consulting firm that provides comprehensive assessment, measurement, and evaluation services for organizations. In 1999, PRO was acquired by the Franklin Covey Company and is now known as the Jack Phillips Center for Research. Today the center is an independent, leading provider of measurement and evaluation services to the global business community. Phillips consults with clients in manufacturing, service, and government organizations in the United States, Canada, Sweden, England, Belgium, Germany, Italy, Holland, South Africa, Mexico, Venezuela, Malaysia, Indonesia, Hong Kong, Australia, New Zealand, and Singapore. He leads the Phillips Center in research and publishing efforts that support the knowledge and development of assessment, measurement, and evaluation.

Phillips's most recent books include *The Human Resources Scorecard: Measuring the Return on Investment* (Boston: Butterworth-Heinemann, 2001); *The Consultant's Scorecard* (New York: McGraw-Hill, 2000); *HRD Trends Worldwide: Shared Solutions to Compete in a Global Economy* (Boston: Butterworth-Heinemann, 1999); *Return on Investment in Training and Performance Improvement Programs* (Boston: Butterworth-Heinemann, 1997); *Handbook of Training Evaluation and Measurement*

Methods, 3d edition (Boston: Butterworth-Heinemann, 1997); and *Accountability in Human Resource Management* (Boston: Butterworth-Heinemann, 1996).

Phillips has undergraduate degrees in electrical engineering, physics, and mathematics from Southern Polytechnic State University and Oglethorpe University; a master's degree in decision sciences from Georgia State University; and a Ph.D. in human resource management from the University of Alabama. In 1987 he won the Yoder-Heneman Personnel Creative Application Award from the Society for Human Resource Management.

Phillips can be reached at the Jack Phillips Center for Research, Box 380637, Birmingham, AL 35238-0637; phone: 205.678.8038; fax: 205.678.0177; email: serieseditor@aol.com.

The Value of Belonging